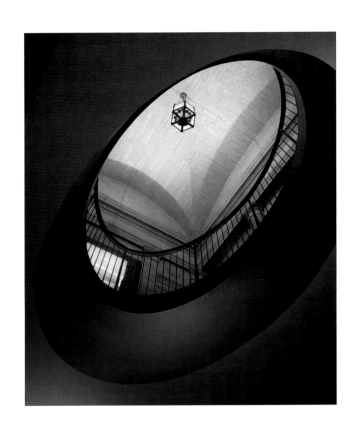

A Noble Task

A Noble Task

THE SAINT PAUL PUBLIC LIBRARY CELEBRATES 125!

BILOINE W. YOUNG

Foreword by Patricia Hampl

AFTON HISTORICAL SOCIETY PRESS

AFTON PRESS

is grateful to

**THE FRIENDS
OF THE
SAINT PAUL
PUBLIC LIBRARY**

*and the following
generous donors
who have made possible
the publication of*

A Noble Task

THE SAINT PAUL PUBLIC
LIBRARY CELEBRATES 125!

Elmer L. and Eleanor J.
Andersen Foundation

Katherine B. Andersen Fund
of the Saint Paul Foundation

F. R. Bigelow Foundation

Harlan Boss Foundation
for the Arts

Joan Duddingston

Howard and Betsy Guthmann

Hubbard Broadcasting Foundation

John and Ruth Huss

Art and Martha Kaemmer
Fund of HRK Foundation

Robert and Alexandra Klas

George and Dusty Mairs

Malcolm and Patricia McDonald

Richard and Nancy Nicholson

Connie Otis

Daniel and Kathryn Rominski

The Saint Paul Foundation

Bill and Susan Sands

Front cover, opposite half-title page, and frontispiece: Photos by Farshid Assassi of Assassi Productions, Meyer, Scherer, and Rockcastle, Architects. *Back cover:* St. Paul Public Library, St. Paul, Minnesota.

Edited by Michele Hodgson
Designed by Mary Susan Oleson
Production assistance by Beth Williams
Printed by Pettit Network, Inc., Afton, Minnesota

Library of Congress Cataloging-in-Publication Data
Young, Biloine.
A noble task : the Saint Paul Public Library celebrates 125! /
by Biloine Young.—1st ed.
p. cm.
Includes bibliographical references and index.
ISBN-13: 978-1-890434-72-4 (hardcover : alk. paper)
ISBN-10: 1-890434-72-8 (hardcover : alk. paper)
1. Saint Paul Public Library—History. 2. Public libraries—Minnesota—
Saint Paul—History.
I. Afton Historical Society Press (Afton, Minn.) II. Title.

Z733.S149Y68 2007
027.4776'581—dc22

2006101279

Printed in China

*Afton Press receives major support for its publishing program
from the Sarah Stevens MacMillan Foundation
and the W. Duncan MacMillan family.*

Patricia Condon McDonald
PUBLISHER

AFTON HISTORICAL SOCIETY PRESS
P.O. Box 100, Afton, MN 55001
800-436-8443
aftonpress@aftonpress.com
www.aftonpress.com

Contents

DIRECTOR'S NOTE *8*   PRESIDENT'S NOTE *9*

ACKNOWLEDGMENTS *10*

FOREWORD by Patricia Hampl *11*

PROLOGUE	THE FIRE	*15*
CHAPTER 1	"A TEACHER COMING SHOULD BRING BOOKS"	*21*
CHAPTER 2	ST. PAUL'S FIRST LIBRARIAN	*33*
CHAPTER 3	TOWARD A FREE PUBLIC LIBRARY	*41*
CHAPTER 4	THE REIGN OF HELEN McCAINE	*47*
CHAPTER 5	BUILDING THE CENTRAL LIBRARY	*53*
CHAPTER 6	TAKING THE LIBRARY TO THE PEOPLE	*71*
CHAPTER 7	A PERIOD OF DECLINE	*81*
CHAPTER 8	SURVIVING THE DEPRESSION	*89*
CHAPTER 9	COLLECTIONS AND THE FRIENDS	*101*
CHAPTER 10	PROGRESS, TO A POINT	*123*

THE BRANCHES *143*

CHAPTER 11	LONG-TERM PLANNING	*153*
CHAPTER 12	CENTRAL LIBRARY'S RESTORATION	*169*
CHAPTER 13	BECOMING LEARNING CENTERS	*187*
EPILOGUE	THE FLOOD	*195*

NOTES *204*   ILLUSTRATION CREDITS *206*   INDEX *207*

Library Director's Note

IN 2007 THE SAINT PAUL PUBLIC LIBRARY celebrates 125 years of service in this community. From humble beginnings, when the reading room of the YMCA merged its services with the Saint Paul Library Association in 1882, we have evolved into a national leader among urban libraries. That evolution—much of it outlined in this book—has seen many incarnations, but one thing has remained constant: We have always been in the business of making the lives of St. Paul citizens better.

With such a proud and sturdy heritage to guide me, I have the daunting and exciting task of helping to envision the future of our library system. I have two predictions about that future to boldly share with you. First, the experience you have in our libraries will be more important than the materials on our shelves or in our computers. With information being so readily available via so many avenues, it is how that information is shared and how learning is facilitated that will become essential to our surviving and thriving.

The second prediction is that, while it will no longer be necessary (or enough) for libraries to be repositories of facts and information, it will be critical for libraries to be centers of culture. We must reflect the spirit and resources deemed most important to our community members, and that will require us to think beyond the inventory we possess and focus on the services we provide.

To do these things well—to make these predictions reality—the Saint Paul Public Library must continue to evolve, to learn, and to always, always focus on our core business of making the lives of St. Paul citizens better.

Melanie Huggins
DIRECTOR, SAINT PAUL PUBLIC LIBRARY

Friends President's Note

THE FRIENDS OF THE SAINT PAUL PUBLIC LIBRARY has a proud sixty-two year tradition of supporting this great institution. Since its inception in 1945, The Friends has raised tens of millions of dollars for books and materials and special programs and projects. From its formative years under head librarian Perrie Jones to the years it was housed at and nurtured by the Saint Paul Foundation, to its present status as an independent nonprofit, one guiding principle has kept The Friends organization true to its mission: being as responsive as possible to the library's needs to help it meet the needs of a changing community.

As the Saint Paul Public Library begins its next 125 years, The Friends will build on the library's successful service to the St. Paul community. As the library works to make the lives of St. Paul's citizens better, The Friends renews its commitment to supporting that effort and helping the Saint Paul Public Library continue to be one of the country's best.

Peter D. Pearson

PRESIDENT, THE FRIENDS OF THE SAINT PAUL PUBLIC LIBRARY

Acknowledgments

IT IS THE LIBRARIANS of the Saint Paul Public Library whom I must acknowledge for their assistance in the writing of this book. Active and retired librarians happily shared with me their memories, memorabilia, and fond anecdotes of life within what they call the "people's university." Scarcely missing a beat for more than a century, all stayed abreast of their patrons' needs, incorporated new technology into their work and—by reaching out to diverse communities—made each new advance accessible to everyone in the city.

Saint Paul librarians quietly persevered when official indifference would have discouraged less determined individuals and, in so doing, solidified the central role libraries play in our communities. An amazing percentage of these professionals devoted their entire careers to the Saint Paul Public Library, thus providing Minnesota's capital city with 125 years of unparalleled and exceptional library service.

I am especially grateful to librarian Kathy Castillo, who put in many hours of work on research; to former Central Library director Kathleen Flynn, who gave me access to materials and a place to work; and to librarian Fran Galt, who carefully read the manuscript and corrected spellings as well as my many misplaced punctuation marks.

This history of the Saint Paul Public Library owes its publication to Chuck Johnston and Patricia McDonald at Afton Historical Society Press. They, like all of the individuals who have been involved in celebrating the library's 125th anniversary, believed from the start that the story of this extraordinary institution, beloved by generations of its patrons, richly deserved to be told. That this book reaches Afton's high standards for literary excellence is due to editor Michele Hodgson, a wordsmith beyond compare. That is it also exceptionally beautiful is the work of graphic designer Mary Susan Oleson, who conceived its overall design and meticulously created each and every page.

B.W.Y.

Foreword

A WINTER AFTERNOON, piercing cold, early in 1973, and I was standing in the main Reading Room of the Saint Paul Public Library downtown, waiting for a book I had requested to be brought up from the stacks. I was only a year or so out of university, and I'd just returned to St. Paul after a string of cheerless temp jobs in California. I'd come home—I calculated for maybe a year—to save enough money to launch into what I thought of vaguely but intensely as my *real* life, which, of course, would transpire far—far!—from my old hometown. Paris figured in my plots, and of course New York winked and beckoned.

Strictly speaking, I wasn't really in St. Paul—I was hovering in a holding pattern till I could wing off. I hadn't even bought a winter coat—who'd want a down jacket in Paris? I just piled on extra sweaters, over that a heavy Peruvian alpaca job, and wrapped myself in a bright shawl as the bitter Minnesota cold drove deeper. I looked like a Russian peasant fleeing for my life.

This attitude of temporary residence made me sulky and inattentive. I lived my days in what Virginia Woolf called "moments of non-being," those nothing patches of time when consciousness nods off while the clock ticks relentlessly on. I might be here, but real life was elsewhere—and Elsewhere was my destination.

I was deep in this chilly state of non-being as I stood by the library checkout desk, waiting impatiently for my book to arrive. Idly, I noticed an older man, dressed in a shabby jacket, seated nearby. He was applying for a library card, apparently for the first time in his life. *Name, address, phone number, signature here, please*—he obediently followed the directions of the librarian on the other side of the table, pressing hard on the paper before him. She then handed him a brochure and a map of the library, along with a small sheet of paper that, she said, would allow him to begin taking out books that very day. His library card would be sent in the mail within two weeks, she told him. She smiled, clearly expecting him to scrape his chair back and go about his business.

But he didn't move. He looked down at the handful of paperwork and then up at the woman's face.

"How much?" he asked.

She looked back, not tracking. Then she laughed. "It's *free!*" she said. "This is a *public* library."

"Free?" he said doubtfully, as if the woman were demented. His face, worn and gray, had the cast of someone who'd never had occasion to believe anything was free. The beautiful big room, the massive arched windows with their mullioned glass, the marble floors, the purposeful hush of patrons fiddling at the wooden card catalog drawers—all this was *free?*

The look he gave the librarian wasn't one of delight but of disbelief.

Maybe a library, any library, *is* unlikely. How improbable, really, that a city should build a mansion for books and then let anybody troop in to use them, even to take them away for a while. Crazy! It goes against every Western cultural assumption about ownership and real estate, about possession and value. Civic buildings usually have to do with control and order, law and just punishment. Objects are *owned,* money and memberships and fees decide what you can have, what you can use. In a sense, ownership decides what you *are.* What's he worth? we say callously, demeaning even the rich.

To argue that, after all, we do "pay" for a public library—in tax levies—proves nothing. For the fact of unquestioned civic agreement about this shared expense returns to the public library its sovereign quality of being free, open, and *ours*—that is, everyone's.

The disbelief—a look of rare wonder—on the old man's face that day, his utter astonishment,

snapped me out of my own impatient non-being, my far-away fantasy life as I stood there watching him shamble off, holding his temporary card.

I wanted to write books, as well as read them. To be a writer—that was my real Elsewhere. Another thing that seemed unlikely. I wanted to claim some kind of homestead in the world of books, some ownership of the unreal estate of literature.

I was probably in kindergarten when my mother said we were going downtown and I would get a library card. That big pearly-white building, she said, as we walked from the St. Clair bus stop across Rice Park, is full of books. "I think you're going to like it there," she said.

I didn't read yet, but she said that didn't matter. There were books for people who didn't read, and soon I *would* read (this was going to happen, she seemed to suggest, by pure magic— *you'll be reading in less than a year*). How I would achieve this astonishing ability that she and my father and my older brother possessed was a complete mystery but still a certainty, apparently. I sat straight in a chair at home, holding my brother's books upside down and pretended to read, and he teased me. This was awful. It was clear that just *holding* a book carefully and with deep attention didn't seem to do the trick.

We went straight to the Children's Room, the low woody shelving making soft curving patterns in the room, the puppet theater curtained and tantalizing in the corner, and Miss Della McGregor bearing down upon us with her alarming makeup and her great shelf of bosom. She was an astonishing spectacle, all smiles and immense Eleanor Roosevelt teeth. But no—not someone to fear. This was the librarian, the woman in charge of all the children's books. My new best friend. My mother handed me over to her.

And what kind of books do you want to read? she asked, looking at me with adult regard, as if she and I understood I knew what I wanted and had business here. The inconvenient detail of my not being able to read didn't seem to play into the situation.

Fairy tales, I said. I should say I confided. Because fairy tales—weren't they the best, really the only point of learning to read?

Della McGregor nodded, the way waiters in gourmet restaurants nod when you have made a wise choice. She led me past her desk to a niche, a whole corner devoted entirely, she said, to fairy tales. *Think you'll find many things of interest here.*

So this was how you became a reader. By walking into the library.

Miss McGregor and my mother talked, and I paged and paged, sitting on what could only be called a tuffet, a little leather-covered stool on wheels that was set in front of the fairy tale bookcase. I amassed a pile of ten thin books, all with gorgeous pictures, and, yes, Miss McGregor confirmed, I could take them all home. Unbelievable.

Maybe that winter day in 1973 it wasn't the disbelieving old man in his shabby coat, but me in my arty Russian shawl who took in and marveled, as I hadn't since that day in the Children's Room, at the glory of the beautiful room, the ranks of the great arched windows marshaled along either side, letting in the dull gold late afternoon winter light that fell on the sheen of the stone floor. At the far end of the immense room, a phalanx of stacks formed a kind tunnel to the glass door leading to the yet more hushed galleries of the Hill Reference Library, where I used to sit at a dark wood table writing my high school term papers. It was the room where, in a way, I first was a writer, bent to my task, closed into another majestic room lined to the ceiling with books,

books, books. The most beautiful room I'd ever sat in—and somehow, it was mine. I could come in, claim my place, snap on the study lamp, and be—at home and also off to the wonderful, otherly Elsewhere I longed for.

It's a life, the habit of reading. And to be a civic benefit, reading must be part of civic life, a publicly shared habit, even though reading a book is probably the most private cultural act possible, one voice speaking directly to the eye and ear of a single individual.

We have to agree on what matters. That's what a culture is, after all. If we decide that books don't belong to us all, that reading is only a private business—there is no civic will for a public library. And that decides the public life we will give ourselves. Even more, it decides who we think we are, who we wish to be. And if reading matters in this communal way—then writing matters too. Each reader implicitly, inwardly knows that reading a book is not a spectator sport, but a participant sport, an active, not passive, activity. In a real sense, the reader *is* the writer too.

If there is a civic home where we can settle in and be ourselves, it is not in our courthouse where we judge and are judged, not in our places of worship where, inevitably, we divide ourselves into sects, and not in the malls and shops where we turn ourselves into the ultimate figure of individualism—the consumer.

The only civic home we can really claim together is here, in our library, the house we've made for books and music, magazines and films, all the ways we tell each other our stories and our news, our discoveries and uncertainties, the beautiful building where we are quiet in order to hear all the noise and news of the wide world beyond us, the great world we think is elsewhere but which beats along our very pulse.

Patricia Hampl

B

The Market House at Wabasha and Seventh Streets housed the Saint Paul Public Library on its second floor from 1900 until the building "burned like kindling" on the night of April 27, 1915.

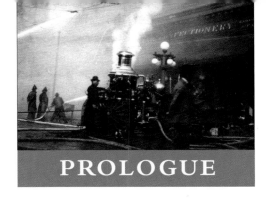

PROLOGUE

The Fire

TUESDAY, APRIL 27, 1915, dawned clear, sunny, and fragrant as only a spring day in Minnesota can be. The residents of the city on the white bluff overlooking the Mississippi were, for the most part, bustling and optimistic. Ever since its designation in 1849 as the capital of Minnesota Territory, St. Paul had experienced phenomenal growth, and civic leaders were convinced that energy and enthusiasm were all that were needed to propel their city toward ever greater eminence.

Two buildings, one commercial and the other judicial, dominated the center of town. Both were built on the farm once owned by pioneer settler Vital Guerin and purchased by the city in 1858, the year Minnesota entered the Union as its thirty-second state. At the northern edge of the property, located at Wabasha and Seventh Streets, stood the Market House. Thousands milled around when the market was open,[1] making the intersection the busiest in St. Paul. The oblong, two-story red brick building was built in 1881 on the same site as its original structure. The ground floor of the first Market House, built in 1853, had accommodated venders of meat and vegetables, while the second floor served as a center of government until a Territorial Capitol was constructed in 1854 at Tenth and Cedar Streets.

In 1881, a week after the second Market House opened, the Capitol burned down. Once again the Market House became a temporary home to offices of the state. Even after the second Capitol opened two years later, municipal judges S. W.

Flint and W. T. Hurr continued to hear court cases in the Market House until a splendid new Ramsey County Courthouse went up in 1885 at the southern edge of Guerin's former farm land.

With municipal services moved to their new home, the second floor of the Market House became St. Paul's convention hall. Mark Twain spoke there, and William Jennings Bryan thundered at audiences with his "Cross of Gold" speech. In 1900, the second floor of the Market House became the home of the Saint Paul Public Library. It was the library's third home. The library had first resided in the Ingersoll Building on Bridge Square, beginning in 1863, before moving in 1889 to four rooms on the third floor of the new courthouse. One room was for books, another was the reference room, and two more provided separate reading rooms for ladies and gentlemen. After outgrowing that space, the library moved to the Market House.

While most of St. Paul's citizens applauded the library's move to larger quarters, the chair of the library board did not. With eerie prescience, former Minnesota governor Alexander Ramsey pointed out to his fellow library board members that the move "would be from a fire-proof building to constant risk of fire."[2] A wooden awning, supported by poles handy for tying up a horse or team, shaded the sidewalk around the Market House. First-floor tenants included Clark's Restaurant, the Sharood Shoe Store, Boe's Millinery, Toumley's Cigar Store, the Central Clothing Store, and, fatefully, the Bosalis and Papas Confectionary.

Sam Craidone was stirring up a batch of candy in the basement kitchen of the confectionary store around nine o'clock on the night of April 27, 1915, when he smelled smoke. Racing up the wooden stairs, he shouted, "Fire!" A score of patrons in the confectionary rushed into the street. Employees grabbed the cash register and carried out tables and chairs. By the time the fire department arrived, the landmark Market House, one of the oldest buildings in St. Paul, was engulfed in flames. One witness said it "burned like kindling." A crowd estimated at twenty-five thousand gathered to watch, including young Alma Schmidt, who could see the blaze from her room at the YWCA. "Somehow one loves a library and it seems awful to have it burn," she later wrote to her mother. "It is so much more human than any other building."

Everything that could go wrong did. Firefighters struggled to enter the burning building but were driven back by smoke. Hoses burst. Assistant Fire Chief Miles McNally arrived at the scene in his chauffeur-driven auto and immediately sent his driver, Thomas Maloney, off to requisition more hose. The excited Maloney crashed the chief's car into the back of the Number 2 fire engine, snapping off a valve and sending a blast of steam forty feet into the air. The automobile then careened off and struck three firefighters, breaking Lieutenant John Costello's collarbone and wrist, shattering Captain Enoch Melander's leg, and injuring Detective Herman Vall. By the time the fire was put out, sixteen firefighters had been injured. One, Martin Kane, was reportedly near death from ulcers irritated by nine hours of exposure to smoke and lethal gas. Assistant Chief McNally was confined to his bed the next day, suffering from injuries

received when a stream from a fire hose struck him full in the face.[3]

Two heroes—John Conway and Clarence Thompkins—emerged from the disaster. Along with thousands of others, they were watching helplessly as the library burned when they suddenly remembered and resolved to save the "jade books." The jade books were a two-volume, limited-edition catalog titled *Investigations and Studies in Jade* and printed in 1906 on handmade paper. The catalog told the story of the more than one thousand pieces of nephrite jade in the Herber R. Bishop Collection in the Metropolitan Museum of Art in New York City. The press run consisted of one hundred copies only; after the books were printed, the type was scattered and all of the materials used in preparation of the books were destroyed. Bishop, an East Coast railroad and steel baron, died four years before the catalogs were printed, but he did designate the recipients, which included the British Museum and the Prince of Wales. Set number 26 found its way to the Saint Paul Public Library.

Clarence Thompkins was the superintendent of the Market House and knew of an unused stairway to the second floor of the burning building. He and Conway made their way upstairs, broke through windows and storage crates, and found the two jade books. As they started back the way they came, they were almost overcome by smoke and had to crawl out of the burning building on their hands and knees. Not an easy task, even under normal circumstances, given that each volume weighed about one hundred pounds, but their efforts saved the books. Neither the gold leaf on the cover nor the scarlet watered-silk endpapers were marred. Only a deep scratch on the red

Fire consumed the landmark Market House and most of the library's books and equipment on the night of April 27, 1915.

The Bosalis and Papas Confectionary shop where the blaze began was reduced to rubble.

leather binding of the first volume attested to the men's difficult rescue mission.[4]

Looking for a good story, newspaper reporters wrote that these two books were the only ones saved from the Market House fire. Yet the Saint Paul Public Library annual report for 1915 states that, of the 158,180 books in the library's collection, approximately 34,000 escaped the fire. Of these, 13,218 were in the schools, 12,734 were in the branches and stations, 7,143 were in the hands of library borrowers, 73 were in storage, 719 had been stored elsewhere, and 615 were at the bindery. Another 8,458 were "salvaged." Presumably, the books that were

salvaged were waterlogged volumes that had not been consumed by the flames.[5]

The loss to the library was estimated at $287,000 on the books and $20,160 on the furnishings for a total of $307,160. Unfortunately, the insurance on the building and contents was only $262,000. Another great loss was one of history. Dr. William Dawson Johnston, the library's director, had just completed years of work on a manuscript titled *A History of University Libraries.* At the time of the fire, it was ready to send to the publisher. The only copy was in Dr. Johnston's office, and it went up in flames with everything else.[6]

The embers from the fire were still hot when Thomas Barlow Walker, president of the Minneapolis Library board, wrote Mayor William Powers of St. Paul to offer St. Paulites the use of the Minneapolis library. Walker pointed out that, although the legislative act creating *his* city's library specified that its facilities "shall be forever free to the inhabitants of Minneapolis," the act did not prohibit extending its service *outside* the city limits. Therefore, Walker reasoned, it was within the bounds of the Minneapolis Library's authority to offer its services to St. Paul residents. University of Minnesota librarian J. T. Gerould circumspectly announced to the press, "If St. Paul's loss shall result in an increased demand for our facilities, we will be glad to do what we can to meet it."[7]

Three days after the fire, the Saint Paul Public Library reopened in temporary quarters at the House of Hope Presbyterian Church, then at Fifth and Exchange Streets in downtown St. Paul. In a symbolic gesture reflective of the religiosity of the age, the first book taken

On the third day following the fire, the Saint Paul Public Library reopened in temporary quarters at the House of Hope Presbyterian Church at Fifth and Exchange Streets.

into the new location was the Bible once owned by Captain Charles Sigsbee of the USS *Maine*. The Bible had been rescued from the battleship after it hit a mine in 1898 and sank in Havana Harbor, precipitating the start of the Spanish-American War. The Bible was later presented to the St. Paul Commercial Club.[8]

When it reopened in the church at noon on April 30, the library did a "rushing business," reported the *St. Paul News*, and within minutes of opening, thirty books had been returned.[9]

The burned-out Market House did not remain vacant for long. Construction began immediately on the Hotel St. Francis, considered to be the latest in modern hotels. When the hotel opened in December 1916, the press noted that "there will be electric lights in the clos-ets which make the carrying of lighted matches into the closet unnecessary, thus the elimination of one great source of fire."[10]

The *St. Paul Pioneer Press,* in an editorial titled "Out of the Crucible," sounded the prevailing note of optimism. "Out of the ashes of the 160,000 books destroyed by the fire Tuesday night there will arise, Phoenix-like, another and greater St. Paul Public Library." Praising Director Johnston's efforts to reopen the library so soon after the devastating fire, the editorial writer went on to philosophize, "It is not buildings or books but living men that make the world go round, develop it, educate it and better it. As long as St. Paul has these, she need fear not moth nor rust nor the fires of destruction. When a disaster serves to bring forth the power of a personality, it is not a loss but a gain."[11]

The library staff at House of Hope Church, June 15, 1915. First row, from left: Mildred Neal, Lucy Rahn, Helga C. Benson, Grace Fifield, Josephine Mann. Second row: Elizabeth W. Clute, Marie Oman, Isabelle Kay, Julia Hess, Stella Courteau, Edah F. Burnett, Ethel Jackson, Pearl Moore, Clara Bryan, Ethel Jensen. Third row: Bertha Buehrer, Hulda Paulson, Emily Pope, Bertha Barden, Marie Sprague, Della Edmunds, Adelaide Apfeld, Belle M. Owens, Myra Buell.

Little Crow's Village *by Klein Rabendorf (1854). The first of a succession of Dakota chiefs, each known as Little Crow, established the village of Kaposia on the east side of the Mississippi around 1750. The village moved to the west bank following the Treaty of 1837. The city of St. Paul grew up across the river from Kaposia.*

ONE

"A teacher coming should bring books"

EDUCATION MATTERED to the pioneers who traveled up the Mississippi River to seek their fortunes amid the hills and ravines where St. Paul now stands. In the spring of 1845, a young woman named Matilda Rumsey corralled the handful of children running around the settlement and brought them together in a primitive log building near the upper levee for classes. The makeshift school closed a few months later when, on June 23, Rumsey married, thus ending both her teaching career and the school. Her departure caught the attention of Dr. Thomas S. Williamson, who headed a mission to Little Crow's Kaposia band of Sioux living in a village across the river from St. Paul. Williamson wrote to William Slade, a former Vermont governor and now president of the National Popular Education Society, about his concerns.

"My present residence is on the utmost verge of civilization," he wrote, "within a few miles of the principal village of white men in the territory. . . . I have had frequent occasion to visit the village and have been grieved to see so many children growing up entirely ignorant of God and unable to read His word, with no one to teach them. I suppose a good female teacher can do more to promote the cause of education and true religion than a man. A teacher coming should

Teacher Harriet Bishop came to St. Paul in 1847.

bring books sufficient to begin a school as there is no bookstore within three hundred miles."

Williamson's letter to Slade resulted in the arrival, two years later on July 16, 1847, of teacher Harriet E. Bishop, a pupil from Catherine Beecher's Training School for Teachers at Albany, New York. While Bishop admired the Minnesota scenery— "all was wild and picturesque; bluffs rose abruptly to a height of 50 or 60 feet"—she was not impressed with the village. "Turning from nature, what a cheerless prospect greeted this view," she later wrote. St. Paul, when Bishop stepped out of the dugout canoe that bore her to the muddy landing, consisted of three American families, about forty Indians and French Canadians, and fewer than twenty log hovels. She began her career instructing nine pupils, two of them white, in a primitive bark-roofed blacksmith shop at the corner of Third and St. Peter Streets. The Dakota people called Bishop's school "Good Book Woman's House."

By the fall of 1847, the American population in Bishop's school had grown to six families. She noted, "The first winter closed in upon us . . . the river was fast bound in ice fetters . . . books were the companions that enlivened the solitude of our evenings."[12]

A member of the Minnesota Territorial Legislature, William Rainey Marshall authored the bill incorporating the St. Anthony Village Library Association, the first such attempt by Minnesotans to provide library services. Born in Missouri, Marshall had staked a claim at St. Anthony Falls in 1847 and afterward moved to St. Paul, where he engaged in several businesses, including hardware sales, surveying, banking, and newspapers. He served as a brevet brigadier general for the Union Army in the Civil War, and in 1866 was elected governor of Minnesota. Marshall urged passage of a black suffrage amendment and when it passed declared that the state is "now altogether free."

PUBLIC EDUCATION IN THE TERRITORY

The idea that all children should receive an education at the expense of the public was still new when Minnesota became a territory in 1849. Massachusetts, in 1837, had established a state board of education to coordinate its public school system, and soon other northern and western states adopted the Massachusetts model. Responding to the concerns of the settlers for the education of their children, Minnesota's first legislative assembly passed an act in the fall of 1849 to establish and maintain common schools.[13] In 1851, Governor Alexander Ramsey suggested that the Office of Territorial Superintendent of Schools be established. Slowly the concept of public libraries, as essential adjuncts to education, began to emerge.

In a move that was to later benefit St. Paul, the Peterborough Library, founded in 1833 in the small town of Peterborough, New Hampshire, became the first library in the United States to provide tax-supported free service to the general public. In 1854, the year St. Paul was incorporated as a city, the Boston Public Library began offering free services to local citizens. Many residents of St. Paul had roots in New England, and the two conflicting streams of their Puritan heritage, conservatism and enlightenment, flowed with them when they migrated to the West.

The year 1849 was likewise significant for Minnesota. Regular steamboat service began on the Mississippi, enabling more and more immigrants to find their way up the river to where the Falls of St. Anthony made navigation farther north impossible. In that year, the Minnesota Territorial Legislature not only created the Minnesota Historical Society, which quickly organized its own library, but also passed an act incorporating the St. Anthony Village Library Association. Though St. Anthony failed to act on the enabling legislation—it spent no money on books—the bill, authored by William R. Marshall, marked the first attempt by Minnesotans to band together to provide library services.[14]

COMPETITION OVER CULTURE

While the St. Anthony Library Association never circulated books, despite the word "library" in its name, it did present a lecture series— a "lyceum," in the parlance of the time. The lyceum in the village of St. Anthony aroused the competitive spirit of its larger neighbor, St. Paul. The writer of an editorial in the *St. Paul Chronicle and Register* complained, "Lieutenant Johnson, U.S.A., delivered a very interesting lecture before the St. Anthony Library Association on Thursday evening. . . . It is a burning disgrace to St. Paul, the capital of Minnesota, that our sister village of St. Anthony is allowed so far to outstrip us."[15] Though it lacked a lyceum, St. Paul *was* a city of readers, supporting four daily papers in 1854 at a time when the city's population did not exceed four thousand. No more than forty-five thousand people lived in the entire Minnesota Territory.[16]

Minnesota was soon to experience a flurry of educational activity, much of it generated by religious organizations. The Methodists established Hamline University in Red Wing in 1854; the Benedictine Fathers founded St. John's University in Collegeville in 1857; and in 1885 the Presbyterians organized Macalester College and Catholic Archbishop John Ireland opened the College of St. Thomas, both in St. Paul.

Regents chartered the University of Minnesota in 1851 and put up a building, but did not admit the first class of students until 1869. Reflecting the level of education in Minnesota at the time, the first class at the university consisted of thirteen freshmen and 217 preparatory students.[17] Professional associations came together. The Ramsey County Agricultural Society was chartered March 6, 1852, and the Minnesota Medical Society held its first annual meeting on January 7, 1854.

St. Paul's reputation for culture, diminished in the press by St. Anthony's lyceum program, was partially redeemed when, on August 11, 1856, the newly established YMCA came to the rescue. Following the example of the Boston YMCA, which in 1851 established a free library, the St. Paul YMCA opened a free reading room. This was an ambitious undertaking as the St. Paul Y had only eleven members at the time of its founding. However, in boldly opening a reading room, the organization was riding the crest of the times.

LIBRARIES AND REFORM

Nineteenth-century reformers, in their zeal to fight poverty, ignorance, and crime, identified the library as one of the agencies that would contribute to social betterment. These reformers were of old New England stock, graduates of eastern colleges who believed that their mission—a potent amalgam of self-interest, class fear, and humanitarianism—was to uplift and educate the poor. They firmly believed that Puritan-inspired moral standards were the rules by which people should govern themselves.

In the past, the social status of a lady or a gentleman had been determined at

birth by that of one's parentage. Now, in America's democratic society, gentility did not depend on one's lineage or wealth so much as by one's adherence to a recognized code of values and behavior. Reformers argued that books offered both a tutorial on how to behave and an escape to a better world for workers whose jobs barely provided a meager living. Approved fiction included the works of Horatio Alger, who wrote stories of hard-working, poor, but deserving lads (never girls) who acquired the skills and manners that admitted them to the world of the respectable. The moral was that gentility could be taught. Libraries were institutions that countered unwholesome pastimes, improved the moral lives of the poor, combated evils, and offered healthy spare-time activities. Libraries offered a way to arrest lower-class alienation from the values of traditional culture.

The Red Wing Building of Hamline University was constructed in 1855, thanks to a gift of land and a grant of $10,000 from the citizens of Red Wing, Minnesota. The building contained a chapel, library, laboratory, and dormitory, as well as recitation and reading rooms. Seventy-three students enrolled at Hamline its first year. Though the catalog referred to them as "ladies and gentlemen," they were, in fact, children or adolescents enrolled in preparatory courses. Hamline introduced its collegiate program in 1857; in 1859, it conferred degrees on Elizabeth and Emily Sorin, the first graduates of any college or university in Minnesota.

The first bookstore in St. Paul was opened in 1850 by General William Gates LeDuc, an attorney from Ohio who had moved to St. Paul to practice law. After successfully representing a client who paid him in land, LeDuc moved to Hastings, Minnesota, where he built a mansion that would later become the first site acquired by the Minnesota Historical Society (in the late 1950s).

A resident of Lowell, Massachusetts, in a typical argument for a free library, urged, "Let the library be free to all and then, perhaps, there will be one young man less in the place where intoxicating drinks are found. Make the library free to all and then, perhaps, there will be one young woman less to fall from the path of purity and goodness."[18]

The old idea of the library as a collection of musty, leather-bound classics, guarded by librarians and reserved for the exclusive use of a sophisticated, educated, male elite, was giving way to the concept of the library as a community resource that provided enlightenment for all levels of society. The role of the librarian was changing from that of a guard to watch over books to that of a guide to the world of wholesome reading.

But not just any books. Fiction was highly suspect. In 1881 the Boston Public Library was asked to exclude all fiction from its holdings on the grounds that the works were corrupting public morals. It was feared that a skillful writer of novels might arouse sympathy for sinners. For many years the Saint Paul Library would allow patrons to take out two books at a time on the condition that only one was fiction. The leading librarians of the country were unwavering in their belief that the role of the public library was to enforce moral orthodoxy.[19] The books housed in the library were to be the time-proven classics, serious, ponderous, and, above all, uplifting. Their aim was to instruct and elevate the public. Books and medicine were thought to have similar attributes: the more disagreeable the taste (or difficult a book was to read), the better it probably was for you.

The mere presence of a library in a community conveyed the idea that education need not end with formal instruction, but could continue throughout life. The library was to provide a way for the mass of citizens who had received only rudimentary schooling in childhood to continue their education.

Books were to be respected. State Representative Lona Schrieber, reared by her Finnish grandparents in Hibbing, Minnesota, remembers, "We had to wash our hands before we could read a book. And we'd never, never write in a book."[20] By 1856 three bookstores were in business in St. Paul.

THE MERCANTILE
LIBRARY ASSOCIATION

It didn't take long before the St. Paul YMCA's free library had competition. On September 18, 1857, thirteen months after the founding of the YMCA library, a group of young men organized a subscription library called the Mercantile Library Association. Mechanics and Apprentice Libraries had developed in the late-eighteenth and early-nineteenth centuries to "promote the orderly and virtuous habits, diffuse knowledge and the desire for knowledge and improve the scientific skill of mechanics and manufacturers."[21] Benjamin Franklin, that American apostle of self-improvement, had been among the first in the New World to foster libraries in which patrons paid a fee or dues for the privilege of membership. While Franklin's purpose was more recreation than education, these early societies kept the idea of libraries and the importance of access to information alive.

Mercantile Library Associations became popular in large eastern cities, where they were formed to offer educational facilities to young clerks and merchants as well as to apprentices whose parents could not afford to educate them. The Mercantile Library Association of New York was established in 1820 and quickly became the largest and most successful of all membership libraries. By 1871 it was the fourth largest library in the United States, exceeded in size only by the Library of Congress, the Boston Public Library, and the Astor Library in New York City—the predecessor of the New York Public Library. The Mercantile Library Center for Fiction, founded in 1820, still occupies an eight-story building in Manhattan.[22]

St. Paul's Mercantile Library Association got its start at a meeting in 1858 at Dr. T. D. Simonton's office in downtown St. Paul. Organizers quickly collected three hundred donated books and housed them in a reading room just above Wabasha on Third Street (now Kellogg), which the association opened to the public in early 1859. The press reported that "it is the intention to make it as attractive as possible by means of numerous files of papers as well as works of various kinds, periodicals. Chess will also add its charms." It appeared at first that the library was to be an all-male affair, but the newspaper went on to report that, "in time, it is the desire to open the room to the reception of ladies so that none shall be debarred the privilege of using the same."[23]

The association charged its members an initial fee of $5 and an annual subscription fee of $3. The first officers were Harwood Iglehart, president, and J. W. Cathcart, treasurer. The organization operated with a seven-man board of directors, a Library Committee of six, a Lecture Committee of five, and a Finance Committee of three. The constitution read, in part, "We, the subscribers, Merchants, Clerks and Business Men of the City of St. Paul, being desirous to adopt the most efficient means to facilitate mutual intercourse . . . have associated ourselves for the purpose of collecting and establishing a Mercantile Library and

Charles Edwin Mayo was active on the Saint Paul Library board and in the Minnesota Historical Society and served as president of both organizations. Mayo was born in 1827 in Brewster, Massachusetts, and was a lineal descendant of nine passengers on the **Mayflower.** *The son of a sea captain, Mayo joined the Boston Mercantile Library before moving in 1853 to St. Paul, where he went into the hardware business. His interests, however, were principally intellectual. He was active in the Mayflower Society, the Cape Cod Historical Society, and the Pilgrim Society of Plymouth, the organization that created the Faith Monument to commemorate the landing of the pilgrims.*

Reading Rooms to be appropriated to the use of young men engaged in mercantile and other pursuits."

The association published strict rules for the reading room in a small red handbook that was given to members:

No person shall be permitted to sit in the Reading Room with his hat on. No conversation shall be allowed in the Reading Room otherwise than in a whisper. No person shall be permitted to smoke, spit on the floor, damage or injure the furniture thereon or conduct in any way inconsistent with decorum. Any member may have the privilege of introducing a friend, not a resident of the city, whose name shall be registered by the Librarian in a book provided for that purpose and who will receive a ticket of admission to the Reading Room for the term of four weeks.[24]

Initially, the Mercantile Library Association prospered, evidenced by its fifteen-page booklet listing all of the volumes in its collection. Late in 1859 the association moved its library to what the press called "a spacious and airy room . . . adjoining Greenleaf's Jewelry Store on Third Street." The *Daily Pioneer and Democrat* noted that the new space was heated and open to members from 4:00 to 8:00 p.m. every day except Sunday. Authors represented in the library included American writers Washington Irving, James Fenimore Cooper, and Nathaniel Hawthorne and such Old World writers as Charles Dickens, Charlotte Brontë, and "Miss Austin."[25] Within a year the Mercantile Library moved yet again, to a building at Cedar and Third Streets.

The early libraries were a combination of a gentlemen's club and a home away from home. The early handbook for the St. Paul YMCA urged that the library reading rooms be carpeted because "there is an air about a bare floor exremely repulsive to many young men."[26]

After its first year of operation, Colonel D. A. Robertson assumed the Mercantile Library Association presidency, with Charles E. Mayo serving as vice president. Mayo was a tall, Massachusetts-born man who was president of the Minnesota Historical Society and a member of the National Academy of Natural Sciences. A local writer commented of Mayo, "He has never dealt in politics and consequently has saved himself many hours of humiliation and regret." Secretary R. F. Crowell and Treasurer R. O. Strong completed the roster of officers. When the Civil War began depressing the economy, the officers found it necessary, in 1860, to reduce the library membership fee from $5 to $3 and the annual dues from $3 to $1.50. Fees to attend lectures dropped to $1.

The YMCA library was also feeling the effect of the war on spending and dropped its lecture fees to ten cents. Competition from the Mercantile Library eventually proved to be too much for the YMCA library and its officers closed it in 1858, only to reopen it in 1861 when an anonymous benefactor arranged for the YMCA to receive "five years' lease of part of the second story of Ingersoll's magnificent building for a Hall and Library room—the only condition being that the estimated amount of rent therefore (two hundred dollars per annum) be raised by them and expended in the collection and maintenance of a public library."

Daniel W. Ingersoll was a busy reformer and educator whose limestone building housed the Second National Bank. He served on St. Paul's Board of Education for twelve years, as president of the State Temperance Society, and on the board of the Reform School of Minnesota. The library was a welcome tenant in his building.

This timely gift allowed the YMCA library to move its collection of books to the Ingersoll Building and conduct its regular Bible classes and other religious meetings in the space. The library was open on Tuesdays and Saturdays from 1:00 until 5:00 in the afternoon, with T. D. Simonton serving as librarian. The press expressed its approval of the new library:

> The arrangements of the Young Men's Christian Association for the convenience of the reading public deserve special notice. The Library and Reading Room will be opened this evening and continue accessible. By a late regulation, any person, male or female, on the payment of one dollar yearly, secures the freedom of books. Among 350 volumes, there are many attractive works. Ladies will find the library a very agreeable resort.[27]

Depressed economic conditions had forced the YMCA to reluctantly abandon its original ideal of a free library and charge its patrons a one-dollar annual fee. It was not alone in having difficulties. The Mercantile Library Association was also experiencing financial problems and, for a time in 1861, closed its doors for lack of funds. The closing of the library attracted the attention of the press. "Whatever has become of the Mercantile Library Association? We know the library is in existence and on the shelves in the rooms of the association, but what has become of the association?"[28]

Mercantile Library Association president J. W. Cathcart was quick to reply that the association was very much alive and that the reading room had been closed in October because of insufficient funds, but would soon be open to the public again. "The Association is entirely clear of debt and a determination to keep it so was the reason of closing the room. . . . During these war times it is not surprising that difficulty is experienced in meeting expenses."[29]

It was not easy to be an enthusiast for a library in a frontier town preoccupied with fighting a civil war. Historian J. Fletcher Williams noted that "continuous efforts were made by its directors to keep up an interest in the association but their efforts were not fully appreciated by the public. The society lingered along until 1862 when the directors made a more vigorous and successful effort and raised enough funds to purchase about 400 new books, making altogether about 1000 volumes in the library at the commencement of the year 1863."[30]

St. Paul had two tottering libraries, each competing with the other and each struggling to survive. No sooner would the YMCA library announce that twenty new volumes had arrived than the Mercantile Library Association would counter that forty new books would soon be ready for circulation from their organization. One writer lamented that in this small city of ten thousand residents there were two associations, each asking for the

Daniel W. Ingersoll was born in New Jersey in 1812 and moved to St. Paul in 1855. His dry goods business, the first in the state, ultimately occupied the first floor of his Ingersoll Building, while the second floor became the first public hall of note in St. Paul. Ingersoll was instrumental in organizing the St. Paul Chamber of Commerce and, for thirty years, served as an elder in the Presbyterian Church.

The Ingersoll Building on Bridge Square was built in 1860 and became a popular venue for speakers and entertainment. When Fort Sumter was fired on, Captain W. H. Acker used the hall to drill members of Company C, First Regiment of Minnesota volunteers. In February 1861, the ladies of the city's Protestant churches, in cooperation with the YMCA, gave a social in the Ingersoll Building to raise funds to establish the Saint Paul Library. The event was the building's dedicatory program.

support of the public for the same objects, each having its own friends and each a rival of the other.

THE MERGER

The obvious solution was to merge and consolidate the two libraries. The YMCA made the first overture. Delegates from each library agreed to meet on a Friday evening, October 30, 1863, under the temporary chairmanship of Daniel Ingersoll and secretary Charles E. Mayo. Representing the YMCA in the merger discussion were Ingersoll, H. M. Knox, George W. Prescott, the Reverend Edward Eggleston, W. S. Potts, D. D. Merrill, H. Knox Taylor, and T. D. Simonton.

On the side of the Mercantile Library Association stood D. A. Robertson, William Dawson Johnston, J. P. Pond, R. F. Crowell, W. B. Dean, R. Ramaley, R. O. Strong, and Charles Mayo. The men went to work, and by the end of the evening they had merged the two libraries into the new St. Paul Library Association, to be housed in the YMCA space in the Ingersoll Building on Bridge Square. Each library brought about a thousand books to the merger. Daniel Ingersoll was elected president of the new association, with Robertson vice president, Mayo recording secretary, Johnston treasurer, and Eggleston corresponding secretary and librarian. The annual cost of a "managing partnership" in the new library was set at $5 and a "reading membership" was $2. The press reported approvingly that "the Provisional Board of Directors organized harmoniously and set themselves about the noble task of founding a public library worthy of the intelligence and enterprise of St. Paul."[31]

The St. Paul Library Association opened the newly merged library on November 11, 1863. Among the holders of more than $100 in shares were several financial leaders of St. Paul, including John Nicols, iron trader and later a regent of the University of Minnesota; James C. Burbank, who was engaged in lumber, banking, and railroad concerns; John L. Merriam, Burbank's partner and organizer of two banks in St. Paul; and Daniel Ingersoll, merchant and president of the St. Paul Warehouse and Elevator Company. The new association's first annual report, issued in January 1864, noted that 448 shares in the library had been subscribed. While the library was, for the present, on a sound fiscal footing, the number of financial subscribers far

outnumbered the library's users. In a town of 10,401, fewer than three hundred had registered to take books from the library.[32]

Despite its meager membership, by 1870 the St. Paul Library Association had increased its book collection to more than four thousand volumes. Reflecting the firm control by the shareholders over book purchases, the collection was an assortment of conservative reference material and well-known literary works. An 1866 article in the *Pioneer Press* praised the purchasing committee's selections, and, reflecting St. Paul's no-nonsense community values, added, "The committee certainly deserves praise for selecting such a valuable lot of works, instead of the trashy novels that fill already too much space on the shelves."[33]

By 1865 residents of St. Paul were exhibiting literary ambitions. Mrs. W. J. Arnold edited and published a collection of poetry with the title *Poets and Poetry of Minnesota*. Though the quality of the verse was mixed, as local critics were quick to point out, the fact that a book of poetry was published and became popular at all indicated a degree of literary interest in the community.

THE MINNEAPOLIS LIBRARY
While St. Paul was merging two small libraries in an attempt to create one stronger institution, book lovers across the river in Minneapolis were likewise working to establish a library. In 1865 boosters had founded the Athenaeum, a subscription library, and housed it in a building with the Minneapolis YMCA. By 1875 the city had 32,000 inhabitants, but only 279 of them had become Athenaeum subscribers. The lack of interest in the library reflected the ponder-

A Visit from the Sage of Concord

RALPH WALDO EMERSON came to speak in St. Paul on February 1, 1867, by way of invitation from the Mercantile Library Association's lecture series and was paid a fee of $147. "The distinguished lecturer is not what the ladies would call a handsome man," reported the *Pioneer Press*. Noted another paper, "More than half the people who go to see him go to see his nose." Emerson spoke on the topic "The Man of the World." The philosopher-poet-essayist arrived in St. Paul by sleigh after one of the most tremendous snowfalls in the history of the state.

From an undated, unsigned typescript in the scrapbook of the Saint Paul Public Library's fiftieth-anniversary celebration.

ous nature of the books in the collection. Most were reference works written for the few scholars who might have occasion to engage in serious research.[34]

Realizing that the Athenaeum Library, as it was constituted, was fulfilling a limited role in the community, Charles A. Pillsbury organized the Mechanics Library Association in 1873 to provide for the reading needs of workers who, after all, made up the bulk of the population in Minneapolis. Henry Stimson, though an officer of the Athenaeum, reflected the prevailing attitude when he commented, "The Athenaeum has done good service but the town has outgrown it. This movement . . . of the mechanics . . . is only an expression on their part of what most of us feel, that the existing library privileges of the city are not what they should be."[35] Pillsbury's action precipitated the bitter dispute that broke out in the mid-1870s over the Athenaeum Library's future direction.

Born in Xenia, Ohio, in 1840, Thomas B. Walker was president of the Minneapolis Library board at the time of the 1915 fire at the Saint Paul Public Library. The timber and logging millionaire amassed one of the great private art collections of the Gilded Age. Contrary to the custom of the time, which aimed to create social barriers between the classes, Walker was committed to freely opening his gallery, located in his home in Minneapolis, to the public. He also provided free, comprehensive catalogs to his collection.

Chicago art critic William Curtis wrote of Walker in 1911: "Anyone, citizen or stranger, is at liberty to call at his residence on any week day, morning and afternoon, and inspect the gallery at leisure, and thus far this year more than 65,000 persons have taken advantage of the privilege. The rooms are so crowded, however, that there is not an inch of spare space upon the walls, and you have to squeeze between tall cases of matchless curios, as rare and as valuable as can be found in the Metropolitan Museum at New York or at the Kensington in London."

The Athenaeum librarian, Thomas Hale Williams, was a representative of the old school, and led the fight to preserve the status quo. He vehemently rejected the idea of making his beloved Athenaeum a "free" public library and opening its stacks to the unsophisticated and unlearned. Thomas Barlow Walker, who had made a fortune in lumber and now wanted a voice in civic affairs, led the opposition to Williams's position. Walker believed "that the rapid growth of the city called for a library which would meet the wants of a mixed population and be free to all."[36] It was the ancient elitist versus populist argument, this time over books and culture. The *Minneapolis Tribune* weighed in on the side of Williams and recommended in 1884 that Minneapolis not follow the example of St. Paul, where the library was merely full of popular fiction because of the lack of funds for more costly reference volumes.[37]

The battle raged for a decade and a half, and when it was over, Walker emerged the victor. The Athenaeum library board cut Williams's salary in half, he resigned the next day, and the board replaced him with a young Harvard graduate, Herbert Putnam, who immediately began planning for a free public library for Minneapolis.

THE LECTURE SERIES

The St. Paul Library Association continued to support the library through membership fees and the lecture series, which proved popular with Minnesotans isolated on the Northwest frontier. The series brought in such luminaries as Horace Greeley, Ralph Waldo Emerson, Henry Ward Beecher, Frederick Douglass, Bret Harte, Elizabeth Cady Stanton, and Susan B. Anthony, as well as Christopher Columbus Andrews, a writer and pioneer in Minnesota forestry. Minnesota lawyer and statesman Ignatius Donnelly was among the speakers who enthralled St. Paul audiences, whose fees helped pay the library's bills.[38]

The St. Paul Chamber of Commerce was quick to recognize the public-relations benefits of the library to the city's growing commercial sector:

The room has made more friends for St. Paul among weary and care-worn travelers than any other institution in the state. Nearly all of the prominent cities in the Union and Canada are here represented by their best Dailies; and many a weary and homesick invalid has had his aching heart warmed to cheerfulness by daily reading in the room the local news of his home paper. . . . One writer in a Southern Journal noted that "The St. Paul merchants have a larger number of papers in their free reading room than can be found in any other one room in the world, thus daily extending to hundreds of weary travelers a genuine hospitality and proving that kind politeness among strangers is *first cousin to Christianity.*"

The notice ended on a practical note:

As there is no intelligence office in this city for the male sex, our business men are strongly urged to promptly leave word at the Reading Room whenever they are in want of clerks, mechanics or daily laborers. By doing so they will accommodate themselves, kindly convenience strangers looking for work and greatly add to our present just reputation for cordiality to strangers.[39]

Notwithstanding the popular lecture series, the Reading Room—with its collection of out-of-town newspapers to cheer visiting salesmen and thousands of books on its shelves—the library had still not succeeded in capturing the imagination of the public. On at least two occasions the press commented on St. Paul residents' indifference to the library. "It is a lamentable fact," a writer editorialized in 1872, "that in a city of 25,000 inhabitants of the energy and intelligence of Saint Paul there are not at least 500 families that are willing to pay the small sum of $3 for the use of 5,400 volumes for one year." With a moralist flourish the writer added, "A public library should be a public educator rather than a supply depot for vitiated tastes."[40]

Six years later, in 1878, though St. Paul's population had almost doubled, attitudes toward the library had not changed. The editor of the *Pioneer Press* noted that "326 [library shareholders] for 40,000 intelligent and enterprising people at the head of navigation of the Mississippi river is not what it should be."[41] In the years between 1863 and 1880, the population of the capital city quadrupled to 41,473. But the St. Paul Library Association still had fewer than four hundred subscribers. That was about to change under the leadership of a soapmaking Methodist minister from Indiana.

Born in New Hampshire, Christopher Columbus Andrews studied law at Harvard and in 1857 came to Minnesota. He settled in St. Cloud, where he practiced law, and was elected state senator in 1859. During the Civil War, Andrews was taken prisoner for several weeks in 1862 near Murfreesboro, Tennessee. He rose to the rank of brevet major-general and was given command of the district of Mobile, Alabama, and later that of Houston, Texas. The author of several books, including **Minnesota and Dacotah** *(1856) and* **History of the Campaign of Mobile** *(1867), Andrews was a guest speaker at the Saint Paul Library lecture series. He served as U.S. minister to Sweden and Norway from 1869 to 1877 and as consul general in Rio de Janeiro from 1882 to 1885.*

Minnesota Prairie, *by Thomas P. Rossiter (1865), an example of one of those "great rolling land-scapes" to be seen nowhere as well as in Minnesota, said head librarian Edward Eggleston.*

TWO

St. Paul's First Librarian

AMONG THE YMCA LIBRARY and Mercantile Library Association board members who met for the fateful merger meeting in 1863, there was no more ardent bibliophile than the Reverend Edward Eggleston. It was not surprising that, before the end of the evening's discussion, he had been named the first librarian of the newly created St. Paul Library Association and given the task of cataloging its two thousand volumes.

Books had always been important to Reverend Eggleston. The Saint Paul Library's first librarian was born in 1837 in Vevay, Indiana, to a household with the largest private library in town. His father was a lawyer, an honor graduate of the College of William and Mary, a member of both houses of the Indiana Legislature, and a Whig candidate for Congress.[42] Too ill to attend school as a boy, Edward Eggleston spent his childhood reading Virgil, Pope, Homer, Emerson, the British poets, and Methodist theology from the books in his father's library.

Edward Eggleston, 1837–1902.

SEEKING HEALTHIER CLIMES

In the spring of 1856, Eggleston's already fragile health worsened. His lungs began to hemorrhage and, fearing he would soon die of consumption, his mother took him on a voyage down the Ohio River to St. Louis, Missouri. There, Eggleston met a group of fellow consumptives who, having heard reports that the air in Minnesota was healthful, were on their way up the Mississippi River. If the reports were true, this was an opportunity for him to save his life. Though he had barely enough money to pay his fare on the boat, nineteen-year-old Eggleston said goodbye to his mother and joined the group.

When his steamer, the *Ben Bolt,* arrived at Hastings, Minnesota, he disembarked and, after resting for a day, took a coach to Cannon City, where he had heard that jobs working in the open air were plentiful. In quick succession Eggleston became a chain-bearer for a surveying party, an amateur surveyor, the driver of a yoke of oxen breaking the prairie sod, and the vender of a recipe for making soap. He would later write of the area, "It marks an epoch in a man's life when he first catches sight of a prairie landscape, especially if that landscape be one of those great rolling ones to be seen nowhere so well as in Minnesota."[43]

At the end of the summer, his health vastly improved, Eggleston returned home, walking four hundred of the approximately one thousand miles to his southeast Indiana home. There, he resumed his studies for the Methodist ministry and did so well, despite his lack of formal education, that he

PREFACE.

A NOVEL should be the truest of books. It partakes in a certain sense of the nature of both history and art. It needs to be true to human nature in its permanent and essential qualities, and it should truthfully represent some specific and temporary manifestation of human nature: that is, some form of society. It has been objected that I have copied life too closely, but it seems to me that the work to be done just now, is to represent the forms and spirit of our own life, and thus free ourselves from habitual imitation of that which is foreign. I have wished to make my stories of value as a contribution to the history of civilization in America. If it be urged that this is not the highest function, I reply that it is just now the most necessary function of this kind of literature. Of the value of these stories as works of art, others must judge; but I shall have the satisfaction of knowing that I have at least rendered one substantial though humble service to our literature, if I have portrayed correctly certain forms of American life and manners.

BROOKLYN, March, 1873.

7

Preface to Eggleston's **The Mystery of Metropolisville,** *which he wrote in 1873 following nine years' residence in Minnesota.*

was ordained and assigned a circuit of ten preaching stations in southwestern Indiana. Eggleston plunged into the work, apparently with too much energy, for he soon became ill again. Convinced that he would die if he stayed in Indiana (he wrote in his journal that he was a "candidate for the grave"), he resolved to return to Minnesota. His brother, George, who became his biographer, wrote that Edward was not motivated to go to Minnesota in hope of gaining land or riches, as were others. "The only fortune he sought," George wrote, "was the privilege of living, the ability to go on breathing in spite of the condition of his lungs. It was the quest for health that led him to Minnesota—as it had Thoreau."[44]

THE ACCIDENTAL MINISTER

The summer of 1857 found Eggleston back in Cannon City, Minnesota, where, on July 4, a boating accident on the Mississippi claimed the lives of four people. When the local minister failed to appear for the funeral, Eggleston, a thin young man of twenty, stepped forward, said he was a Methodist minister, and offered his services. The boating accident later became a pivotal incident in Eggleston's only Minnesota-based novel, *The Mystery of Metropolisville.*

When the Minnesota Methodist Conference met in Winona in August 1857, the assembled elders accepted Eggleston on probation. His ordination papers had not yet arrived, but he dazzled the ministers of the church. The Reverend William McKinley of the examining board said of him, "There was something about him that attracted people at once. His powers of observation, description and conversation were phenomenal. He could talk better than any man I ever knew. His geniality, natural eloquence and magnetic personality made him a favorite everywhere."[45] The Methodist Conference assigned Eggleston to minister to two Minnesota towns: St. Peter and nearby Traverse des Sioux and much of the surrounding territory.

In 1850, the white population in Minnesota Territory was about 6,077, almost entirely confined to the small area between the St. Croix River on the east and the Mississippi River on the west. Stillwater, St. Paul, and St. Anthony were the only settlements of any size in the territory. The Treaty of Traverse des Sioux, signed in 1851, opened to white settlement an empire of twenty million acres west of the Mississippi. The ink was scarcely dry on the treaty before settlers stampeded in, cutting down the trees, plowing the prairies, building houses and barns, and laying out new towns. In 1860, just two years after Minnesota became a state, the population was 172,023, an increase of 2,700 percent in a decade. It was to this exploding frontier population that the young Methodist minister dedicated himself.

In preparation for what must have seemed a daunting task, on New Year's Day in 1858, Eggleston composed resolutions for himself that were reminiscent of those written by Benjamin Franklin and Cotton Mather. More monkish than Methodist, the resolutions outlined a strict regimen:

Rise at 4:30.
Devotion until 6.
Read the Bible until 7 (20 chapters).
Breakfast and exercise until 9.
Study until 11:30.
Five minutes of private prayer at the
    close of every hour.

The duties went on in similar fashion until the end of the day. As if this list did not cover enough aspects of his life, Eggleston composed another set of resolutions:

I will be neat and cleanly.

I will not eat or sleep more than is necessary.

Treaty of Traverse des Sioux *by Frank B. Mayer (1885) depicts the signing of the 1851 treaty with the Sioux.*

Purple Prose

"METROPOLISVILLE is again the red hot crater of a boiling and seething excitement. Scarcely had the rascally and unscrupulous county-seat swindle begun to lose something of its terrific and exciting interest to the people of this county, when there came the awful and sad drowning of two young ladies, Miss Jennie Downing and Miss Katy Charlton, the belles of the village, a full account of which will be found in the *Windmill* of last week, some copies of which we have still on hand, having issued an extra edition. Scarcely had the people of Metropolisville laid these two charming and much-lamented young ladies in their last, long resting-place, the quiet grave, when there comes like an earthquake out of a clear sky, the frightful and somewhat surprising and stunning intelligence that the postmaster of the village, a young man of a hitherto unexceptionable and blameless reputation, has been arrested for robbing the mails. It is supposed that his depredations have been very extensive and long continued, and that many citizens of our own village may have suffered from them. Farther investigations will doubtless bring all his nefarious and unscrupulous transactions to light. At present, however, he is under arrest on the single charge of stealing a land-warrant."

From The Mystery of Metropolisville *by Edward Eggleston.*

I will study every subject that comes to my notice thoroughly, avoiding superficiality.

I will preach without fear of man.

I will keep my responsibilities ever before me.

I will do or say nothing that would possibly bring reproach on the cause of Christ.

I will seek for zeal.

For a year Eggleston preached every Sunday in either Traverse des Sioux or St. Peter. During the week he hiked to villages farther west, making friends with the Native Americans and picking up legends he would later use in his children's stories. He walked because he was too poor to buy a horse. Stipends for Methodist circuit-riding ministers ranged from $9 to $40 a year, and many of them survived on the rabbits and squirrels they shot for food.[46]

While at Traverse des Sioux, Eggleston lived at the home of Thomas McGraw, a bricklayer, and while there came down with typhoid fever. Before his illness, he had become interested in another resident of the house, a young widow named Lizzie Snider. Believing that he was near death he confessed to Lizzie his feelings for her. Lizzie, who had been at his bedside almost continually during his illness, replied that she reciprocated.

Somewhat to his surprise, Eggleston recovered and a month later he and Lizzie married. Following their marriage he was appointed state Bible agent, which put him back on the road, once again covering the territory on foot. During a spring flood, he crossed a raging icy river by walking on the top of a submerged wooden fence. Seeking to spend more time with his bride, he resigned his Bible salesman job, moved to St. Paul, and accepted the pulpit of the Market Street Methodist Church. At the age of twenty-one, Eggleston had become the pastor of one of the largest Methodist churches in Minnesota. It was not an easy task.

FROM PASTOR TO PITCHMAN
The Market Street congregation had broken away from the larger Methodist

Church in St. Paul. The city was barely large enough to support one Methodist Church, let alone two, and Eggleston was not always able to collect his $400 annual salary. Nevertheless, he faithfully delivered two sermons every Sunday, taught Sunday school (which he thoroughly enjoyed), conducted the Wednesday evening prayer meetings, and was on call at all times for his parishioners. In his spare time he taught himself French.

From the Market Street Methodist Church, Eggleston was called, a year later, to a church in Stillwater, Minnesota, was named to the board of Hamline University, which had moved from Red Wing to St. Paul, and was ordained an elder. It was during his stay in Stillwater that Eggleston began to amass his own library, perhaps as a way to take his mind off the problems he faced with his congregation. His predecessor at the Stillwater church had made it his habit to knock at the back doors of his parishioners' houses when making pastoral calls. This gesture of humility was not Eggleston's style. He entered the homes of the members of his congregation by the front door and, as a result, got a reputation for being a snob and much too forward for a minister.[47] Eggleston endured the situation for a year and then asked for a leave of absence from church affairs to go into the soap manufacturing business.

It is probable that Eggleston needed the money as his family grew. A few months after his resignation from the Stillwater church, a Mankato newspaper carried an advertisement for Economic Soap. It read, in part,

> The Economic Soap saves Rubbing
> The Economic Soap saves Boiling
> The Economic Soap saves Bleaching
> It saves Work
> It saves Time
> It saves Trouble
> It saves Patience
> It saves Health
> It saves Everything.[48]

Despite the extravagant benefits Eggleston claimed for his product, Economic Soap did not sell well. Although the business made a bare living for his family, the effort required to sell

Market Street Methodist Church in St. Paul, ca. 1860.

soap was distasteful to him. He discovered that he was not a businessman, and so, after struggling with it for a few months, he abandoned the enterprise.

After recovering from a long illness, Eggleston accepted the post of pastor of St. Paul's Jackson Street Methodist Church. His health was never robust, and he expended it so recklessly that he had to take periodic long rests if he were going to continue at all. The Jackson Street Methodist Church was a large and prosperous congregation and the parishioners, noting their pastor's threadbare clothes, presented him with a fur-trimmed and fur-lined overcoat, overshoes, cap, and gloves. They were the finest clothes Eggleston had ever owned.

The Jackson Street church was the most important Methodist church in Minnesota, with 120 members and property valued at $5,000. Eggleston's annual salary was $600.[49] Under his administration, the Jackson Street Sunday school increased in popularity and Eggleston became known as the "Sunday School Man." When he was occasionally ridiculed for his short-lived enterprise in selling soap and the process for making it, he replied, "I am prouder of my soap recipe than I am of my preaching; for the soap was above criticism while the sermons certainly were not."[50]

In the early spring of 1863, Eggleston began taking some small but significant steps to change his life. He jotted down in a notebook every Hoosier expression he could remember from his childhood, phrases like "right smart" and "mighty purty." And then, perhaps for the first time in his life, he read a novel. While Eggleston had grown up with books and

had been an avid, if not compulsive, reader all of his life, all of the books he read had been classics. From childhood he had been told that novels were evil and a waste of time. Reading fiction at this point in his life reawakened his desire for a career as a writer, an activity to which he had been drawn for much of his life. That he had a writer's aptitude should have been obvious to anyone who listened to the stories he told his Sunday school classes or observed his students' rapt attention. The reports Eggleston wrote to his supervisors during his circuit-riding days had been far superior to those composed by others.

A MODEL LIBRARIAN

In May 1863, Eggleston resigned his church post and became a writer by night and operator of a stereopticon exhibit by day. It was an attempt to provide for his family without totally exhausting himself. Using a large canvas measuring 225 square feet, he gave illustrated lectures with views of Windsor Castle, Melrose Abbey, and other famous scenes. His first performance in Ingersoll Hall did not go well; his gaslight ran out of fuel and the projected images were dim and blurred. Fortunately, most of his audience was pleased with the novelty of the performance and were too inexperienced to complain. Later on, he resolved most of his technical difficulties. The *Pioneer Press* declared the entertainment to be an unqualified success: "He had got his instrument to complete working order now and it threw up the views on the canvass last night with wonderful effect."[51]

Eggleston's performances were popular in St. Paul because he included pictures of local personalities and scenes, but when he toured Minnesota with his slides, he found that fewer people were interested. It was at the end of 1863 that he became librarian for St. Paul. He brought to the post energy and dedication. The *Pioneer Press* noted that "Mr. Eggleston, who had charge of the arrangements and classification of the volumes, has peculiar talents as a librarian. We wish his services may be secured permanently in that capacity."[52]

That was not to be. Though Eggleston is identified as a director of the library at a meeting in late January 1865, he is not mentioned in connection with the library again, and by June Evan E. Edwards had become the librarian. The large Methodist Church at Winona, Minnesota, had offered Eggleston its pulpit and he accepted. He stayed for two years, was active on numerous committees, built up attendance in the Sunday school, and then resigned, again because of poor health. Also influencing his decision to depart was his desire to write. He had sold several children's stories to America's first periodical for children, *The Little Corporal*. When he was offered the associate editorship of the magazine in Chicago, he jumped at the chance.

Eggleston's fellow clergymen were dismayed at his decision. The reading and writing of novels was not considered wholly respectable. One of Eggleston's colleagues, the Reverend Cyrus Brooks, wrote, "His present occupation, novel writing, seems out of harmony with the ministerial calling and has brought upon him severe and perhaps not wholly unmerited censure. But those who know him best will be slow to believe him mercenary or false to his convictions of right."

In his luggage, as he packed to leave Winona in 1866, Eggleston carefully placed his dictionary of Hoosier expressions along with an outline and the first chapters of a book titled *The Hoosier Schoolmaster*. Published in 1871, the book would rocket him to international fame and prosperity.

Though he served only a few months as the Saint Paul Library's first librarian, Eggleston was a model for librarians of the future. He brought to the task his love of books and their orderly organization so that they could be made available to the public. His notebook, in which he painstakingly cataloged his own private library during the year he lived in Stillwater, is in the collection of Cornell University.

Historians of American culture credit Eggleston with pioneering the writing of realistic, regional literature. He was among the first, in his book *The Hoosier Schoolmaster,* to write about American scenes and themes. Generations of children read his popular "Chicken Little" stories. When Eggleston left Minnesota, he went on to help secure the passage of an international copyright law, write books of history, and become president of the American Historical Association. He never lost his concern for children. The work he began in Minnesota churches to humanize the Sunday school continued throughout his life and he promoted the cause of kindergartens when others regarded them with derision and ridicule. Edward Eggleston shared in Minnesota's heroic age. The pen that wrote a nineteenth-century literary classic was also the pen that cataloged the first two thousand books of St. Paul's new library.

The Saint Paul Library's circulation desk in the Market House with its closed shelves behind it.

THREE

Toward a Free Public Library

THE FINANCIAL STRAIN of the Civil War drained the resources of the patrons of St. Paul's library. Subscription fees could not keep up with expenses. For four years the fledgling Minnesota Historical Society rented a small room adjoining the library's two rooms in the Ingersoll Building to house its own collection and paid the St. Paul Library Association $10 a month. While welcome, this financial help was not enough. Struggling to remain solvent, the library board raised the price for reading memberships in November 1864 from $2 to $4 a year and charged shareholders $2 a year in addition to their annual payment of $5. When the increased fees did not bring in enough funds, and with the financial situation of the library growing ever more dire, the board experimented further with fees. In 1866, the library reduced the membership fee to $3 a year and raised the annual cost to shareholders from $2 to $3.

Besides losing money, the library was losing its librarian and many of its books. Evan Edwards resigned as librarian in early 1866, and Josephine Kelly took his place. Kelly found the library in deplorable condition. Books were disappearing, either through theft or carelessness, and many that were returned were defaced with scribbling and notes. From its inception the library had operated with a system of open shelves. Patrons browsed through the shelves of books, took what they wanted, and wrote the names of their selections on a piece of paper for the librarian to record. It was time to change the system. To the ire of many of

the patrons, Kelly, with the approval of the library board, closed off access to the shelves of books. She explained the new system in a memorandum to subscribers: "A new and complete catalog has been furnished members from which they may select their books using a blank slip provided for that purpose. The charge will be made and the book delivered at each end of the librarian's desk."[53] She softened the blow by stocking the most recent arrivals on shelves at each end of the librarian's desk, "so arranged that the books can readily be seen by visitors and selections made from them."

The efficient and determined Josephine Kelly resigned in December 1869, to be replaced by Maggie E. Creek. Creek served until May 1871, when her post was taken by her sister, Mary S. Creek, who was to stay for six years, until 1877. Under the direction of Mary Creek, the outlook for the library began to improve. The book collection continued to grow, the lecture series brought in a little more than $2,200 in one year, and, despite public indifference, St. Paul managed to put together the second largest collection of books in the state. The board reported, "We believe in the sympathy and confidence of the community and so possess more elements for the successful prosecution of our work than at any previous date in our history."[54] The *Pioneer Press* added its accolades: "If there is an institution in this city that deserves support, and a good generous support, it is the St. Paul Library. . . . It has been kept alive by a few able, plucky and persistent citizens who have been determined that it shall be a permanent institution."

In 1879, when Alexander Ramsey was president of the St. Paul Library Association, his proposal that the institution become a public one was rejected. Ramsey, a native of Pennsylvania, is the only man to have served as both territorial governor and governor of Minnesota. His administration was known for sound economic management, especially of the state's school lands. While in office, he offered the first Union Army volunteer regiment to fight in the Civil War. Before becoming governor, he was superintendent of Indian Affairs. Ramsey (1815–1903) was elected mayor of St. Paul in 1855 and later elected to the U.S. Senate.

Charles J. Ingles, an enthusiast for the library from his youth, remembered when the library annual fee was $3. "Five dollars bought a double ticket and a life membership was granted for fifty dollars. This last was offered yearly as a prize to a high school pupil graduating with the highest honors. My own first membership was given me as a Christmas present in 1877. It was the most highly prized of all my presents for that year."[55]

TAX SUPPORT

Once people accepted the idea of compulsory education and tax support for schools, public support for libraries became the logical next step. (The number of public schools in Minnesota was increasing; by 1870 there were seventeen high schools in the state.) Massachusetts and New Hampshire led the way in legislating public support for libraries, passing laws in 1847 and 1848, authorizing towns to tax themselves to finance libraries. Maine, Vermont, Rhode Island, and New York soon followed.[56]

Despite the Civil War and the hard times associated with it, the number of libraries in the United States continued to grow. Between 1825 and 1850, 551 libraries were established while 2,040 were opened from 1850 to 1875. While most were still the dues-paying, subscription-type of library, by 1876 there were 188 free municipal public libraries supported by taxation in eleven states, from Massachusetts, which had 127, to Iowa and Texas, with one library each.[57]

Despite Minnesota's population of New England transplants, it was not until 1879 that the state adopted Chapter 106 of the General Laws, which permitted communities to levy taxes for the support of public libraries. Within months

of the passage of Minnesota's library law, Zumbrota became the first city in the state to establish a free public library. Within two years, Fairmont, Sauk Center, Jackson, and Alexandria followed Zumbrota's example. Noting what was happening in neighboring communities, former governor Alexander Ramsey, president of the St. Paul Library Association, proposed in September that the St. Paul City Council take over the subscription library and run it as a free public library. The council turned him down. One member scornfully referred to the library, which at that time had 6,000 volumes, of which 971 were reference works, as "light, useless reading."[58]

Three years later the Library Association's board of directors again went to the city to petition it to accept the library and finance it under the 1879 general library law. This time the economic climate of the city was better. The Northern Pacific Railroad connecting Minnesota's capital with the West Coast was almost completed. The seven-story Ryan Hotel was under construction at a cost of a million dollars, and Macalester College, formerly the Baldwin School, was soon to open with seventy-five students. A mood of optimism prevailed.

OPENING A FREE PUBLIC LIBRARY

On September 5, 1882, the St. Paul City Council passed a resolution that appropriated $5,000 to establish a public library in the capital city, to be supported by taxation. The vote was 8 to 2.[59] The mayor appointed a new city library board, composed of the same men who had been active in the old association, and they wrote a new set of bylaws. Alexander Ramsey continued as president, Maurice Auerbach was vice president, and William H. Kelley served as secretary of the nine-member board. Each member was to serve for three years. The Saint Paul Public Library was officially organized on September 25, 1882, and opened for service to the community on January 2, 1883.[60]

When the board members of the St. Paul Library Association looked back on their eighteen years of struggle to reach this point, they found many accomplishments to be proud of. They had kept a reading room open, supplied with the best periodicals and magazines published in the United States, and regularly added new books. They had published three catalogs of the library's books (in 1864, 1868, and 1872), and introduced a growing number of children to the delights of a library. Almost 75 percent of the library's patrons were "of the juvenile class," and book purchases reflected children's interests. The library they turned over to the city in the fall of 1882 contained 8,051 books stacked on shelves in rooms in the Ingersoll Building. To manage the enterprise they also bequeathed to the city a capable librarian, Helen J. McCaine.

Opening day for the new library was momentous for St. Paul schoolboy Charles Ingles, who had received a library card as a Christmas gift. Ingles had taken an after-school job with the library in May 1882, staffing the library from 6:00 until 9:00 in the evening. On Saturday mornings he came to the library to do the sweeping and dusting. "Our location was on the second floor of the Ingersoll Building," he remembered. "The Reading Room was on the Third Street front while the book stacks were in the rear and extended further west toward Bridge Square. The rest of the floor was occupied by doctors' and dentists' offices. The third floor [at that time] was vacant."

On January 2, 1883, the day the new city-supported library opened, Ingles rushed to his post from school and arrived at 2:00 p.m. "Rather to my surprise I found things very quiet," he wrote. "In those days every patron signed his name in a register, of which there were two, one for men and one for women, the odd numbers being given to the men and the even numbers for the women. . . . The first card was issued to Col. Henry L. Carver, an old resident and a member of the Library Board. The second . . . was given the Rev. J. Nattrass, a retired Presbyterian minister. It shows how slowly things moved when I say that by the afternoon I had issued the sixth card to Mr. John Walker Adams, now a resident of New York City."[61]

The slow start on opening day was not indicative of the public's response to the free public library. "People soon learned that they could draw books free of charge and soon we were abounding with

Saint Paul Public Library vice president Maurice Auerbach emigrated in 1857 from Germany to St. Paul. He became a community leader involved in every large financial undertaking in the city.

patrons," Ingles said. "In a short time another clerk was employed, Miss Grace Spaulding (later Mrs. Edward Randall). We also acquired a janitress, in the person of Miss Mary McCloskey, who remained with us for two or three years."[62] The St. Paul Chamber of Commerce noted the increased use of the library. "The free circulating library on Third Street is most generously patronized, the number of daily visitors averaging 100. It has a collection of 12,000 volumes."[63]

Every resident or individual with a permanent place of business in the city could register to borrow books. Cardholders could take out two books at a time and keep them for two weeks. Exceptions were recently purchased books, which could be taken out for one week only and could not be renewed. Fines for overdue books were three cents a day. If it became necessary for the library to send a messenger to collect the overdue book, the delinquent borrower was charged an additional twenty cents. By

the end of 1884, 3,492 people had become cardholders of the library.[64]

The librarians continued to see themselves as guardians of public morals. Books considered not suitable for the library's readers were hidden or given away. When Ingles worked at the library he noted, "On a lower shelf were placed a number of volumes which had been removed by Miss Creek, I believe, as unfit for circulation. Among them were a number of Ouida's novels, which were given to a young high school friend who assisted at night, while I chose the first and only volume of the essays of Montaigne. This I took because of the date, it having been published in London in the year 1700. I never read it. Later I was amused when a set of the essays, in three or four volumes, an unexpurgated edition, was placed upon the shelves and no comment was made. It illustrates the mental attitude of the day."[65]

The popularity of the library soon overwhelmed the two rooms on the second floor of the Ingersoll Building, and in June the library moved up to the third floor, occupying the entire space of what had been Ingersoll Hall. The room had high ceilings and was lighted on three sides by tall windows providing views of the river as far downriver as Newport and upstream to Fort Snelling. The ceiling of the hall was a source of pride to Daniel Ingersoll, an impressive figure with a long, white beard. He had had a paper hanger divide the space into panels and outline them with crimson-colored paper. Ingersoll would bring friends to the third floor, grasp them by the arm, and exclaim, "Look aloft and admire."[66]

The new third-floor quarters were heated with stoves, but because of the many windows, the space was drafty and cold

The floor plan of the Saint Paul Public Library when it was housed on the third floor of the Ingersoll Building. The sketch was made by Charles J. Ingles for the observance of the library's fiftieth anniversary.

in winter. The librarian's desk was located in the southwest corner of the space. A small reference room took up the northwest corner and was scantily stocked with dictionaries, encyclopedias, atlases, a gazetteer, and *Alibone's Dictionary of Dates*. The room was occupied most of the time by a retired schoolteacher who used it as a retreat. He dozed there by the hour, accompanied by a small dog that would curl up under a table and join him in going to sleep.[67]

TO THE COURTHOUSE
Even the additional third-floor space in the Ingersoll Building was makeshift, so in 1889 the city decided to move the library to the west side of the third floor of the newly built courthouse, between Cedar and Wabasha and Fourth and Fifth Streets. The Chamber of Commerce, always a booster for the library, reported that "the St. Paul Public Library has a collection of books that have been chosen with rare discrimination. Many of the books are of a class to be found only in the best libraries of the country. The General Laws of 1879 authorized a tax levy of half a mill on the dollar for a library fund, only a portion of which has been used thus far. Large and well-lighted rooms have been secured in the new Court House into which the Library will be moved early in the spring of 1889."[68]

While the move to the courthouse provided the library staff with the advantages of steam heat in winter, electric lights, and an elevator, and was an improvement over the Ingersoll Building, which had housed the library for twenty-eight years, the rooms in the courthouse were poorly arranged for a library and badly ventilated. The librarians made the best of it. Despite the cramped nature of the space, in the ten years that the library was in the court-

house, the librarians increased the collection from 26,000 volumes to 51,000 and book circulation from 100,000 to 261,000. Politicians did what they could to help.[69] When the room set aside for children's books was needed for other purposes, Mayor Andrew R. Kiefer donated his office for the children's room.

Nevertheless, scarcely a year after the move, it was obvious to the board of directors that the courthouse space would quickly become inadequate. And so began the lengthy effort to find permanent, or failing that, improved housing for the Saint Paul Public Library. That effort would be preceded by expansion of services via library branches, or stations, and by a school outreach program, all ably led by head librarian Helen J. McCaine.

This imposing St. Paul City Hall/Ramsey County Courthouse, with its fifty gargoyles peering down from the walls, was built in 1889. Designed by Edward Bassford, it stood on Fourth Street between Wabasha and Cedar. A muddled attempt at Richardsonian Romanesque architecture, it was described in 1925 as "antiquated, inconvenient and an architectural mistake." The building had so many faults—terrible acoustics in the council chamber, poorly laid out rooms, expensive to maintain—that, with few regrets, it was torn down in 1933.

Helen McCaine,
1835–1922.

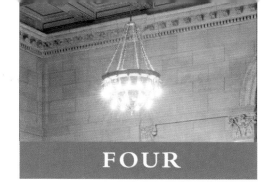

FOUR

The Reign of Helen McCaine

IT WAS A REMARKABLE coincidence that the woman who was the first librarian of St. Paul's free public library came from Peterborough, New Hampshire, the community credited with being the first in the nation to establish a free, city-supported public library. Born Helen J. Gray on June 16, 1835, in Peterborough, she attended the Peterborough Academy, a college established in 1837 by Nathan Ballard, a graduate of Dartmouth. She moved with her husband, William McCaine, to St. Paul in 1874. His work with the Bensteinite Manufacturing Company took him away from his wife for long periods of time.

With no children, nor close relatives in St. Paul, Helen McCaine had time on her hands. Possessed of a love of reading and libraries, particularly public libraries, she began volunteering her time at the subscription library. She moved quickly up the ranks to assistant librarian and then, in 1877, when Mary S. Creek resigned, to the position of head librarian.

PROTOTYPICAL FEMALE LIBRARIAN

McCaine took over the Saint Paul Public Library at a time when very few women were active in the business and professional world. In the Victorian Age, it was believed that women were handicapped in their work because they had a more delicate physique than men and were unable to endure continued mental strain.

With the "the calm, quiet dignity and strength which we associate with New England women,"[70] McCaine embodied the genteel Victorian belief in a woman's superior sensitivity and spirituality (a rationalization for a woman's secondary status) and personified the position of the lady as the custodian of culture and morality. Melvil Dewey, a later president of the American Library Association, held that women librarians had a greater opportunity to do good work than did either teachers or clergymen. The librarian, he argued, could reach those who never entered a church or attended school. When such opportunities for altruistic service lay before her, what woman librarian would stoop to a vulgar discussion of money? Women in general were expected to accept lower salaries because they did not have a family to support, a rationale accepted by men and women alike. In 1884 the combined annual salaries for St. Paul's head librarian, three full-time assistants, one part-time assistant, and a janitor was $2,427.70.[71]

The self-abnegation expected of women librarians was expressed by Mary Ahern, editor of the journal *Public Libraries,* who wrote, "No woman can hope to reach any standing . . . in the library profession . . . who does not bring to it that love which suffereth long and is kind, is not puffed up, does not behave itself unseemly, vaunteth not itself, thinketh no evil."[72]

A tireless worker, McCaine operated on the premise that she was discharging a sacred trust for the public, one that used her full knowledge of literature as well as her strength and conscience. Genuinely modest, she had a low estimate of her powers and abilities and was truly unconscious of the place she came to fill in her profession. She would not tolerate any publicity about herself and even restricted the circle of those who knew and appreciated her.

A typical turn-of-the-century librarian, McCaine kept her personal publications to a minimum. They were a modest assortment of book lists she wrote on such topics as *Selected Books on Gardens and Gardening, Select List on Fungi and Mushrooms,* and *Select List of Books for Sunday School.* Writing anything additional would have looked, to her, as if she were seeking publicity.

MENTORED BY POOLE

McCaine had been in her post but a few weeks when the superintendent of schools suggested that the city send her to the Chicago Public Library for three or four weeks to study library management. The Chicago Library did not offer formal training in librarianship, merely an opportunity to observe head librarian William Frederick Poole, one of America's most prominent librarians, in action. McCaine's brief apprenticeship under Poole was the only library instruction she received. No other librarian in the United States fared any better, however. Melvil Dewey would not found the nation's first library school, at Columbia University, until the late 1880s.

A tall man with walruslike whiskers that flowed down past his coat collar, Poole had headed the Chicago Library since 1874 and had impressive credentials. Before moving to the Windy City, Poole had been librarian of the Mercantile Library Association of Boston, librarian of the Boston Athenaeum, and librarian of the Cincinnati Public Library. Poole was the originator of *Poole's Index,* a guide to periodical literature, and had

developed a system of book arrangement by major subject headings.

In 1885, Poole was elected the second president of the American Library Association, which was founded in 1876 in Philadelphia during that city's centennial celebration. During that event, 103 of the nation's 209 librarians gathered to form the association. Again, New England dominated; 99 of the librarians were from Massachusetts or New York. The members elected Justin Winsor, head of the Boston Public Library, as its first president. Winsor, who went on to become head of Harvard's library, was succeeded after nine years by Poole, the acknowledged elder statesman of the profession. The third president was Charles Cutter, librarian of the Boston Athenaeum.

Winsor, Poole, and Cutter were the old guard of the library profession, intent on shaping the moral values of society. Their social beliefs, which dominated library philosophy at the time, were that family, education, and righteous behavior were the marks of a gentleman or lady in the community. Genteel, urbane, and ceremonial, Poole was reluctant to give up old methods of administration and was suspicious of new ideas. Only after a protracted battle with these older elements of the association did Melvil Dewey, with his new ideas on cataloging, come to dominate the American Library Association in the mid-1880s.

Poole's work and attitudes greatly influenced Helen McCaine, who held lofty standards for what a library should be. Poole was opposed to open shelves at the Chicago Public Library, so the shelves in the Ingersoll Building remained closed. Poole was opposed to the idea of public access to a card catalog of books; so was

William Frederick Poole of the Cincinnati and Chicago Public Libraries mentored St. Paul's Helen McCaine.

Justin Winsor was a founder of the American Library Association in 1876 and was superintendent of the Boston Public Library as well as librarian of Harvard University.

McCaine. In its early days the Saint Paul Public Library had not had a card catalog and instead had issued printed lists of books from which readers could make their selections. The first card catalog consisted simply of slips of paper filed in a cardboard shoebox. During the early years, Helen McCaine had the staff keep track of the circulation by dropping peas in the compartments of a tin box that had divisions for the various kinds of books.[73] As the collection grew, she had no recourse but to introduce a card catalog on which the title, author, and subject of each book was listed, but for several years she reserved the cards for the use of the staff only.

McCaine's management of the Saint Paul Public Library reflected her profound conservatism and adherence to traditional ways. Reflecting her New England background and Poole's influence, she was never the first to try out a new idea, and would institute changes only when they had been proved successful by others. Despite her adoption in 1900 of Dewey's decimal system of cataloging—a radical step on her part because Poole largely opposed it—McCaine continued to be distrustful of anything new.

She and Gratia Countryman, her counterpart in Minneapolis, were entirely different individuals. When Countryman was appointed head librarian in 1904, she immediately created an open-shelf room in the Minneapolis Library. Across the river in St. Paul, McCaine remained cautious and did not move toward open shelving until 1910. Countryman, who was a leader in librarianship and later became president of the American Library Association, had more foresight and imagination. She was dedicated to taking the library out to the people and

believed in expanding the services and facilities of the library to match the explosive growth of Minneapolis. McCaine also had leadership abilities. She was one of four librarians who met at the Minnesota Historical Society offices on December 29, 1891, to form the Minnesota Library Association and was elected vice president. McCaine did not, however, become overly involved in plans to build a new facility for the Saint Paul Public Library, leaving that, more or less, to the library board for much of her tenure. She was more dedicated to building a high-quality collection of books.

McCaine's strength and expertise was in selecting books for the library, a skill that earned her a nationwide reputation. To the library world's amazement and admiration, she personally scrutinized and partially read almost every one of the tens of thousands of volumes that entered the Saint Paul Public Library. She regularly wrote up lists of titles she suggested be purchased and submitted them to the library board for their approval. There is no record of a board member ever failing to approve her recommendations. During her tenure the library collection grew from 6,000 books in 1877 to 148,000 in 1913. There were 608 periodical titles and 82,000 clippings on 1,200 subjects in the newspaper clipping collection.[74] Only twenty-one libraries in the entire United States had larger collections.

LIBRARY STATIONS AND SCHOOL OUTREACH

McCaine preferred to busy herself with book selection and management than to put her efforts into outreach programs. Still, in 1885, she began sending discarded library books to the city jail, workhouse, and hospitals, where she thought they could be of benefit. She inaugurated a

Charles Cutter was the librarian of the Boston Athenaeum and developed the Cutter Expansive Classification System, which influenced the development of the Library of Congress.

Gratia Countryman was a nationally known librarian who led the Minneapolis Public Library from 1904 to 1936.

picture collection in the children's department for teachers' use, organizing the pictures alphabetically in vertical files, and provided portfolios for borrowers to use in taking the pictures home. While the library was still located in City Hall, she also organized a separate room for children, in part to make the general circulation room more convenient for the adult patrons but also to give the children's books—which were popular—more space. In 1909 she initiated weekly Saturday story hours, which drew an average attendance of more than one hundred children for each session, the majority boys.

Between 1880 and 1890, St. Paul's population increased by 100,000. Residential neighborhoods expanded into outlying areas and residents wanted more convenient access to books. In response to repeated requests from the Sixth Ward, the library had established in 1891 a "station"—a place where orders for books could be left to be delivered later from the main library. Helen McCaine was not in favor of the idea, and after six months she closed the station. But the pressure for stations continued.

In 1894 the citizens of the Sixth Ward in St. Paul applied to the city and library board for assistance in establishing a branch library in their community. It was their second request for library services. The board's reply was no. Ideas had to be well developed, tested, and proved beneficial before St. Paul officials would adopt them. The library's conservative ideology did not foster consideration of expanding or changing the library.

By 1904 Minneapolis had ten delivery stations in operation as well as three branch libraries. Succumbing to community pressure, in 1905 the Saint Paul Public

Library board opened five stations: two in the Sixth Ward and one each in the First Ward, St. Anthony Park, and Merriam Park. Drugstores predominated as station sites. Among the station locations were Neighborhood House, Bastyr Drug Store, Bodin's Drug Store, Fieseler's Drug Store, the Midway YMCA, Weiler's Drug Store, the Universalist Church reading room, Fuch's Drug Store, McArdell's Bakery, and Hall's Millinery Store.

The stations were an instant success, each year circulating from one thousand to seven thousand books per location. In 1906, McCaine recommended to the board that six additional stations be established. She sent a collection of two hundred books to each of them, rotating the collections every three months. The library gave a messenger his bus fare and paid him 25 cents per station per visit. Messengers visited each station once a week to supply orders for books. By 1913, 17 percent of the library's total circulation was accomplished through the delivery stations.[75]

Minneapolis led the way in a second major library service, the provision of books to the schools. The library began sending books to the Minneapolis schools as early as 1893, and by December 1904, Countryman was distributing collections of one hundred books each to forty Minneapolis schools. It was not until 1907 that McCaine sent out the first collections to St. Paul schools, a box of fifty books for grades four to eight to each of the ten largest schools. The circulation for the first eight weeks was a remarkable 2,732. To her credit, McCaine recognized the success of the program and added to the service. By 1913, the Saint Paul Public Library was serving forty-three public schools with 10,085 books. The school circulation that year was an astounding 133,313—an increase over 1912 of 25,855.

THE McCAINE ERA ENDS

Because she did not want to supervise the move to the new library then under consideration, Helen McCaine resigned as head librarian of the Saint Paul Public Library in 1913. J. G. Pyle, one of her board members and head of the James J. Hill Reference Library, said of her, "Because she was modest and unassuming, because she belonged here and would not have dreamed of accepting advancement elsewhere, because she shrank from every form of publicity, St. Paul did not know for many years that it had the rare good fortune to possess one of the ablest librarians in this country. . . . On one point nobody could make her yield. If she believed a book to be intrinsically unfit for general circulation, it would not go on the shelves. She had the conscientious sense of duty that we associate with sterner times and communities than ours." Said Minnesota lawyer Pierce Butler, who became an associate justice of the Supreme Court, "By appearance and learning she gave suitable tone and atmosphere to the library." McCaine had been the perfect, genteel library hostess. One of her staff members said of her, "Kindly, courteous though firm, clear and precise in her direction, unwavering in her loyalty to the library and the patrons of it, a woman above all most conscientious and sterling in character and strong in mind."[76]

A photograph of Helen McCaine shows an erect, dignified, unsmiling woman who gazes sternly at the camera. There is a slight downturn to the edges of her mouth and no hint of humor in her direct gaze, which she may have assumed was the proper aspect to present to the photographer for a formal portrait. With

The Art of Womanhood

IN 1908 THE ST. PAUL INSTITUTE of Arts and Letters maintained an art gallery in a room provided by the city on the third floor of the Saint Paul Public Library, then located in the Market House. The art displayed in the gallery consisted almost entirely of needlework and stitching. All genteel Victorian ladies of a household occupied their time with needlework in colored silk, woolen knitting materials, and cotton thread-making embellishments for their surroundings. Stitchery was one of the few outlets for women's energy and creativity. During the decorous days before World War I, the social customs were strictly observed in St. Paul. A woman did not eat dinner in a public restaurant lest she be considered "fast." Oddly, hotel dining rooms were a different matter. It was entirely proper for a woman to have an occasional meal in a hotel—particularly if she were traveling.

Source: St. Paul: Saga of an American City *(1980) by Virginia Brainard Kunz.*

her hair piled on top of her head, a high-collared blouse, and a brooch at her throat, she radiates Victorian competence, rectitude, and strength of will.

At her death in 1922 at age eighty-six, the *Pioneer Press* noted, "Thorough knowledge of books, of the widest scope, and of what a library ought to be, she added a rare and ripe judgment; a capacity for meeting the public in her own gracious way and winning its confidence and esteem. . . . She knew how to make order and discipline blossom into affection."[77]

For thirty-seven years, Helen McCaine had been the human incarnation of the Saint Paul Public Library. During her tenure she built a solid institution for the next librarian, her dynamic successor, to take beyond its walls to all of the citizens of St. Paul.

Electus D. Litchfield's architectural drawing for the new Saint Paul Central Library.

FIVE

Building the Central Library

FOR ALMOST FOUR DECADES, Helen McCaine devoted herself to the internal workings of the Saint Paul Public Library, content to leave political and business matters to the library board. As head librarian, however, McCaine undoubtedly participated in discussions over the proposed new home for the library. The discussions lasted for nearly two-thirds of her tenure, beginning in 1883 and not ending until 1917, four years after her retirement, with the new building's grand opening.

Almost as soon as the Saint Paul Public Library had moved into its cramped Ramsey County Courthouse quarters in 1889, the library board and its ally, the St. Paul Chamber of Commerce, were focused on the dream of constructing a new library building. It galled them to look across the river and see, completed in 1889, Minneapolis's monumental new public library building, the pride of the city. The board knew better than to look to its own community for help, however. The 1890s were not good years for St. Paul. Bonds had come due and, though provision had been made to pay them off, the political mood favored retrenchment rather than investment. Officials reduced the tax levy to a level so low that basic services to maintain the city were threatened.

In 1891 the city adopted the Bell Charter, which changed the way library board members were chosen and put strict limitations on expenditures of public funds. Instead of being named by the mayor, library board members were now chosen by judges of the district court. In addition, the city was not allowed to spend more than $15,000 per year on the library, regardless of its need.[78] The budget restrictions would last nine years, until a new charter removed the limit. Nonetheless, between 1890 and 1900, thanks to small donations to the library that collectively, in some years, totaled more than the city appropriation, the book collection doubled.

Minneapolis Public Library, Hennepin Avenue at Tenth Street, Minneapolis, ca. 1890s.

JAMES J. HILL AND MACALESTER'S LIBRARY

Faced with St. Paul's budget restrictions and the conservative mindset of its politicians, library board members realized it was futile to talk with city officials about financing a new building for the library. Instead they turned their attention to St. Paul's most noted private benefactor: James J. Hill. They were aware that, as early as 1887, Hill had talked with Edward D. Neill, head librarian and professor of history, English literature, and political science at Macalester College, about building a library.

Hill's own education had been cut short at an early age, and to compensate for that lack, he had been an avid reader all of his life. When St. Paul proposed to put on a lavish celebration to recognize the completion of his Great Northern Railway to Seattle, "the Empire Builder" responded that he would prefer that St. Paul put the money toward a public library. "I will add twice as much more and a good library building can be put up at once," he declared. Struggling to survive the severe Panic of 1893, the city had turned down Hill's offer.[79]

Taking note of Hill's interest in helping finance a library, Edward Neill suggested to him that he put up his library at Macalester College. Neill pursued the idea with enough success that on July 10, 1888, Hill wrote to him:

> The proposition to establish a library of reference in the arts, sciences and literature, open to all investigators, in connection with Macalester College has been considered. If the trustees will erect a fire-proof building, to cost no less than $20,000, upon the completion of the same I will give $5,000 with the understanding that $2,500 shall be expended for books by the librarian at that time and that the balance shall be safely invested and the annual interest expended for the library. Until the completion of the building the librarian is authorized each month to draw on me for $30 for the purchase of important books and material, said sum to form a part of my contribution.[80]

On July 30, Neill, impatient to get started, wrote to Hill:

> This summer I desire to make a beginning for the Hill Reference Library and it would gratify me if, in accordance with the terms of your kind letter, you would send a check for $30 drawn somewhat as on the form enclosed.[81]

It appears that, at heart, all parties to the transaction, with the exception of Neill, were lukewarm about the library project. Hill's promised contribution was meager, the Macalester trustees failed to take any action, and the project was quietly dropped. Neill never did get his monthly stipend of $30 for books, and instead Hill gave $500,000 to the Catholic Church for the construction of the St. Paul Seminary, two miles west of Macalester College. The word around City Hall was that Hill had first offered the half-million dollars to St. Paul for a library on the condition that the city pay a part of the cost. When St. Paul officials allegedly refused, other eager recipients stepped forward and Hill gave his money to further the education of priests.[82]

Long before the library moved into the courthouse, the St. Paul Chamber of Commerce had championed the cause of a new building for the library. Acting on its own, because the City Council would not, the chamber succeeded in getting a bill passed in the state legislature on February 26, 1889, authorizing St. Paul to issue bonds in the amount of $50,000 to purchase a site for a new library. As soon as the bill became law, the library board and the chamber formed a joint committee to find a suitable location.

The Reverend Dr. Edward D. Neill was the first superintendent of schools for the Minnesota Territory and the first president of St. Paul's Macalester College. He tried but failed to interest James J. Hill in locating his reference library at Macalester; it went instead to the Saint Paul Public Library. Neill also served as a chancellor of the University of Minnesota, an assistant secretary under President Abraham Lincoln and an aide to President Andrew Johnson, and founding pastor of St. Paul's First Presbyterian and House of Hope Churches. Neill was a strong supporter of education so long as it taught Christian principles. He was unalterably opposed to coeducation.

LIBRARY PLANNING BEGINS

The question before the committee was a legitimate and significant one: How big a plot of land did the library need? To answer it, committee members played at being architects. Their thinking went like this: They all agreed that the "stack system" of storing books was the most efficient. So they measured a double-faced bookcase and found it to be ten feet long and seven feet high, and to hold, on average, nine hundred volumes. If the cases were three-and-a-half feet wide—which included the space between the cases—and if two feet of space were allowed at the ends, they reasoned that a building two stories high would hold 180,000 books. If the rooms were sixteen feet high, with galleries built half way up the walls, 100,000 more books could be accommodated. A building 150 feet by 50 feet with wings extending 30 feet in front for the reading rooms would require a plot of ground about 154 feet in length by 64 feet in width!

They soon realized that this amateur method of designing a library was generating neither confidence nor enthusiasm among the library's patrons. Taking a different tack, several members of the committee suggested that the library be built as a wing on a proposed auditorium building, ignoring the lack of compatibility between cheering sports fans and readers seeking the quiet of a reading room. That idea, while much discussed, also did not gain traction.

A year later, in 1890, in a move to compel the city to take some action, the St. Paul Commercial Club organized a mass meeting at which citizens passed resolutions urging the Common Council to issue the bonds the legislature had authorized two years earlier to buy a site for the library. A second resolution asked the city to petition the legislature for permission to sell the Market House (which the city owned) and use the proceeds to build the library and an auditorium—not necessarily conjoined.

The public clamor spurred St. Paul officials into action, and permission to sell the Market House was quickly granted by the legislature. The Commercial Club then began an intense lobbying effort to persuade the city to sell the Market House and use the proceeds to build the new library. Before the Common Council could act on the suggestion, the financial panic of 1893 and resulting five depressed years lowered property values to such a level that selling the Market House would not have brought in enough funds to build the new library. To add to the library board's frustration, the Common Council then refused to authorize the sale of bonds to purchase a site, insisting that the board had to first find the money to build the building.

The library board felt itself blocked at every turn. When they could think of little else to do, they formed another committee. In 1896 the board organized the St. Paul Library Association and gave it the express charge to find a building to house St. Paul's growing library. Again, nothing happened. With the construction of a new building for the library an apparently hopeless cause for the present, the board turned to an examination of existing space downtown for the library.

MOVING TO THE MARKET HOUSE

In 1898 Edward Feldhauser, a member of the library board, had a novel idea. He suggested that, instead of waiting for the

The Reverend Dr. Edward Neill at home with his wife and children. As befitted family members of a famous educator, all are industriously reading.

real estate market to go up so the Market House building could be sold for a respectable sum, the Market House be remodeled and used for the library. The first-floor space could be rented to stores and the second floor given over to the library. Feldhauser estimated that the remodeling would cost $40,000. To get the fund-raising going, he started a chain-letter project and asked each recipient on his mailing list to contribute twenty-five cents. One of his letters ended up on James J. Hill's desk. Hill sent back a curt reply:

> Replying to your letter of the 11th instant, I beg to say that under the present condition of the library, I could take no interest in the matter and it would be a loss of both your time and mine to make any appointment.[83]

It was obvious to all that Hill was in no mood to do anything on behalf of the Saint Paul Public Library. Though Hill did not contribute, others did, and Feldhauser's letter campaign brought in $565.

At last, on February 10, 1899, after a decade of letter writing and lobbying, the St. Paul Common Council passed an ordinance transferring the Market House property to the Saint Paul Public Library. In reality, the city was relieved to get the Market House off its hands as, due to its poor construction, the building had proved to be a liability. It took $98,359[84] of remodeling, under the direction of architect J. Walter Stevens, to make the building habitable for the library and to provide housing for tenants on the first floor, whose rentals, projected at $20,000 per year, would pay back the city's investment. On July 23, 1899, the library opened to the public

with a "book reception" in the Market House given under the auspices of the Commercial Club. In 1900 the library moved into half of the second floor of the Market House and, in 1908, expanded into the rest of the floor.

Library board members had no illusions that the Market House would be the final home for St. Paul's library. Feldhauser had told Hill in 1898 that the Market House would be temporary quarters. The books had barely been settled onto the shelves in the Market House when the board began a three-year campaign to build a new library. Since James J. Hill had taken himself out of the picture, they aimed their appeal at one of the world's richest men, a steel magnate turned philanthropist who had already funded two Minnesota libraries, one each in Duluth and Mankato.

APPEALING TO CARNEGIE

Andrew Carnegie was a likely prospect for funding the Saint Paul Public Library. Between 1886 and 1917, Carnegie alone would give a total of $41 million to the construction of public libraries in 1,420 American towns and cities, including sixty-four in Minnesota.[85] The most active member of the City Development Committee of the Commercial Club, St. Paul attorney Edwin Chittenden, led the campaign to win over Carnegie. Early in 1901, Chittenden wrote to the philanthropist in New York with the proposal for a St. Paul library. To increase his chances of getting Carnegie's attention, Chittenden sent a second letter to the New York office of Cass Gilbert, the architect of Minnesota's Capitol Building, which was then under construction. A third letter went to Dr. J. S. Billings, director of the New York Public Library. At the time,

While laying plans for a grand new building of its own, the Saint Paul Public Library occupied the second floor of the Market House from 1900 to 1915.

A view of the Reference Room of the Saint Paul Public Library, taken in 1910 when it was housed on the second floor of the Market House. Hats were considered necessary attire for ladies when they ventured into public areas.

Billings was negotiating with Carnegie for $5.2 million to build sixty-five branch libraries in New York. Chittenden hoped that, because of his presumed close relationship with Carnegie, Billings could be helpful in advancing St. Paul's petition.

At Chittenden's request, Cass Gilbert, who grew up in St. Paul, set up a meeting between Chittenden and Billings to discuss the matter. Billings, fearful of jeopardizing his efforts for New York by pleading St. Paul's case, was of little help. Gilbert, however, remained involved. He sketched preliminary drawings for a St. Paul library and sent them, along with a request from Chittenden for $500,000, to Carnegie, who was now in residence in Skibo Castle in Scotland for the summer. On June 22, 1901, James Bertram, Carnegie's private secretary, who was in charge of planning for the Carnegie libraries, replied to Chittenden:

> Your letter of April was laid before Mr. Carnegie this morning, but he feels that it would be indelicate for him to become the donor of your libraries in St. Paul when the late Judge Hale, a resident, left the residue of his estate for this purpose. The memory of the citizen who does this should in Mr. Carnegie's opinion be held in grateful remembrance and his action commemorated. Otherwise he should have been pleased to consider the matter favorably.[86]

Judge Henry Hale had moved to Minnesota in 1856 from Vermont, where he had been secretary of state and editor of the *Burlington Free Press*. Hale had erected more than fifty substantial buildings in St. Paul. When Hale died in 1890

he left a portion of his estate, the Hale Memorial Fund, to the library. But his will stipulated that the funds could not be used for twenty-five years.

There were other problems as well. Most of Hale's wealth had been in real estate in St. Paul's Lower Town, around Jackson and Third Streets. Three years after his death, in the aftermath of the Panic of 1893, the property lost value. In fact, it might have been foreclosed if his widow, Mary Hale, a woman of independent means, had not invested large sums of her money to rescue her late husband's real estate. Moreover, the terms of Hale's will were convoluted. It provided that one-half of the excess of his income over and above the cost of maintenance of his various holdings through a term of years should be put under the charge of a board of trustees and, when a sufficient fund had accumulated, it could be used for the erection of a central public library. This was no financial foundation on which St. Paul could build a public library. What was Carnegie thinking?

Chittenden immediately prevailed upon Mrs. Hale to write Carnegie and explain the limitations of the Hale bequest, but her letter and others did not dissuade him. Cass Gilbert, who saw a major commission slipping away from him, continued to nurture his contacts with Billings and Carnegie. Billings backed further and further away from any involvement with St. Paul, but in February 1903 Gilbert reported an encouraging rumor: that Carnegie had changed his mind and was now looking favorably on St. Paul's request. Chittenden's spirits soared, only to be dashed a few weeks later when a letter arrived from James Bertram:

Mr. Carnegie has gone over the papers about the Saint Paul Library several times and definitely stated he did not see his way to do anything in the matter, the Hale bequest, etc, being in the way.[87]

It was clear that Andrew Carnegie would not change his mind about helping to finance St. Paul's new library. Chittenden was convinced there was more involved in Carnegie's rejection of the request than just the Hale affair and the meager details stated in Bertram's letter. He was right. Rumors soon revealed details of Carnegie's thinking, as Chittenden explained in a letter to Gilbert in the fall:

Since I last wrote you, Mr. D. R. Noyes [founder of the St. Paul drug firm Noyes Brothers and Culter] has told me that Mr. Carnegie directly told some of [Noyes's] friends that the reason why he does not give St. Paul a library is that J. J. Hill lives here and is fully able to provide one for the city.[88]

A SITE IS CHOSEN

It took Mayor David W. Lawler of St. Paul to break the impasse that the Common Council's chicken-or-egg decree had imposed on the library board. The mayor proposed selling the Market House for whatever it would bring and using the money as the nucleus for a library building fund. In the meantime, the city still needed to select a site. The board responded in September 1910 by appointing a committee, chaired by F. J. Clemans, to accomplish the task. In October the committee endorsed a suggestion by A. W. Lindeke that the block on the south side of Rice Park be acquired. A part of it was owned by the

Gordon and Ferguson Company and the remainder by the city, which had purchased it for the Central Police Station. The block was approximately 200 feet square; Gordon and Ferguson's piece of it could be purchased for $250,000.

The library board quickly agreed on the Rice Park library site, but just as quickly disagreed on how to raise the necessary funds. One faction on the board wanted to raise all of the needed money for the site and building, estimated at $500,000, through popular subscriptions. A second group wanted to raise the money by selling the Market House property. A third faction wanted to sell bonds to finance the library and, rather than sell the Market House, keep it and use rental income from the property to pay the interest on the bonds. Mayor Lawler, the president of the library board, and other influential citizens favored the third approach.

Then, in December, David Chauncey Shepard, who had made his fortune as a railroad contractor, offered to give $100,000 toward the $500,000 needed for the library site and building on the condition that the rest of the money be contributed by individuals who were or had been residents of Minnesota. He further stipulated that no other monies, neither from the sale of the Market House nor taxation or bonds, be used to build the library. Shepard's money was tempting, but his conditions were onerous.

HILL COMES THROUGH

The library board was still mulling over Shepard's offer when, in August 1911, James J. Hill, perhaps not wanting to be outdone by the generosity of one of his friends in his adopted hometown, suddenly offered $250,000 on essentially the

For two generations, the family of David Chauncey Shepard (1881–1956) was involved in railroad construction and expansion. Chauncey, a graduate of the University of Minnesota, became president of the Empire National Bank of St. Paul and a director of the Northwest Bank Corporation. He offered funding for the city's new library building, but his terms were deemed too conditional.

James J. Hill funded both the Saint Paul Public Library and the reference library that bears his name. A native of what is now Ontario, Canada, Hill moved to St. Paul when he was eighteen and quickly learned all aspects of the freight and transportation business. In 1893 he completed his Great Northern Railway from St. Paul to Seattle—the nation's only privately funded transcontinental railroad.

League, the Federation of Grade Teachers, and the Federation of Women's Clubs all pledged their support.

Then, in another surprise announcement, Hill declared on March 5, 1912, that instead of giving $250,000 on condition that $400,000 be raised by popular subscription, he would give $700,000 for the building and endowment of a library, no strings attached. Furthermore, if the city would acquire the balance of the Gordon and Ferguson plot and proceed with construction of the new public library building, Hill would make his reference library a part of it.

The logjam was broken at last. The St. Paul Chamber of Commerce sprang into action and pledged itself to raise, through public subscription, the $100,000 needed to purchase the site. A gift from the estate of Minnesota Supreme Court Justice Greenleaf Clark, who died in 1904, added another $30,500. In June the state legislature authorized the city to issue $600,000 of thirty-year bonds at 4.5 percent for a new library building in St. Paul. The Common Council gave its approval on July 27, and the project was finally on its way.

same conditions: that St. Paul raise an additional $400,000 by popular subscription. While these offers were tempting, Lindeke and Lawler continued to hold out for the sale of the Market House and issuance of bonds to finance the library. To bring everyone's plans together, the committee negotiated a final wrinkle to the plan: that bonds be issued, that the Market House property be leased instead of sold, and that the income from the lease be used to pay the interest on the bonds. This plan met with everyone's approval. The library board, Hill, Lindeke, Lawler, the Women's Civil

The library board, exhausted from its decade of struggle to get the Saint Paul Public Library's new home built, was relieved to have Hill take over. Though he was seventy-three years old and nearing retirement, no one was surprised at the energy he invested in his leading role in the design of the new building. Hill was known to be a hands-on manager, involved in the smallest details of his many endeavors.

Politically speaking, the board was wise to let Hill take the lead, since the project had unprecedented complications. St. Paul's new library was not going to be one library, but two—one public, the other private, operating under different governing boards and different financing. "It was a combination under one roof of a public library, built and administered by the city, and a reference library, built and administered by the generous gift of a private citizen."[89] No dual-purpose library like this existed.

St. Paul businessman Lucius Pond Ordway, who had recently rescued a financially crippled 3M, gave impetus to the movement to raise the required $100,000 by popular subscription when he declared, "All this talk is not bringing us to anything. Let's get busy. I obligate myself to raise $5,000 for this project. If I can't raise it, I'll dig it up."[90] He and eight other members of the Association of Commerce, including Theodore Griggs, Webster Wheelock, and A. W. Lindeke, joined in matching Ordway's promise.

Nine days later, when Hill raised his pledge another $50,000, St. Paul became giddy with excitement. Headlines read, "Mr. Hill Announces That He Will Spend $750,000 on New Library," "Boosters Cheer Wildly and Bring in $16,629 More," and "Optimism Rampant as Canvassers Compare Notes at Luncheon." Hill's spokesperson, Charles W. Gordon, said, "This means $1,500,000 for St. Paul's Library and of this the subscribers pay only $100,000. It is the best investment the city has ever had a chance to make."

The announcement caused "the wildest enthusiasm." Committee women organized to raise money, doctors subscribed, and schools sent solicitations home with the students. "Nearly one-eighth of the money reported today for the new

library site fund was pledged over the names of 2,055 school children of St. Paul." The youngsters, undoubtedly with the collusion of their parents, raised $1,521.24.[91] St. Paul citizens had reason to be pleased with themselves. The story of Hill's gift of three-quarters of a million dollars for a library appeared in the same newspaper that advertised men's suits and overcoats for $10, oak kitchen cabinets for $14, and women's shoes for seventy-five cents.

HILL CHOOSES AN ARCHITECT

The news of Hill's involvement no sooner hit the streets than the Reverend William C. Pope, pastor of the Church of the Good Shepherd, who ministered to the homeless of St. Paul's downtown, approached Hill and urged him to consider Pope's nephew, Electus Litchfield, as the architect for the project. Electus Litchfield was the son of William B. Litchfield, the president of one of the predecessor companies of the Great Northern Railway and a friend of Hill's. Though Hill probably could have chosen Litchfield on his own, and without opposition, he followed the process and asked Litchfield, who had built several public libraries, to present his credentials to the library board. Cass Gilbert was apparently not considered for the commission. In 1912, the library board of St. Louis, Missouri, hired Gilbert to design its Central Library building.

The board readily accepted Litchfield as architect on December 18, 1912, as well as Charles C. Soule, a Boston publisher, library planner, and author of *How to Plan a Library Building,* who was brought in as a consultant on the interior design. Soule urged his clients to "plan always from the inside outward. Do not consider any feature of the exterior or of construction

The library's Reference Room was named for Greenleaf Clark, an associate justice of the Minnesota Supreme Court.

St. Paul businessman Lucius Pond Ordway advanced $14,000 to the fledgling 3M Company, thus rescuing it at a crucial time in its history. Ordway later became president of 3M.

In December 1912, the library board commissioned Electus D. Litchfield to design the new Central Library.

until the problems of administration and growth for libraries . . . have been thoroughly examined and understood."[92]

Helen McCaine's mentor, William Frederick Poole, had crusaded to reform library architecture. Eastern libraries had been designed to resemble cathedrals with high vaulted spaces and vast galleries. Poole called for a practical approach to library design, at least on the interior. The exterior could resemble a Gothic church, if that was what a community desired, but he believed the inside should be functional. "In libraries abundant light is more essential than facilities for fortification," he dryly observed. Poole favored well-lighted and ventilated small rooms filled with books organized by subject. His ideas on library architecture, widely known but also locally filtered through the diffident McCaine, no doubt had

some bearing on the design of St. Paul's new library building.

As if he had a premonition of his early demise, Soule went to work immediately and within a few weeks of his hiring wrote Hill, "The building committee of the Public Library Board has accepted my tentative sketch of the interior as their first step in planning the new library. . . . If, however, you wish to further talk with me about any phase of library work, I am at your call."[93] But Soule died on January 7, 1913, a few weeks after his tentative sketch had been accepted. The interior of the library would follow a plan nearly identical to the one Soule outlined in his book.

As soon as Litchfield's appointment was approved by the library board, Hill contacted him and, as builders often do at

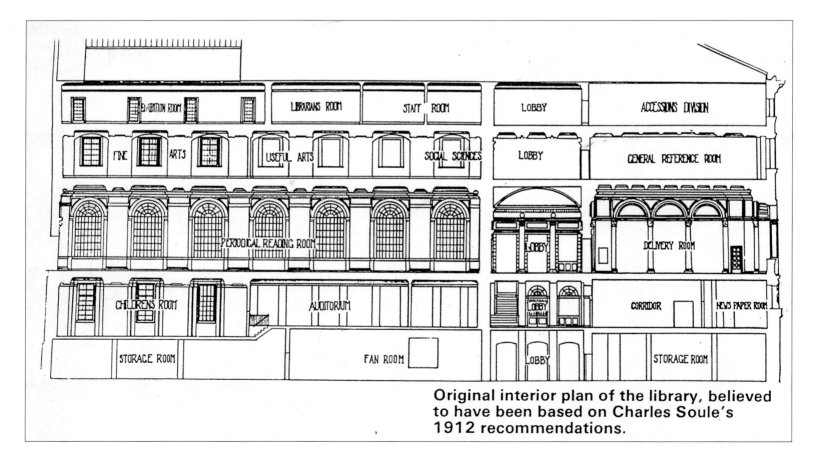

Original interior plan of the library, believed to have been based on Charles Soule's 1912 recommendations.

the beginning of a project, sketched out a bare-bones proposal. "My idea," Hill told the architect, "is to have good material and plain design avoiding all useless ornamentation." That Hill really wanted a far more exuberant design was revealed in a letter he sent to his long-time financial partner and the country's leading investment banker, J. Pierpont Morgan. Wrote Hill: "I am getting ready to build a reference library in St. Paul and to help me in the matter of architecture I would be greatly obliged if you would send me a photograph showing the general outside appearance of your library [in Manhattan]." Morgan sent Hill the photograph and Hill passed it on to Litchfield, telling him to use it as the model for the St. Paul project. Litchfield must have gasped when he saw the picture, for he wrote back to Hill, "You have set us a high standard in taking this building for comparison but I shall do my durndest."[94]

Litchfield came well equipped for the job. Born in New York in 1872, he graduated from the Brooklyn Polytechnic Institute at age seventeen and went to work for the prestigious New York architectural firm of Carrere and Hastings, which had won the competition to design the New York Public Library. He was a dashing young professional with society ties and a knack for attracting media attention. While with the firm of Lord and Hewitt, he collaborated on the U.S. Department of Agriculture Building in Washington, D.C. Among his other notable public buildings were the U.S. Post Office and Courthouse in Denver and the Brooklyn Masonic Temple in New York City. Litchfield would later become famous for the design of an entire community, called Yorkship Village, near Camden, New Jersey.

CLASSICAL INSIDE AND OUT

Workmen broke ground for St. Paul's new library building in 1914, but it was not fully completed and occupied until 1917, the year American troops under Brigadier General John Joseph Pershing landed in France to fight in World War I. The building, whose shape was a hollow rectangle, faced south toward the Mississippi River. Built in a Northern Italian Renaissance style, it was reminiscent of the palaces of Florence and Genoa. Its exterior was encased in pink Tennessee marble, one of the most beautiful and durable of marbles, while the interior was Mankato stone from Minnesota. The maple woodwork was stained gray. A grand flight of steps led to the lobby, where, over a floor of blue Rutland and golden vein Formosa marble, surrounded by polished columns of Mankato stone, visitors entered the library through an outpouring of classical symbolism.

The portal to St. Paul's new library announced to the world that this was no longer a rough frontier city, but one that had grown from the great classical civilizations of the past. Facing the entrance,

James J. Hill admired the look of J. Pierpont Morgan's library (now the Morgan Library and Museum), which the New York banker built in 1906 to house his extensive collection of books, rare manuscripts, prints, and drawings. Charles McKim, of the architectural firm of McKim, Mead, and White, designed the building at a cost of $1.2 million. The library is located on Thirty-sixth Street in New York, which, at the time, was just east of Morgan's residence, a brownstone house built in 1880. His home was torn down in 1928 to make room for an exhibition hall and a reading room, also designed by McKim. Morgan's son, John Pierpont Morgan Jr., made the library a public institution in 1924.

The site of the new Saint Paul Public Library, looking north-east from Washington Street, November 25, 1913. The Saint Paul Hotel is at the upper right.

The laying of the cornerstone for the new library in 1914. The Minnesota Club is at the top left.

The new library under construction, May 1, 1915. The architect was Electus D. Litchfield; the builder, the Thomas J. Steen Company.

The main Reading Room at the new library, nearing completion in 1916.

65

high on the wall, was a panel in relief showing "Instruction" sitting upon a throne. On the opposite panel a central winged figure bore two tablets with images of Knowledge, the Torch, and the Sphinx. Other figures graced the lobby, including those representing Science and the Arts, as well as Architecture, Philosophy, Music, Poetry, the Arts of War, the Arts of Peace, and Aeronautics. Additional panels contained figures representing Science and the Fine Arts on the one hand and Agriculture and the Domestic Arts on the other. All had been sculpted by New York's Ulysses Ricci. While few in St. Paul could identify or even pronounce the names of the Greek muses painted on the nine beams over the circulation desk, they knew they were important.

The south wall bore the inscription "The Public Library of the City of St. Paul founded as the St. Paul Mercantile Association, September 18, 1857." (The YMCA efforts, which had preceded the Mercantile Association by several months, evidently had been forgotten.) The north wall contained quotations from the Book of Proverbs: "Keep fast hold of instruction; let her not go; keep her for she is thy life." Also, "Wisdom is the principal thing, therefore get wisdom and with all thy getting get understanding."

The largest room was the Periodical Room, followed by the Circulation or Delivery Room. Smaller rooms were set aside for the fine arts, science and technology, and social science. The Newspaper Room, the Children's Room, and the Office of the School Department occupied the basement. Very little of the building was actually open to the public, as the major portion was given over to the rows upon rows of closed stacks of books.

The façade of the Saint Paul Central Library is of pink Tennessee marble. Matching entrances usher the public into either the James J. Hill Reference Library on the left or the public library on the right.

The New York firm of Sherwin and Berwin was engaged to decorate the ceilings in a style reminiscent of the twelfth and thirteenth centuries. The artist, Frank Fairbanks, who was from Boston but had studied at the American Academy in Rome, explained the design:

> There are just three rooms under consideration, the reading room, the delivery room and the Greenleaf Clark room. The beamed ceilings are to be treated with color in a manner perfectly consistent with the Italian renaissance style of the building. . . . Subdued tones of gray and blue with some gold will be used in the delivery room, a general effect of dignity, repose and seriousness. For a library, both from the architectural and decorative standpoint, must be treated seriously. It is a place for quiet thought and for study. The reading room will have a good deal of color, though not in the decorative futuristic sense. . . . The Greenleaf Clark room will have more color.[95]

Lee Woodward Zeigler, School of Art director at the St. Paul Institute of Arts and Letters, painted color medallions depicting Muses—Graces, Fates, and Furies—in other areas of the building. Loath to leave any space unembellished, artists added monograms of masters of painting and initials of the architect, builders, and decorators between ceiling beams.

St. Paul's citizens were interested in every aspect of their new library. They marveled at the bronze elevator doors, decorated in Renaissance designs and containing the acronym of the library, and approved of the practicality of the cork floors that covered the three principal rooms. The tiles were made by compressing fourteen cubic inches of cork into a one-inch cube and filling it with linseed oil, giving the tiles, according to the manufacturer, the wearing quality of marble as well as the benefit of being waterproof.

Assisted by the Boy Scouts, the Saint Paul Public Library moved into one section of the unfinished building in 1916. James J. Hill's death that year would delay the completion of the interior of his reference library, located in the east section of the building, for five years. Hill's widow, Mary, assisted by their children Clara Hill Lindley, Louis W. Hill, Rachel Hill Boeckmann, and Charlotte Hill Slade, supervised the project after her husband's death. Mary Hill died just one month before the grand opening of the Hill Reference Library on December 20, 1921.

BUILDING DEDICATION

Despite delays in completing the interiors on the Hill section of the building, construction continued on the public library portion. At the dedication of the completed building on October 11, 1917, Marion L. Burton, president of the University of Minnesota, declared it to be the most beautiful library in the country. Its total cost was $770,018, including $130,000 for the site. Of this, $100,000 had been raised by popular subscription and $30,500 was the gift of Justice Greenleaf Clark.

Exercises at 4:00 p.m. and again at 8:00 p.m. formally opened the building. Mayor Vivian Irvin, representing the city, entrusted the library key to Commisioner of Education Harold Wunderlich. In a repetition of the ceremony that marked the opening of the library's temporary headquarters in the House of Hope Presbyterian Church following the 1915 fire, Wunderlich handed the key and the Bible of the steamer *Saint Paul* to librarian Dr. William Dawson Johnston. The Mohegan Troop of the Boy Scouts raised the flag and the Central High School orchestra played at the evening exercise.

.

In a letter he sent to head librarian Jennie Jennings on the fiftieth anniversary of the library, Electus Litchfield recounted his memories of the building of the library:

> I was indeed fortunate in the personnel of this Board and in particular in the Building Committee with which I had most to do. I shall never forget my delightful relations with Mrs. E. A. Young, Mr. F. A. Fogg and Mrs. Robert E. Olds and the others associated with them. No architect had a more loyal or helpful committee.
>
> The plans were prepared in consultations with Mr. Soule of Boston, the leading library expert of his time, and the building embodies his theory of correct library administration. The stacks, in direct communication with delivery, reference and work room and extending the full height of the building, had, it was believed, ample capacity for many years to come and provided the opportunity for additional book space without disturbance of the various functions of the building.

Litchfield believed that the Tennessee marble he had chosen for the exterior was "an aristocrat among building materials" and the Mankato stone created "an important monumental interior. In the design and execution of the ceilings I had the assistance of Mrs. Frank Fairbanks, who, for many years has been Director of Painting in the American Academy in Rome, and of Mr. Lee

The library's acronym is centered on each of the ornate panels decorating its bronze elevator doors.

Woodward Zeigler, at that time Director of the Art Institute of St. Paul."[96]

Not everything had gone smoothly during construction. There was controversy and delay in purchasing furniture, for example. There were arguments over the balustrade around the library grounds, with one private citizen threatening court action. City Commissioner of Education Anthony Yoerg and city architect Charles A. Hausler disagreed over construction details. Meanwhile, W. C. Handy, the comptroller, held up payment on some invoices when costs overran the estimates. For some reason a door connecting the library reading room and the Hill Reference Library had not been drawn in the original plans. It took an act of the City Council and the authorization of an expenditure of $1,255 to get the door installed.[97]

Critic Robert Hale, writing in the *Pioneer Press,* found fault with the furnishings:

> The only flagrant defect in the interior appears in one item of the furnishings. . . . Just how an architect of Mr. Litchfield's standing who carried out innumerable details with discrimination, would choose a Gothic type of seat for a secular Renaissance building is one of those strange perversions of taste, or should we say "temporary aberrations," which sometimes afflict men whom the gods favor. The pointed, curious reinforced backs of the chairs have no relation whatsoever with a renaissance or Roman structure, howsoever appropriate they may be in a Gothic Guild or Chapter House, such as the House of Hope.

Hale may have felt defensive about his critique, for later in his article he writes:

Why notice flaws? Many people are apt to stand pat or fall down in worship without understanding. By being cognizant of defects, St. Paul will be in a position to make the next municipal edifice more perfect.[98]

In 1917, two years after the big fire, St. Paul's new public library was in operation. More than 70,200 people held library cards. The library's reach was so extensive that even eight playgrounds in the city received library service. By 1921, annual circulation would climb to 1,222,409, or 5.11 books for every man, woman, and child in St. Paul. Credit for much of that growth was due to Helen McCaine's successor: Dr. William Dawson Johnston.

The painted ceiling in the Greenleaf Clark Reference Room, restored in 2002.

The Greenleaf Clark Reference Room on the third floor of the Saint Paul Public Library as it looked in 1924. Clark, a Minnesota Supreme Court associate justice, was a major donor to the library's construction. The room, which features a small, elegant alcove entered through three arches, later became the Science and Industry Room.

Dr. William Dawson Johnston came to St. Paul with exceptional credentials when he was recruited to assume the position of head librarian in 1914.

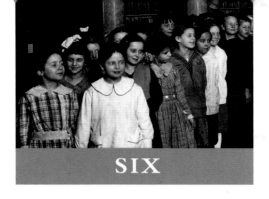

SIX

Taking the Library to the People

IT WAS THROUGH PURE LUCK, or perhaps inadvertence, that St. Paul readers had experienced, in Helen McCaine, thirty-seven years of extraordinary library service. Fortunately, members of the library board understood how important her talents had been to the success of the Saint Paul Public Library and they were determined to replace her with the best librarian they could find. After a nationwide search, the board persuaded Dr. William Dawson Johnston, the head librarian at Columbia University since 1909, to accept the position.

Johnston was born June 11, 1871, at Essex Center, Vermont, the son of a clergyman. He had graduated from Brown University, studied at the University of Chicago, and earned a master's degree in history from Harvard. He taught history at both Brown and Michigan before his interest in bibliography led him into librarianship. In 1900 he began work at the Library of Congress, where he wrote the *History of the Library of Congress, Volume 1,* published in 1904. From the Library of Congress he went to the Brookline Public Library and then to Columbia. In 1911 Rutgers College conferred a doctorate of literature on Johnston for his work as a librarian and writer. His reputation was known throughout the profession as exceptional.

Johnston arrived in St. Paul on January 1, 1914, to take up his duties. He was a frail-looking, gentle, quiet-mannered man who nevertheless exuded nervous energy. His hair was parted in the middle, in the fashion of the time, and in his pictures he has a half-smile on his lips. He owned a car, yet he walked seventeen miles a day to work up an appetite.

Johnston was a marked contrast to Helen McCaine. A member of the "new school" of librarians who had departed from the conservative philosophy of Winsor, Poole, and Cutter—the founders of the American Library Association—Johnston believed in taking the library to the people. He wanted to put a sign on every lamppost, saying, "Your book is at the library." He believed that "the book should seek the reader . . . the book that's on the shelf might as well not be a book at all."[99] On another occasion he remarked, "I wish that every book was out, except those in the reference room." He held that a library was to be used, not treasured. Johnston was another Gratia Countryman: like his counterpart in Minneapolis, he believed that a librarian should be involved in the community.[100]

ONE-MAN PUBLICITY MACHINE

Johnston started the most active publicity campaign for the library that St. Paul residents had ever experienced. He was an excellent speaker and spoke constantly to groups. Ahead of his time in promoting the library's services, he circulated fliers to more than 30,000 homes via water-meter readers and arranged for telegraph messengers to carry library brochures on their rounds to downtown stores and offices. He printed blotters with facts about the library and gave florists lists of books to send to their customers with the flowers. To get more books into homes he started a telephone-

order program to deliver books within a two-mile radius of the library for a charge of five cents and sent 20,000 fliers about books for children to the schools. Johnston increased the library's registration by 4,000 in his first year alone.

He also sent library-related notices to trade periodicals. The electricians' *Buzzer* and the lumberjacks' *Pine Cone,* along with churches and clubs, received lists of recommended reading. In 1920 Johnston established the first industrial book stations, placing collections locally at the American Hoist and Derrick Company and in the clubrooms of the St. Paul City Railway. This was followed by industrial stations in the Great Northern Railway offices, the Christ Child Society's Home, and the Community Food Center.

Taking note of the new interest in recorded music, Johnston started a phonograph collection in the Fine Arts Room that soon contained more than four hundred records. He added a "lantern slide" collection, used mainly by professional artists. To better serve children, he expanded the "story time" to two sessions per week, instituted contests and gave out prizes, started a reading club, and awarded certificates to those who read a dozen books. A child who read thirty books earned a pin. In 1915 juvenile books made up 53 percent of the total library circulation. Johnston also set up a Schools Services Division. By 1917 the library was serving fifty-two public schools and fourteen parochial schools. During 1918, 1,337 pupils, accompanied by their teachers, trooped through the Central Library.

Johnston not only brought children to the library, he brought the library to them. A picture in the *Pioneer Press* showed the public library truck, staffed with two storytelling librarians, at a city playground. The accompanying article reported:

Once every week this edifice of knowledge visits each playground whereupon all games are abandoned, swing and sand piles are deserted while the children gather around to select their reading and to hear the wondrous tales with which the Story Ladies are equipped. This is the first step toward cooperation with the city playground system taken by Dr. Dawson Johnston, librarian, and it is proving of immense value in correctly directing younger minds of the city and turning the playground into a place of learning as well as a place of play.[101]

It is little wonder that Johnston was popular with the press, which gladly gave him publicity. In 1916 he got the *St. Paul Daily News* to institute a column called "Library Corner" in the Sunday paper. In 1920 the *Pioneer Press* inaugurated a new book review column, unique because it was "edited by a city librarian."[102]

CARNEGIE FUNDS THREE BRANCHES

Aware of the strong demand from the city's neighborhoods for branch libraries, Johnston contacted the Andrew Carnegie Foundation for a grant for St. Paul soon after his arrival. He was aware that Carnegie had slowed his investment in public libraries because some communities, given free libraries, had failed to maintain them. When Johnston pointed out that St. Paul, through neighborhood subscriptions, had donated the land for

These children are viewing an early audiovisual presentation at the Saint Paul Public Library in the 1920s.

Schoolchildren tour the library's marble-columned Greenleaf Clark Reference Room, ca. 1920.

the libraries, Carnegie gave him a grant of $75,000.

On September 16, 1914, Johnston presided over the laying of the cornerstone for the new Central Library. Mayor William Powers used the occasion to announce Carnegie's grant for building three branch libraries, in St. Anthony Park, Riverview, and Arlington Hills. After struggling for more than a decade to put up one library building, St. Paul would soon have four libraries under construction. The branch libraries would be designed by city architect Charles Hausler, who had worked under Louis B. Sullivan in Chicago. The elegantly homey interiors would follow the pattern of other Carnegie libraries. In 1917 all three branches were opened. Circulation in the branch libraries' first year of operation was Arlington Hills, 69,996; Riverview, 56,721; and St. Anthony Park, 26,656.[103]

Feeling expansive and goaded by Johnston, the library board extended the privileges of the Saint Paul Public Library to all of the residents of the state, charging a fee of five cents for each book borrowed. There was, however, an exception. Books deemed to be "needed by citizens of St. Paul" and books purchased in the current year were not to be lent to nonresidents of the city.

Johnston was proud of St. Paul's generosity. In *Western Magazine* he wrote:

> The service of the St. Paul institution is remarkable in still another respect. It is not limited to its citizens but extends throughout that great territory of which St. Paul is the center. Its discarded books are sent to outlying lumber camps and frontier villages and towns where they in many cases become the nucleus of community libraries. . . . Today anyone in the state or in adjoining states who is unable to secure the books or the information which he needs from a local library or from the state library commission may obtain the use of any book in the Saint Paul library or may secure any information in its

The Riverview Branch Public Library at 1 East George Street is one of the three Carnegie libraries in St. Paul. City architect Charles Hausler designed all three libraries. Riverview is noted for the tall Palladium-arch windows that line all four sides of the building.

Librarians Marion Lambert, Ethel Bruckner, and Myra Buell on the steps of the Central Library, ca. 1924.

possession by applying through his local library or through the state library commission.[104]

Johnston mined library cards for data that revealed the breadth of membership. He noted that 76 percent of the high school teachers in St. Paul had library cards, as did 71 percent of the grade school teachers. In checking the clergy, 44 percent of Episcopal ministers were found to have cards, as were 56 percent of the Methodists. Businessmen fell somewhat behind; only 33 percent of them were registered with the library.[105]

STORMY TIMES

Not all of Johnston's tenure was sunny. The first major crisis of his career at the Saint Paul Public Library was the Market

House fire in 1915. Though the fire was a disaster for the city and an enormous personal loss for Johnston, whose printer-ready *History of University Libraries* was consumed by the blaze, he and the library bounced back. Within days of the fire he reopened the library in the House of Hope Presbyterian Church, using the main auditorium for readers and the basement for the accession department and children's book area.

Public support for the library reached an all-time high following the fire. The Commercial Club issued a call for books to be donated, the Minnesota Historical Society gave several thousand of its duplicate books to St. Paul, and the Society of Civil Engineers offered to transfer its library of about 3,000 volumes

to the city. Joseph A. Wheelock's son, Webster, donated a part of his late father's collection. Citizens holding books that had been checked out at the time of the fire were urged to return them and not keep them as souvenirs of the disaster. By the end of 1915 the collection had reached 66,500 volumes. Two years after the fire the Saint Paul Public Library had 3,000 more books on its shelves than it had had before.

Five months after Johnston's arrival, a new charter commission that had been adopted by St. Paul went into effect. Though he may not have realized it at the time, the new commission form of government would greatly complicate his stay in St. Paul. Under the provisions of the charter, the duties of the library board were given to a single individual, the commissioner of education, who was a member of the City Council as well as the administrative head of the Department of Education. The charter also provided for a complicated and cumbersome library advisory board composed of the superintendent of schools, the principals of all of the high schools, a teacher who was to be elected by the entire body of teachers in the public schools, and one representative from each ward of the city. The library was also made subject to the city's Civil Service Commission and newly established general purchasing department.

Johnston's troubles began with the purchasing department. In the fall of 1915, Commissioner Anthony Yoerg warned that "Dr. Dawson Johnston may resign unless he is assured by Mayor Powers that the purchase of books for the public library will not be retarded by Purchasing Agent Hohenstein." The newspaper story went on to report:

A committee headed by W. A. Hardenbergh is expected to call on the mayor soon to ask him to take a hand in the differences which have existed for months between the librarian and the city's purchasing department. The quarrel apparently originated because Mr. Hohenstein does not approve of the purchasing of books by the librarian before orders or requisitions are delivered to the purchasing department. "They will not tell us what kind of bindings they want or anything else that we should know." Meanwhile Johnston asserts that the purchasing department does not buy the books he requisitions and often pays excessive prices in addition to delaying deliveries.[106]

Hohenstein's resignation ended the dispute.

When World War I ended in 1918, it was suggested that the Civil Service Commission's advisory committee, named to oversee the purchase of books, look overseas for bargains. They had no scruples in urging that St. Paul take advantage of Europe's postwar economic prostration to line its shelves. As one writer noted:

Europe affords an excellent market in which to buy books. I believe that if Dr. Dawson Johnston was sent there by the city with authority to make purchases he could save St. Paul thirty cents on every dollar expended. In Europe, and especially in England, many thousands of books can be bought at a great sacrifice because the people of that country are eager to part with anything not classed as necessaries. This applies to individuals as well as book dealers and institutions.[107]

Johnston did not raid England's distressed libraries for books but continued to look elsewhere.

Johnston's hiring practices also were at odds with St. Paul's Civil Service Commission. He wanted only the most highly qualified staff members for the library and recruited them from throughout the country. In 1917 he brought in as head of the catalog division (and promoted her in 1919 to assistant librarian) Jennie T. Jennings, who had been chair of the Riverside California Library School and reference librarian at Iowa State College; hired Katherine Dame from the New York State Library to become chief of the reference division; and enlisted Jeanne Griffin, of the Detroit Public Library, to head the Social Science Room.

Johnston's zeal for the library, his impressive administrative talents, and his insistence on quality conflicted with how the Civil Service Commission interpreted the rules. The commission wanted to have input on who was hired at the library and preferred internal promotions. For his part, Johnston wanted the freedom to select the best candidates for the jobs from wherever he could find them. He also believed in specialized training for librarians and started an apprentice program for senior library assistants. A competitive examination selected the five who could take the course. The program was rigorous and involved taking a summer library course offered by the University of Minnesota, working as an apprentice in the library for five months, and taking a Civil Service examination.

The friction between the library and commission grew so heated that, "with

In 1917 head librarian Dr. William Dawson Johnston began sending the first Saint Paul Public Library bookmobile to playgrounds. The press approved, calling the program one of "correctly turning the playground into a place of learning as well as a place of play."

a view to the establishment of better relations between the library and the Civil Service Bureau, a committee was appointed by the Mayor . . . to investigate the relations between the two bureaus." In an obvious effort to keep the problem from escalating and attracting unfavorable press notice, the committee recommended that "publicity not be given to the charges of one department or bureau against another until these charges have been laid before the mayor and their truth investigated in such manner as he may deem best."[108]

Such conflicts were not confined to St. Paul. In 1917 the executive officers of the American Library Association asked Johnston to chair a committee of the association to investigate the Civil Service in its relationship to library service.

JOHNSTON DEPARTS FOR PARIS

By the early 1920s, St. Paul, along with the rest of the country, was responding to the effects of world events and the pull of modern technology. The library ordered books in twenty-four modern languages. The Central Library was equipped with a state-of-the-art, switchboard-operated telephone system that connected the main library with its branches and with the public at large.

In 1921 Johnston was invited to go to Paris for a year to create a library out of the great number of books that had been sent to the American Expeditionary Force in France during World War I. He asked City Commissioner Lee R. S. Ferguson, his nominal boss, for a year's leave of absence, saying, "I should like to come back to my position here in St. Paul at the end of my year. . . . I have become much attached to St. Paul and to the work here and I should be very sorry indeed to give it up."

Ferguson, who, besides being a City Council member and commissioner of education was the rector of the Episcopal Church of the Messiah, denied Johnston's request for a leave. "Dr. Johnston gives the city no assurance that he intends to return to St. Paul and I feel it is decidedly unfair of him to ask us to grant a leave of absence," Ferguson said. "Furthermore I have no right to bind the city longer than my term of office which will expire next June."

The Women's Clubs of St. Paul were furious at Ferguson's decision. The Library Committee of the Fourth District and the State Federation of Women's Clubs joined in requesting that Dr. Johnston be granted the year's leave and be asked to decide, within six months, if he planned to return to St. Paul to resume his duties. They pointed out, quite reasonably, that if Johnston decided to stay in Paris, the commissioner would still have six months in which to select a new librarian. In the meantime, assistant librarian Jennie T. Jennings could take over.

Despite the public clamor, Commissioner Ferguson refused to grant the leave. Johnston regretted the furor his request had caused. "When I asked for the leave of absence I thought it would be quite possible to grant . . . that our present library staff could carry on the work efficiently during my absence. . . . Had I foreseen such a situation I should not have asked for a leave at all."

On September 27, 1921, he wrote a memorandum to his staff:

> Whether I leave St. Paul permanently or not, I hope to maintain in future years the friendships . . . which have meant so much to me since I became librarian. . . . I expect the staff to carry on the work in my absence in the same fine manner in which it has carried on . . . and that the different members of the staff will show the same loyalty to the traditions of the Library in the future which they have during the years when I have been with them.[109]

When Johnston boarded the 8:15 p.m. train leaving St. Paul for New York City, he carried in his waistcoat pocket several calling cards bearing a secret very few in St. Paul knew. The cards read "Sir William Johnston-Gordon." Johnston, indeed, bore an English knighthood as a family inheritance. He did not use it in the United States, but when he went to Paris to head the American Library, he decided to assume the title. Dr. W. Dawson Johnston, an English knight and one of the nation's most extraordinary and able librarians, left St. Paul in October 1921 for Paris, where he became director of the American Library. In 1926 he returned to the Library of Congress as its European representative and was active in that position until his death, at age fifty-seven, on November 18, 1928.

During Johnston's seven years in St. Paul he saw to the completion of the Central Library, three branch libraries, and a book collection of 300,000 volumes. Holders of library cards increased from 33,000 to more than 75,000, and the annual circulation of books went from 488,000 to more than one and a half million. With one exception, most likely Seattle, the city of St. Paul had the largest per capita circulation of books in the country.[110] But within months of his departure, the library that Johnston had elevated to such prominence began to free-fall under a successor who was far from bookish.

Dr. William Dawson Johnston, pictured with the staff of the Saint Paul Public Library in the 1920s.

The Saint Paul Public Library is a ghostly presence viewed through the snow-covered trees of Rice Park on a winter day in 1930.

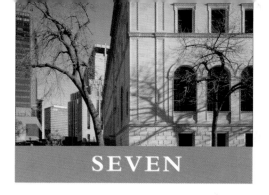

SEVEN

A Period of Decline

IT WAS A SMALL MIRACLE, following the departure of Dr. William Dawson Johnston, that St. Paul's commission form of government did not completely unravel the city's vaunted public library system. Under the provisions of the city charter, each elected commissioner was placed in charge of a city service, regardless of how little that individual knew about its management. The authority vested by the charter in a city commissioner gave him extraordinary powers. As a commissioner, Lee R. S. Ferguson had the authority to name department heads without consultation with anyone else in the city. Although selections were subject to ratification by a majority vote of his fellow commissioners and the mayor, it was the practice among the commissioners not to interfere in each other's domains. A commissioner never knew when he might urgently need the vote of a fellow official for some special project.

When Ferguson was faced with the task of replacing the city librarian, he disdained to follow the earlier example of the library board, which had conducted a nationwide search to fill the vacancy left by Helen McCaine. Instead, Ferguson offered the position to Webster Wheelock, a local man about town.

Webster Wheelock was born December 7, 1870, in a house on St. Peter Street in St. Paul, the son of Joseph and Kate Wheelock. Wheelock's father was the owner and editor-in-chief of the *Pioneer Press* newspaper. Wheelock graduated from Yale University in 1893 with a Phi Beta Kappa key and came home to work as a reporter on the newspaper. He

followed his father as editor and principal owner of the paper for three years until the stockholders sold the *Pioneer Press* to the *St. Paul Dispatch,* thus ending Wheelock's career as a journalist.

With the newspaper sold, Wheelock passed his time playing tennis and hung around the St. Paul Athletic Club, where he hobnobbed with city officials and prominent residents. He did farm-mortgage and insurance business on the side. Webster Wheelock was one of the boys.

OPPOSITION TO WHEELOCK AS CITY LIBRARIAN

When word spread that Ferguson planned to name Wheelock to the library position, professional librarians and educators reacted with outrage. Citizens enlisted leading educators of the city in the movement to prevent the appointment of a city librarian without professional training. St. Paul clubwomen protested Wheelock's appointment, claiming there was "a decided sentiment against the appointment of a man who had not had adequate library training."[111] Circulating a petition against the Wheelock appointment, they obtained the signatures of every member of the Macalester College faculty and many from the faculties at Hamline University and the University of Minnesota's College of Agriculture.[112] Headlines proclaimed "Fight Is Launched against Wheelock as City Librarian."[113] The petition protesting his appointment contained more than one thousand signatures when the women presented it to Commissioner Ferguson, but he was unmoved. He submitted Wheelock's

name for librarian to his fellow city commissioners for their approval. Mayor L.C. Hodgson and Commissioners Ferguson, F. W. Matson, J. H. McDonald, and Wenzel voted in favor. Ferguson claimed to be shocked when two commissioners, A. E. Smith and J. M. Clancy, voted against the nomination.

Ferguson berated Smith and Clancy for questioning his ability to run his department. "I never have interfered in any of your appointments," Ferguson exclaimed heatedly. "I have at all times supported you and given you credit for the ability to handle the affairs of your department. I am surprised that you would not extend to me the same courtesy."[114] The newspaper headline over the story of the council meeting read, "Wheelock Named Librarian After Fight in Council. Ferguson Submits the Appointment, Flays Smith and Clancy, Who Vote Against Selection."[115]

The minimum Civil Service requirements for jobs at the library did not apply to the head librarian position. The only qualifications for the position set by the city charter were that appointees have an education equal to that provided by the University of Minnesota and be familiar with library practice and usage. Clancy and Smith said they voted as they did because "I did not know anything favorable to Wheelock. There have been articles in the paper and if they knew what they were talking about, he was not the man to run the place. There have been people objecting to his appointment and you have never answered them."[116] Ferguson was still outraged and repeated, "In other words, I'm not capable of running my department."

Disregarding opposition to the appointment, the City Council appointed

Webster Wheelock city librarian on February 18, 1922. He was to take office on March 1 at an annual salary of $4,500. He had no training in the field of librarianship and was unprepared to take on the responsibilities of a complex urban library with its branches, station, and multiple services. As the next nine years would demonstrate, Webster Wheelock was clearly not equal to the task.

Wheelock was keenly aware of the opposition against him in the community and knew that he needed to prove himself as an effective leader. He promptly joined the American and Minnesota Library Associations, becoming elected president of the Minnesota association in 1923. He hoped to learn from these contacts, but after only a few months under his leadership, the excellent library organization created by his predecessor began to fall apart. Wheelock's goal was to increase book circulation, but circulation was 31,748 less in 1923 than it had been in 1922. He blamed the decline on radio, saying, "There is no doubt that the popularity of radio, which absorbs many hours previously devoted to reading, played a considerable part in the falling off."[117]

The more likely reason for the decline in visits to the library was the fact that the budget for books was reduced. Expenditures for books decreased from $42,000 in 1920 to $17,000 in 1927.[118] With fewer new books on the shelves, fewer people went to the library. In 1923 Wheelock made a plea for used books to be donated to the library and collected 6,056. He asked citizens to contribute their month-old magazines.

The library was not the only organization to suffer financially. The entire city was struggling for funds. St. Paul needed more and more services, yet the commissioners refused to increase the mill rate. Annual Civil Service pay raises took a greater and greater share of the library's budget, forcing the library to lay off employees to grant raises to the remaining staff.

Wheelock had no interest in outreach and so was unable to keep up the momentum and enthusiasm for the library that Dr. Johnston had generated. Instead of the friendly, welcoming image Johnston had created for the library, Wheelock's attitude was punitive. He sent registered letters threatening court action to borrowers who failed to return books. "Borrowers know the library 'means business,'" he insisted in his annual report. "There have been very few complaints of over-severity."[119]

This belligerent attitude toward delinquent borrowers, many of whom were merely absent-minded, did not endear the library to the public. Instead of being regarded as the affectionate site of story hours for children, the source for recreational reading or research, a place as comfortable and familiar as a living room, the library took on the forbidding aura of a police-state agency, hostile and unwelcoming.

Wheelock distributed no promotional leaflets about the library and gave few talks. He discouraged school visits and did nothing to expand children's services. Despite his journalism background, Wheelock made no contributions to library literature and no donors made major donations to the library during his tenure. He believed that until there was more money for more staff, more books on the shelves, and better service, it was not advisable to publicize the library. He stated that "the policy of the library in respect to publicity is quiescence."[120]

Webster Wheelock headed the Saint Paul Public Library from 1922 until his death at age sixty-one in 1931.

A Demand for Dictionaries

WHEN THE CROSSWORD CRAZE HIT ST. PAUL, dictionaries were so much in demand that the library was forced to impose a five-minute rule on their use. "There is hardly a moment when the dictionaries are not in use, mostly by middle-aged and elderly women," said Marie Bracem, acting chief of the reference section. "There are four large dictionaries in this department, nine in the reading room, one in the industrial arts room and half a dozen or so smaller ones in the circulation department that can be taken out. Yet we have had to order an additional large dictionary for the reference room and may be to get still another."

St. Paul Dispatch, January 10, 1925.

Locked in the Library

SEVENTY-YEAR-OLD FRED FAKEK was deeply engrossed on a paper on grafting fruit trees when the library closed at 6:00 p.m. No one noticed him sitting in a corner reading, and he did not hear the librarian call out that the building was closing. When he finally looked up from his paper, he was alone and locked in. After rattling the doors and finding himself unable to open them, he found a telephone and called the police. Upon their arrival, they too were unable to open the doors. Finally they put up a ladder and an officer crawled into the library through a second-story window. Fakek at first refused to climb down the ladder. Faced with the prospect of spending the night on the cold stone floor of the library, however, he finally allowed First Captain J. W. Harley to coax him down.

St. Paul Pioneer Press, May 30, 1926.

Quiescence led to indifference. If the library did not believe in itself, it was difficult for the public to care about it. Wheelock did not want to promote a library that was not buying many books, believing it was wrong to invite people into the library only to find old titles.

Wheelock's restrictions on publicity created a downward spiral. A reduced staff could not handle an increase in circulation, so he ordered fewer books, with the result that fewer and fewer book lovers crossed the marble lobby into the empty rooms. Residents of St. Paul forgot that the library had once been the cultural center of their city, Everyman's university. Now, more and more of them dismissed it as a factor in their lives and the memory of what the library had once been slowly faded from their consciousness.

The late 1920s and early 1930s were difficult financial years for St. Paul as the city struggled to recover from the war and headed into the Great Depression. While every public institution struggled, the Saint Paul Public Library suffered far greater economic hardship than did Minneapolis's library, which continued under the dynamic leadership of Gratia Countryman. Communities with well-supported, active libraries had constituencies who understood the benefits conferred on cities by libraries and supported them at the polls.

In October 1924, Wheelock proposed closing the school library branches based on his budget projections for 1925. The proposal brought a storm of protest that so overwhelmed him that he reallocated his budget to include funding for the school operations. Financing of school libraries, however, remained a recurrent crisis throughout the 1920s that resulted, in 1927, in the laying off of five library clerks and five assistants and the closing of seven of the remaining seventeen school stations.[121] The closing of the school stations also cut off any library services to the adults in those neighborhoods.

LAWSUITS WIN SUPPORT FOR LIBRARY

Webster Wheelock had a business background that he used to the advantage of the library in two court cases, both decided in the late 1920s. In the first case, the courts decreed that the proceeds of the long-ago bequest of Judge Henry Hale could be used to build branch libraries. Approximately $88,000 became available, which the city would later use to construct the Hamline and Merriam Park Branch Libraries. Both were completed in 1930.

The second court case involved the old Market House property, which many people had forgotten was owned by the library. Walter J. Richardson, along with his father, Harris Richardson, who had been a member of the old library board, questioned who was getting the rental income from the land on which the Market House once stood and was now the site of the popular Hotel St. Francis. Why, they asked, was the library being starved for funds when it should be getting income from one of the most valuable pieces of land in St. Paul? The *St. Paul Dispatch* headlined, "Library in Peril, Petition States: Fund Suit Filed." The story continued, "St. Paul's public library has deteriorated alarmingly and is in grave danger of destruction for want of adequate operating funds."[122]

Edward P. Davis, president of the Northwestern Trust Company, was a member of the Library Advisory Committee. Claiming to represent St. Paul's taxpayers, Davis filed suit against the city to restrain officials from diverting rentals from the old library property at Seventh and Wabasha Streets into St. Paul's general fund. The rentals totaled approximately $50,000 a year. The city charter of 1912 had left ownership of the Market House land with the library, but had assigned its management to the commissioner of education. The rental income had gone into the city's general fund ever since.

Davis told the court that the provision for the operation of the Saint Paul Public Library was so inadequate that it should have the exclusive use of all revenues resulting from the renting of the property. He characterized the library as St. Paul's municipal orphan because of its neglect: "This action is not directed against any individual or group of individuals but against existing, injurious conditions which have created a situation demanding an immediate remedy." Davis declared that the condition of the library was so much worse than the public realized that, unless something was done, the Central Library and some of its branches would be abandoned. Davis's opinion carried weight. He was the oldest man in service with the Northwestern Trust Company and the last remaining individual who had been associated with the regime of James J. Hill.

The suit was settled in favor of the library, but there was a downside. As Wheelock wrote in his annual report, "This property is probably as valuable as any in the city and ought ultimately to provide a substantial fund either for building or endowment purposes." He added, "As was expected, the Council found it necessary to offset this new resource by a deduction in the amount raised by taxation for library purposes."[123]

CITIZENS ORDER FIRST STUDY OF LIBRARY

The newspaper headline writer did not exaggerate when he wrote that the Saint

The Hotel St. Francis was built on the site of the burned-out Market House in 1916 and survives today as Seventh Place, a residential building with 130 apartments. In the late 1990s the St. Paul Port Authority, which owned the building, entered negotiations with the St. Paul Companies to buy the building and the adjacent Orpheum Theater. The company planned to raze both properties for the expansion of its headquarters. When the city's Heritage Preservation Commission recommended that Seventh Place, the Orpheum Theater, and the nearby Coney Island deserved historic designation, plans for the sale were shelved.

Paul Public Library was in peril. In 1928 a group of concerned citizens raised the funds for a survey of the situation. They appealed to the president of the American Library Association for the names of widely recognized librarians who could advise them. Two of the nation's most prominent and respected librarians, Arthur E. Bostwick, director of the St. Louis Public Library, and Carl Vitz, director of the Toledo Public Library, agreed to visit. They studied the Saint Paul Public Library and reached three main conclusions.

First, the library needed more books. "The chief need is a larger appropriation for the purchase of books. Curtailment of service is to be greatly deplored, but the need for books comes first."

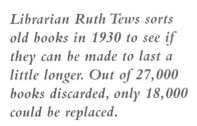

Librarian Ruth Tews sorts old books in 1930 to see if they can be made to last a little longer. Out of 27,000 books discarded, only 18,000 could be replaced.

Second, the citizens had lost interest in the library. The consultants were especially critical of the commission form of government of St. Paul. They recommended that the library be separated from other city departments and run by a governing board as it had been in the past.

Third, the branch system was inadequate. "Instead of four branch libraries, a city with the population of St. Paul should have eight or ten."

The consultants had additional recommendations that they pressed on the committee with just as much urgency:

That the tax levy be raised to the equivalent of one dollar per capita.

That there be more publicity for the library. "The publicity policy seems to have been negative and quiescent. . . . We recommend a more active one but avoiding too much harping on lack of books."

That staff be cut to buy books. "We feel that here is the greatest shortcoming . . . and that further cuts in personnel . . . may be justified if necessary to increase the supply of books, the life blood of a library. We can scarcely dwell on this point too emphatically."[124]

The consultants had done their job. Now, it was up to the citizens of St. Paul to take action to save their library.

Despite Webster Wheelock's good intentions throughout his nine years of stewardship, the Saint Paul Public Library continued on its downward plunge. Citizens who had once expressed pride in their library forgot it existed. Due to a lack of funding (expenditures for books decreased $25,000 between 1920 and 1927), the book collection failed to meet the most basic needs of the patrons.

Wheelock was clearly aware of the deplorable situation of the library. The problem was that he had few ideas of what to do about it. In 1930 he again asked for donations of used books, hoping to receive as many as 100,000 volumes. He sent out a small flier asking that books be brought to the library during Book Week, April 21–26. "For the first time the Saint Paul Library appeals to you for your help," he wrote. "It finds itself in a desperate situation with a very small book fund and readers wearing out 11,000 volumes a year more than it can replace. . . . Please do not bring in old text books or books from long series, such as *Tom Swift,* the *Bobbsey Twins,* the *Elsie* books or long series of Boy Scout or Girl Scout stories. The library needs and wants better books than these."[125] He reported that *Uncle Tom's Cabin* was popular and the library had sixty copies in circulation. Children had worn out 300 copies of *Little Black Sambo.*

In an interview with the press in the spring of 1930, Wheelock sounded both discouraged and resigned. "The library is in a desperate situation," he said. "For seven years it has had a book fund only half large enough for a library in a city of St. Paul's size. As a result it has been reduced to the lowest ebb of efficiency. The burden of carrying on under such discouraging conditions has grown too great. Relief has been sought in vain from the city administration. . . . We are tired of gently reminding the public of our situation."[126]

After a three-month illness, Wheelock died in office on April 1, 1931, at the age of sixty-one.

Head librarian Jennie T. Jennings on the occasion of the fiftieth anniversary of the Saint Paul Public Library, October 1932.

EIGHT

Surviving the Depression

THE CONSULTANTS' REPORT on the condition of the library got the public's attention. The Library Advisory Board, the organization mandated by the city charter, had met only intermittently. Months had passed without a meeting; in fact, no meeting had been held during the entire year of 1928. Editorial writers excoriated the city:

> The experts deplore the failure of the department to make real use of the Library Advisory Board. They charge to this a large part of the responsibility for the indifference which the public shows toward the library. . . . If the library is today suffering from public indifference and lack of adequate support, large part of the responsibility must be laid to the failure to acquaint the public with, and to bring about a sympathetic understanding of the condition.[127]

Abashed by the consultants' report and editorial outrage, the Library Advisory Board hastily reorganized and met on April 2, 1929. Members vowed to turn the board into "an effective and responsible body, thoroughly conversant with the Library, its problems and its needs to the end that there may be a body of citizens well-informed . . . in which the public will have confidence." Members agreed to meet every Tuesday to study the affairs of the library and, in addition, to hold monthly meetings.[128]

The reorganized Advisory Board intended to make things happen. The board organized five perma-

nent committees (Finance and Budget, Personnel and Civil Service, Building Program, Library, and Gifts and Endowments) and began campaigning to remove the professional library grades from the Civil Service. On June 18, 1929, they moved that the City Council proceed immediately with building and equipping two library branches out of the proceeds of the Hale Memorial Fund on sites that had long ago been donated to the city by the Hamline and Merriam Park communities.[129]

The public library also gained a second support group, this one an organization without legal ties to the city. Called the Friends of the Library, it was organized in 1923 to replace the Saint Paul Library Association, which had been formed in 1896 to campaign for the new Central Library building. Organizers of the Friends, concerned about the direction the library had been heading, pledged their help to expand and improve library service. E. P. Davis, who had brought the earlier suit against the city, was the organization's treasurer.

The Friends organization began its efforts by distributing a tiny, four-page booklet titled "What the Public Library Is and Does," with information taken from the library's annual report of 1922. Inside the front cover is a plea for help:

> This little booklet has been designed to give you as briefly as possible a concrete idea of what your Public Library is and does, because we want you as a citizen of St. Paul to realize the necessity of aiding the present movement

to keep this great educational institution from having to curtail its activities.

The portion of the city taxes allotted to the Public Library this year is only sufficient to keep the plant functioning. . . . We are therefore appealing to public-spirited citizens to become members of "The Friends of the Library" by contributing the nominal fee of $1 and endeavoring to obtain new books for the shelves. "$1 and a book" is our slogan and we are suggesting that when you have bought and read a new book you will send it to the library for the benefit of those who are reliant upon this institution for their educational facilities. Any old sets of books you may care to send in will be acceptable. Remember, a book in circulation is worth a dozen on the shelf. Will you help us?

On the following page, next to a photograph of the Central Library, the leaflet advises:

If you Want to Know:
The address of a friend
in another city,
How to can green peas,
What wheat was worth in 1896,
How to take care of the baby,
Who wrote that poem,
Who anyone is or was,

Or anything about
anything or anybody,
Call up the Public Library.

Unfortunately, this first iteration of the Friends of the Library did not last and soon all that remained of the organization was a copy, preserved in the Central Library, of the booklet the Friends had printed.

The Friends of the Saint Paul Public Library purchased this model of a deep-sea fishing boat for the Children's Room in 1925. When it was acquired, the model was believed to be more than one hundred years old.

JENNIE JENNINGS BECOMES CHIEF LIBRARIAN

Assistant librarian Jennie Jennings, brought to St. Paul early in William Dawson Johnston's tenure, had served faithfully as assistant director throughout the troublesome Wheelock years. A consummate librarian, Jennings was the author of several professional articles, among them, "Statistics of Women's Library Work" and "How the Library of Congress Classification Works Out in a Public Library."

Jennings confessed a weakness for western novels: "I suppose my liking to read Western stories will earn a black eye for me from other librarians. Of course I do not believe that Wright and Gray have produced literature. Oh my, no." Jennings traced her fondness for westerns to the years she had spent at a gold mining camp with her husband. "He liked Western stories too and I used to read them to him after his sight failed." She found writer Theodore Dreiser's work "ponderous" and Sinclair Lewis's *Elmer*

Gantry "unfair and untrue." Her "special favorites" in books were Hawthorne, Dickens, and Galsworthy.[130]

Following Webster Wheelock's death, Commissioner of Education Irving Pearce, who had succeeded Commissioner Lee R. S. Ferguson, named Jennings head librarian. "In announcing the appointment of Jennie T. Jennings as librarian, I do so after a complete study and analysis of the position and upon the recommendation of the sub-committee of the Library Advisory Board," Pearce stated. "I believe that Mrs. Jennings' education, character and experience qualify her for the promotion, which is a just one, and should tend to encourage more initiative and closer cooperation in the Department and show that when efficient service is given there is a chance for promotion." Her salary was not to exceed $300 a month.

Jennie Jennings was about to face the most trying period of her entire library career. It was 1932, one of the two worst years of the Great Depression. Since 1929, 10,000 banks had failed, more than thirteen million people had lost their jobs, and almost one-quarter of all Americans were unemployed. Franklin D. Roosevelt was elected president.

Jennie Thornburg Jennings was born in Farmland, Indiana, in the late 1860s. While she was still a child, her family moved to Dallas County, Iowa, where she attended the country schools. She continued her education at Iowa State College, later earning a bachelor's degree in letters at Cornell University. Following her graduation she worked for the Cornell University Library and attended the summer sessions of the New York State Library School. After marrying

Jennie Thornburg Jennings held the Saint Paul Public Library together during the trying years of the Great Depression. Her first job at the library was as chief of the catalog division and head of the training class. In 1919 she was appointed assistant librarian and became head librarian in 1931. During the eleven years that Jennings conducted library apprentice classes, more than one hundred aspiring librarians completed the course. Jennings also taught the summer sessions of the University of Minnesota Library School.

Thomas Brownfield Jennings, she moved with him to Arizona, but an accident to her husband that destroyed his sight brought her back into library work. She taught cataloging and classification at a Riverside, California, school and was appointed head cataloger in Randolph-Macon Woman's College in Lynchburg, Virginia. Two years later she became reference librarian at Iowa State College.

Deeply invested in library work as a profession, Jennings was a member of the American Library Association and attended its national conferences in 1923, 1925, 1928, and 1930. She chaired the Catalog Section of the American Library Association in 1921–1922 and the Committee on Regional Groups of Catalogers. Jennings contemplated the world with a steady, serious gaze through large, round eyeglasses. St. Paul's politically oriented city commissioners did not intimidate her.

STRUGGLING TO KEEP LIBRARIES OPEN

Where Webster Wheelock had been reluctant to draw undue attention to the problems facing the library and ask for public support, Jennings was not. She appealed directly to the conscience of the community. In a "Letter to the Citizens" in 1932, she wrote, "Do you, Citizens of St. Paul, want your library to be closed for a month, as the Comptroller proposes? The responsibility is yours. Will you close the door of opportunity to the children, to the unemployed, to the student and above all to the youth who has found all other doors of opportunity closed? Will you close the library also?"[131]

A year later, in 1933 when city budget hearings loomed, she wrote another eloquent appeal, this one addressed to the "friends of the library." It is unclear if she meant the organization by that name or was including all St. Paul patrons of the library in her salutation. But there was no mistaking her meaning. She pointed out that the library budget submitted by the comptroller cut out $33,269, which was more than the cost of service in all of St. Paul's branch libraries: "It does not seem possible that St. Paul will allow the widest cultural agency in the city to be closed to its citizens and its children in this time of special need."[132]

"Does St. Paul mean to destroy the library service built up with so much care and sacrifice?" she wrote. "While the budget has decreased, the demands upon the Library have increased heavily. In the Central Library and branches the increase in circulation last year was 160,367 more than in 1930." After years of decline, attendance at the libraries was indeed up. Workers who had been laid off in the Depression were haunting the libraries, scrutinizing the help-wanted notices, studying books on retraining, and, in some cases, merely trying to stay warm.

Jennings fought against the idea, promoted by the city comptroller, of temporarily closing the library. "The fact that Minneapolis has closed its libraries for two weeks has been held up as an example to St. Paul. Minneapolis has not cut the salary rate of its staff and is taking this method to avoid such a decrease. St. Paul has cut salaries in 1928, 1931, and 1932 and promises another for 1933."

Her pleadings did not save the library from closure. "The closing of the Public Library and its branches on Thanksgiving and on November 25–26 [1932] as a result of tax delinquencies has been a real hardship on the men and women as well as to the children of St. Paul," Jennings wrote. "This is demonstrated by the crowds which thronged the libraries on Monday, November 28, following the closing days. This was by far the largest day's work in the Library's history exceeding by nearly one-half the preceding largest day, November 12. Over 20,000 volumes were handled in that one day."[133]

Patrons in the Periodical Room of the Saint Paul Public Library, 1933.

Miss Pusin in the Classroom Department types cards for incoming books, which Milton Smith is reshelving. Note the classroom boxes stacked six feet high.

The Classroom Department, where books were selected and packed in rectangular wooden boxes to be sent to St. Paul Public School classrooms.

When the issue of again closing the library came before the St. Paul City Council on September 16, 1933, the newly energized Library Advisory Board issued an impassioned statement to the taxpayers of St. Paul that left no doubt of its position:

The Comptroller has suggested closing the Library for one month. We wish to ask which month of the year the taxpayers of St. Paul are to be deprived of an institution which for the past one hundred years has been recognized as an inherent part of American civilization? We do not believe that the average taxpayer, in order to save three and one-third cents per month, wishes to deprive himself and his children of library service which is an integral force in his business, social and cultural life. We earnestly request that every citizen of St. Paul who believes that the proper functioning of the Library is worth to him three and one-third cents per month, appear at the Council meeting which will be held

at the Council Chambers of the Court House Saturday at 10 a.m. The City Council has the power to minimize the disaster by increasing the Library appropriation by ten percent. Tell the Council to do so.[134]

Despite Jennings's campaigning and the fact that the country was emerging from the Depression, St. Paul's libraries were forced to close, not for a month, but for fifteen days, from August 25 to September 8, 1935. The City Council appropriation for the library, which had been $176,950 in 1930, had shrunk to $154,677. The 1930 appropriation had been down 22 percent from the previous year, despite the fact that book circulation was up 10 percent and Reading Room and Reference Room usage was up almost 40 percent because of the Depression-era need for information on jobs and skills. As Jennings pointed out, "The library has $22,000 less funds in 1935 than in 1934. Ten years ago, in the year 1925 when there were only three branch libraries, the appropriation was $222,376." Jennings noted in her annual report that "your library is now suffering the effects of its years of starvation." More than half of the books added to the library's collection that year were gifts. Rather than lay off staff, Jennings herself made the decision to close the library. By closing the library, "all members of the staff are thus treated alike, all losing their salaries for that time."[135]

When the *St. Paul Daily News* suggested that the closing of the library was not much of an inconvenience because people took out hundreds of books in anticipation, she responded with indignation, insisting that the article gave a wrong impression. "Approximately 48,000 books and magazines, which ordinarily would have been borrowed for home use during

the last two weeks, gathered dust on the library shelves. The Central Library alone would have circulated 15,000 volumes to adults and 3,000 to children," she said, producing figures showing 7,500 patrons had been denied the services of the Reading and Reference Rooms because of the closing.[136] Jennings was not one to let a slight on the library pass without a response.

When the library reopened, books "literally poured over the counter." The press reported triple lines of library patrons returning books. By 6:00 p.m. on September 8 more than 7,500 had been returned, and that total did not include children's books. The librarians had been too busy to keep count.

Notwithstanding the impoverished state of the city's finances, Jennings was unrelenting in bringing the acute financial needs of the library to the public's attention. She pointed out how library services were needed most desperately by people who were out of work. In her budget request for 1934 she wrote, "In the Public Library unemployed men and women find books to improve their equipment for future jobs, the young high school and college graduates, baffled by the closed doors where they vainly apply for work, come to the Public Library, here to continue their studies or to escape from discouragement in books of adventure, travel or romance. The Public Library has over 373,000 books for the use of its citizens. We ask for sufficient funds *to keep the library doors open*" (emphasis in the original).[137]

Throughout the tenure of Webster Wheelock, library attendance had dropped every year. Under Jennings, despite the Depression era's cutbacks, library attendance increased dramatically.

Circulation in 1931 set a record, increasing by 100,000 books over 1930.[138] In her budget request for 1934, Jennings presented the city commissioners with a five-year comparison. "In 1928 our patrons borrowed 1,463,936 books and magazines," she wrote. "In 1932 they borrowed 1,713,493, an increase of 250,557. The Reference and Periodical departments had an increase in readers of 73,026. Does St. Paul recognize this by an increase in the budget? NO, by a decrease of $27,929 in 1933 and a proposed decrease of $11,000 for 1934."[139]

In her 1935 budget request, Jennings noted, "The addition of steel book stacks should be included as the most necessary item. To continue storing books in the sub-basement where mold and dust accumulate or to continue piling books on the floor entails delay in the service, adds to the cost of service and causes deterioration in the books themselves. For nine years this stack unit has been requested. Double the amount now requested will soon be needed. Respectfully submitted, Mrs. T. B. Jennings, librarian."[140]

THE LIBRARY BEACON
In response to the library consultants' call for more public information about the library, Webster Wheelock had launched a newsletter called *The Library Beacon*. In its first issue in March 1929, he had written, "The purpose of this little publication, which we intend to issue monthly except in July and August, is to give to the people of St. Paul information about their library." The first issue listed recent donors to the library and news of new books. The publication of *The Library Beacon,* and later, its absence, became a barometer of the economic health of the library.

The second issue brought the good news of a $10,000 trust fund established by Mrs. James H. Skinner and her son, William W. Skinner, as a memorial to the late James H. Skinner, founder of St. Paul's Merchants Trust and Savings. The library did not have an endowment at the time, and the trust, mindful of the city's tendency to deduct from tax support any contributions to the library, was careful to state that the trust was intended to supplement the amount raised by taxation and not be substituted for any part of it.

The September 1929 issue of the *Beacon* announced, "After a wait of many years the sites donated to the city for branch libraries by the residents of Merriam Park and of Hamline districts are to be utilized. On each of them will be erected a library building large enough to care for the needs of the community for many years and of a type worthy of those two resident districts."

Friendly litigation, overseen by Webster Wheelock, had finally resulted in the allocation of the Judge Henry Hale gift of almost forty years before to the construction of the two branch libraries. The writer

Myra W. Buell, head of the Central Library's branch activities, and Jean M. Christmas set off to deliver books to inmates at the Ramsey County jail, 1935.

Sorting some of the 30,000 worn books in June 1933 are, from left: Mrs. Schulz (standing), Lorraine Schwarz, Mrs. Dolan (standing), Miss Tews, Miss Gebhard, and Dorothy Toomey.

Patrons fill the Greenleaf Clark Reference Room on the third floor of the Central Library in the early 1930s. During the Great Depression, the library was crowded with unemployed workers who were seeking information on jobs and studying new careers.

of the *Beacon* article added, "There is a fly in the ointment, for that branch [Merriam Park] can not be operated until the library appropriation is considerably increased. There is little prospect of that until 1931. Fortunately, the Hamline branch building can be operated with no increase in cost over that of operating the present rented branch." The Hamline Branch Library was an outgrowth of a small station opened in 1908 in a millinery store on Snelling Avenue. By 1918 the station had been moved six times, ending up in a rented storefront a few feet from its first home. Staffing by a professional librarian helped the station to grow into a branch library that opened to the public on September 2, 1930.

The 1931 issues of *The Beacon* reported that the library maintained, in addition to the Central Library, five branch libraries, twenty-seven neighborhood industrial and institutional stations, and gave bedside services in ten hospitals. The issues between April and June 1933 were combined into one four-page pamphlet that contained a plea for borrowers to take better care of the books. Titled "Mending the Libraries' Books," it asked:

> Who tore the pages out of this book?
> Who broke the back of that book?
> Who cooked this book?
> Who underlined these paragraphs?
> Was it the dog?
> Was it the baby?
> Was it you?

It was obvious that money was running out for the publication of the *Library Beacon*.

The next issue of the *Beacon* did not appear until 1934 and covered the months January through March. "During the early months of 1934 the Reading and Reference rooms have been crowded with

The plucky librarians who held the library together during the Great Depression, ca. 1932. Seated, from left: Myra W. Buell, Belle M. Owens, Jennie T. Jennings, Helga C. Benson, and Elizabeth W. Chute. Standing, from left: J. Charlotte Campbell, Elsa E. Juds, Della McGregor, Katherine Dame, Amy C. Moon, and Elsie L. Baker.

readers," it reported. "In these two departments alone the recorded attendance in 1933 was 242,083 as compared with 153,668 in 1928. Men seeking new skills in their trades . . . the unemployed studying to prepare for possible positions or to find enjoyment and escape from anxiety. Of all subjects, economics shows the greatest increase in number of readers."

The *Library Beacon* dated January–June 1936 brought discouraging news. "The year 1935 marks the lowest point in the library's budget for ten years. . . . All library expenditures except bare running expenditures were cut to the absolute minimum for the remainder of the year. The utmost endeavors were made to keep the Library doors open so that the public could use what resources the Library had although few new books could be bought in the last half of the year." The *Beacon* dated July–December 1936 contains no announcement that it is the final issue.[141]

Over in Minneapolis, Gratia Countryman, who had been the dynamic director of the public library since 1904, resigned. During her thirty-two years as head of the library, she had opened 350 book distribution points in the city, including twenty-one branches, fifty-three business and factory stations, and fifteen hospital libraries.[142]

The three worst years of the Great Depression—1932, 1933, and 1934—were also peak years for users of the Saint Paul Public Library. The library was frequented by more readers during the Depression than at any preceding time. Most of the books consulted were of a serious nature, such as nonfiction works on economics and social subjects. Attendance in the Periodical and Reference Departments went up from 153,000 in 1928 to 242,000 in 1933 and 1934. In 1938, library patrons checked out 1,307,703 books.[143]

Of Prohibition and Presidents

IN 1932, ON THE OCCASION of the fiftieth anniversary of the Saint Paul Public Library, Mrs. Janes Randall DeCamp, a former employee, wrote from her home in Berkeley, California:

"Your building today [Central Library] is very beautiful but you have nothing more beautiful than the roof of the Ingersoll Building when moonlight was on the winding Mississippi with the green just showing on the hills of Dayton's Bluff and West St. Paul and Grote's Tivoli all festive with lights and the band playing and the waiters rushing around with . . . oh well, that was before Prohibition anyway.

"Only once did my allegiance to her [librarian Mrs. Helen J. McCaine] go under the smallest cloud. That was when President Cleveland was to address the multitude in Bridge Square, his charming bride at his side, and the directors decreed that the library should be closed that evening and she wouldn't let any of us come down to hang out of the windows and drink in his eloquence. We felt life was hard and that one time our beloved superior could not intercede for us."

The staff of the Saint Paul Public Library celebrates its fiftieth anniversary, October 1932.

A Paean of Praise

"ST. PAUL IS MY FIRST LOVE, first in childhood and first in my library service. I knew the library when it was housed in the Court House; was part of it in the old building at Seventh and Wabasha streets; and grieved with the community when fire swept away its wonderful collection of books. I recall the gallant courage of officials and staff to keep the library spirit awake after the fire, while reorganizing in the old House of Hope church; and I sang a paean of praise with others of the staff and friends who took part in the first Open House of our beautiful new library in 1917. The following year I went to Washington, D.C., to enter war work. In the fall of 1920 I came to take charge of the Periodical Department of the Los Angeles Public Library."

Letter from Blanche E. McKown to Jennie T. Jennings, September 29, 1932.

As part of its fiftieth anniversary celebration in 1932, the Saint Paul Public Library honored eight forty-year patrons of the library. Seated, from left: Mrs. Mary Kellogg McIlrath, Mrs. Ida Wilson Smith, Mrs. Clara Ingalls, and Mrs. W. J. Logue. Standing, from left: E. C. Corridan, W. J. Logue, H. W. Phillips, and Thomas Conway. (Note photograph of Webster Wheelock on wall, top row, second from left.)

Famed children's librarian Della McGregor hands out cookies and punch July 29, 1943, at a party for children and their dolls at the Saint Paul Public Library. The formidable "Miss McGregor" reigned over the department for more than half a century. She was revered by writers of children's literature and their publishers, and through her efforts the children's program at the Saint Paul Public Library became recognized throughout the country.

NINE

Collections and The Friends

POLITICS WAS ALWAYS the shadow looming over the Saint Paul Public Library. As Al Heckman, executive of the Norwest and Grotto Foundations and consummate St. Paul insider, explained in a 1991 interview with editor Virginia Brainard Kunz of *Ramsey County History* magazine:

> You have to remember that in those days we had a form of city government where the councilmen ran at large and the mayor appointed them to positions as full time heads of city departments. Politically, the mayor would tend to appoint councilmen to positions that either would bring someone into the limelight where he would be likely to make mistakes that would be black marks on his career, or he would bury a councilman in a department where he was not very visible.

> Mayor Mark Gehan appointed John Finley as Director of Libraries, Auditoriums and Public Buildings. Finley was a locomotive foreman on the railroad and I think had about a fourth grade education. It was obvious that Mark Gehan was trying to stick him out here where he'd make all kinds of blunders and wouldn't be elected again. But John was a smart man. When John found out what position the mayor was appointing him to, he went over to the University and asked for advice as to who was the best person to head the Saint Paul Library.

The University of Minnesota spokesperson recommended Smith College graduate Perrie Jones.

JENNINGS IS DEMOTED

It had been Jennie T. Jennings's fate to be an administrator of the Saint Paul Public Library through some of its most difficult years, from the decline that took place under Webster Wheelock to the despair brought on by the Great Depression. Through it all, she never faltered in calling on city officials to act responsibly in their support for the library. While it is possible that her unrelenting advocacy may have become too much for city officials, it was also clear that it was time for a change of leadership. "I want a person who can go around and talk to the luncheon clubs and sell the Public Library," said Director of Libraries John Finley on December 16, 1936. He then demoted Jennings back to assistant librarian and named Perrie Jones the new St. Paul librarian.

The Library Advisory Board responded immediately:

> The Library Advisory Board of St. Paul desires to place on record its lasting appreciation for the work which has been done for the Public Library and for the citizens of St. Paul by Mrs. Jennie T. Jennings. . . . As Assistant Librarian and as Librarian, Mrs. Jennings has served the Public Library during one of the most critical and difficult periods of its history. With a budget reduced far below the safety point she has succeeded in maintaining the library as nearly unimpaired as was humanly possible. Faced with public indifference and with all kinds of pressure which demanded still more drastic reduction of services in the library,

The delighted audience at the first of a summer series of puppet plays presented on the library terrace. In this performance on June 14, 1937, puppeteers Mary Alice Kane and Joseph Ryan presented three plays: **Animal Orchestra, The Three Bears,** *and* **Rumpelstiltskin.**

Mrs. Jennings stood firm in her defense of the essential features of library work. For this courage and firmness the City of St. Paul should always be deeply grateful to her. . . . The Board wishes to express its grateful appreciation . . . for her cordial and gracious co-operation with a group of interested citizens who have shared with her a sense of the great importance of the Public Library."[144]

Jennings accepted her demotion with good grace until August 1937, when it was announced that she had resigned and that her position of assistant librarian would be filled by Mary Parson from the University of Michigan. A few days later, word got around that Jennings had *not* resigned but had been dismissed by Perrie Jones so that Jones could bring in Parson to take Jennings's place.[145]

This was a controversy of major proportions. Jennings hired a lawyer to fight her forced resignation and to demand her rights and benefits under the Civil Service System. The city comptroller inserted himself into the controversy by declaring that he would refuse to sign any provisional appointment for Miss Parsons because she was from out of town and that endorsements should be only for persons in line for promotion.[146] Then Finley poured more fuel on the fire by announcing that he was abolishing the position of assistant librarian as an economy move.

The public responded with outraged letters to the editor:

As an employee of the Public Library for eight years it was my pleasure to serve under Mrs.

Jennings in her capacity as Librarian and to be in close contact with her work. Mrs. Jennings had the profound love and respect of the entire library staff and her efficiency as librarian was reflected in the admirable manner in which she guided the library through the trying and lean budget years since 1929, for although Mr. Wheelock was titular librarian until he died, Mrs. Jennings, in fact, conducted the routine work of that office.

Another expressed indignation about the "raw deal" that a public servant of twenty years was receiving. The Minnesota Federation of Women's Clubs wrote, "The Federation condemns as improper, unwarranted and contrary to the spirit of the City Charter any changes in technical or professional positions made by a Commissioner for political or personal whims."[147]

The City Council resolved the situation by reconsidering Finley's decision to abolish the assistant librarian position. In return, Jennings agreed to remain as assistant librarian until August 1, 1938, when she would resign and accept a pension.[148] Jennie Jennings, the librarian who had championed the public library and held it together throughout the years of the Great Depression, lived in St. Paul for another two decades until her death in January 1956 after a long illness. No official note was taken of her passing and she was buried with only a small graveside service in Linden, Iowa.

JONES DEBUTS

The new librarian, Perrie Jones, was born the second of four children in Wabasha, Minnesota, on March 22, 1886, and grew up on the banks of the Missis-

Brontë and Barbers

A REPORTER FOR THE *Pioneer Press* decided in 1938 to find out which books library patrons were reading. He reported on March 20 that one copy of Plato's *Dialogues* had been taken out by the wife of a taxicab driver, two students, and a housewife. C. E. Montague's *Disenchantment,* one of the most trenchant collections of essays on the Great War, had been circulated to the wife of an engineer, an unemployed newspaperman, an usher at a movie theater, the wife of a hospital grounds superintendent, a housemaid, and two students. Emily Brontë's *Wuthering Heights* was taken out by five students, the wife of an editor, a housemaid, an unemployed woman, the wife of a barber, a rental library clerk, and a clerk in a music store. The reporter's article never explained how he determined the occupation of each of the readers.

sippi River. She remembered her childhood with fondness. "I can't tell you how lovely it was. The Mississippi was our back yard. We could sit on the bluffs and look across at the Wisconsin shore which grandmother said always reminded her of Wales. We children loved the river traffic and knew every boat and packet by the sound of its whistle and the shape of its funnels. . . . School was a mile away but we always walked and came home to lunch so we did four miles every day."[149] Jones loved to walk, and later walked to work, thinking nothing of taking twenty-five-mile hikes in Europe and in the Black Hills of South Dakota.

Jones attended the University of Minnesota for three years and then Smith College, where she earned her bachelor's degree. Following graduation she taught school in Rushford, Minnesota, where she also coached the girls'

A patient hospitalized in 1943, following an encounter with a truck, enjoys a book provided by the Saint Paul Public Library Hospital Service.

Lucille Francis, hospital librarian of the Saint Paul Public Library, reads to children at Children's Hospital, 1944.

basketball team. From 1911 to 1915 she managed the Wabasha Public Library. Realizing that she needed more formal training if she were to advance in the field, she enrolled in the New York Public Library School and upon graduation accepted a position as an assistant in the Technology Division. When World War I broke out, Jones was given a leave of absence to go with the YMCA/YWCA to France, where, among other duties, she worked in a hospital identifying name tags on the rows of wounded waiting for medical care.

This experience had a profound effect on her. For the rest of her life she would focus on providing services to people confined in hospitals and other institutions. Finding a way to combine her love of books with the needs of the sick, she pioneered the field of hospital library services. She was among the first to recognize that access to books was as essential for the sick as it was for the well.

At first it was hard for Perrie Jones to return to the United States and work with people who had no idea what the war had been like. She lived for a year with friends in Europe before revealing her plans in a letter to her family. "I have thought the last few days rather seriously of investigating the State Library Commission in St. Paul. I know people there and should like to get a job in the organized end of it."[150]

When she returned to Minnesota, Jones learned that the Wilder Charity (now the Wilder Foundation) had agreed to pay the salary of a hospital librarian for the Saint Paul Public Library for one year and she was chosen for the position. Jones's desire to take the library to hospital patients meshed with Dr. William

Lucille Francis, hospital librarian of the Saint Paul Public Library, brings books to a young patient, 1944.

Below: Patients in the Northern Pacific Hospital receive library service from hospital librarian Lydia Rosander in March 1944.

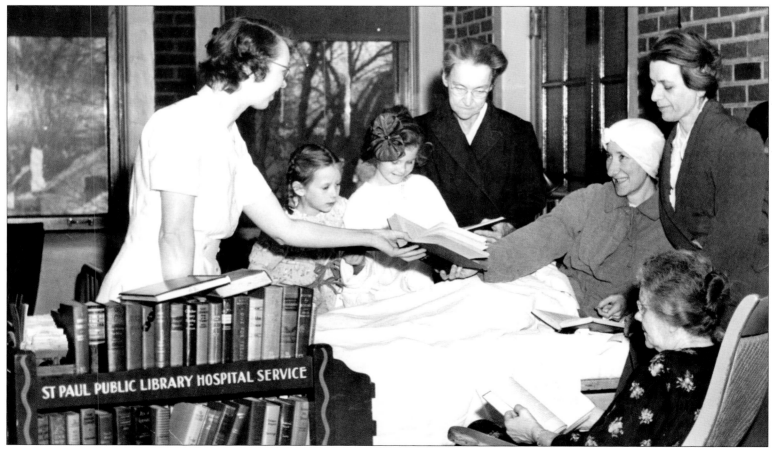

Eighth-grade students from Maxfield School visit an exhibit of "Races of Mankind" at the Central Library in November 1945.

Phyllis Sands examines one of the old musical instruments in the Central Library, November 11, 1946. From the monogrammed jumper and the white shirt with French cuffs that Phyllis is wearing, we know she was a pupil at St. Joseph's Academy.

Dawson Johnston's philosophy of libraries. What began in 1921 as an experiment became, after two years, an accepted part of the library service in St. Paul. A newspaper photo shows Jones in a hospital room standing next to a tea cart of books. The caption reads, "If Soldier is Unable to Go to the Public Library, Presto, Chango, and the Library Comes to Him."[151]

Jones expressed her philosophy in an address. "Sick people are a part of the community," she said. "Is there any reason why the Public Library, reaching out to all parts of the community, should discriminate against a man when he is stricken and in the hospital? The federal authorities are doing a much better job in providing library service for hospitalized veterans than the public libraries are in providing for the civilian sick. Let us include service to hospitals."[152]

Perrie Jones's reports to the Wilder Charity show that the hospital service was popular. During the last nine months of 1921, 12,814 books were circulated. In 1922 the total doubled to 24,704 and in 1923 the figure rose to 35,779. Volunteer assistance by the Junior League helped keep expenses down. The Wilder Charity funded the program for a second year, after which the hospital position was made part of the Civil Service structure of the library.

In 1924 Jones was elected chair of the Hospital Librarian Section of the American Library Association, a position she held for many years. She was also instrumental in developing a course (which she taught) for hospital librarians introduced into the curriculum of the School of Medicine at the University of Minnesota—the first course of its kind offered in any U.S. college or university.[153] The University of Minnesota Press published Jones's fifty-page annotated bibliography titled *One Thousand Books for Hospital Libraries,* in which Dr. Eric K. Clarke is quoted as saying, "Well chosen books can become valuable aids to recovery, while poorly chosen ones may exert a dangerous influence."[154]

In 1928, Jones left her hospital librarian position with the Saint Paul Public Library to become librarian for state institutions, taking books to mental hospitals, prisons, and schools for children who were wards of the state. She had held this job for nine years when Commissioner Finley tapped her for the head librarian position in St. Paul. She began her nineteen-year tenure on January 1, 1937, at a salary of $4,500. The press welcomed her. "She [Perrie Jones] and the Library Board should be assisted by all civic groups anxious to rescue the Library from the period of unavoidable neglect it has undergone in these recent years. Miss Jones undoubtedly will be able to prove to public opinion that it deserves better support."[155]

Perrie Jones opened the Saint Paul Public Library to a continuing series of art and photographic exhibitions and related them to issues of the day. She featured the works of black poet and author James Weldon Johnson and sponsored an exhibition called "Jewish Book Week." In 1939 she publicized Langdon Post's book *The Challenge of Housing,* which dealt with restrictive housing patterns, a controversial subject in St. Paul at the time. She organized a Spring Book Fair and sponsored a Great Books program that, at one time, had ten discussion groups going.

Campaign Promises

DEAR MESDAMES:
Following a conference with several members of your Association: Should I be reelected Comptroller of the City of St. Paul, I am pleased to inform you that I will increase for 1937 over 1936 by at least $5,000 Fund 16A-5 known as "New Books and Periodicals" and that the total amount of the Saint Paul Library appropriations will be at least $5,000 more in 1937 than it is in 1936.

Letter from H. F. Goodrich to members of the St. Paul College Club, April 17, 1936.

Librarians Peggy Haas and Emily Hultgren hang a picture in the Exhibition Room of the Central Library, September 2, 1937.

Above left: Edah Burnett, librarian in the Fine Arts Room, checks out a picture to Mrs. Henry Landreville for her home in November 1945.

Above right: Mrs. William West Jr. and Mrs. O. I. Sohlberg, members of the Library Activities Committee, pose with pottery from the Southwest, ca. 1940s.

THE SKINNER ROOM AND PUPPET THEATER

Perrie Jones quickly recognized that if she were to solve the library's financial problems, she would have to develop and cultivate a support group of bene-factors. She began seeking out private funds. First to respond to her overtures was the St. Paul Garden Club, which landscaped the library courtyard in 1938 and 1939. Earlier, Mrs. James H. Skinner and her son, William W. Skinner, had contributed funds to build the Skinner Room for Young People as a memorial to James H. Skinner, who had been a library benefactor. Architect Magnus Jemne designed the space, which immediately became a national model for library service to teens.

A leaflet announcing the opening of the Skinner Room informed parents that "the need for special work with older boys and girls who have outgrown the children's room but are not yet ready for the larger collections and greater specialization of the adult departments has been recog-nized for many years. . . . The architect . . . has expressed by means of architectural detail and through the use of strong, clear colors some of the vitality and energy of youth. The room with its paneled wood walls, its comfortable chairs and window seats and its gay colors has an informal home atmosphere which will encourage reading, browsing and consultation with the librarian. . . . A small but carefully selected collection of books in literature, arts and sciences . . . will make it possible

The inauguration on June 9, 1939, of the Skinner Room for Young People as a memorial to James H. Skinner. The room was one of the first in the United States dedicated to the interests of teenagers. From left: John C. Feldman, deputy commission of education; Perrie Jones, head librarian; W. W. Skinner; Mrs. James H. Skinner; Axel F. Peterson, commissioner of education; William H. Fallon, mayor of St. Paul; John P. Mullaney, deputy commissioner of public safety; and Mrs. William H. Fallon.

Planting tulip bulbs on the Saint Paul Public Library grounds on October 15, 1948, are Adelbert Fettinger of the Department of Education; Perrie Jones, head librarian; Mrs. B. H. Ridder; and Mrs. Horace Thompson of the St. Paul Garden Club.

Generations of children watched shows performed in the Central Library's puppet theater. Created by Norwegian architect Magnus Jemne in 1949, the stage is made of walnut and features a carved head of Loki, the god of mischief in Norse mythology, over the stage. At least one puppeteer who learned his skills in this theater went on to fame as a puppeteer.

for young people to become acquainted with the best in these fields." The Skinner Room opened on June 9, 1939, under the direction of librarian Eleanor Herrmann, who wrote in her annual report that the purpose of the room was "to provide a reader's advisory service to young people of high school age and encourage reading for pleasure."

A decade later, to the delight of generations of St. Paul children, Jemne designed an elaborate puppet theater made of bleached walnut from southern Minnesota that featured the head of Loki, the god of mischief in Norse mythology. Jemne himself carved the likeness. The Schubert Club furnished the Marion Ramsey Furness Memorial Room for listening to music in 1940, and in 1949 Louise Savage, wife of businessman Arthur H. Savage, financed the remodeling of the Children's Room in memory of her parents, Emilie Belden Cochran and New York banker Thomas Cochran. Magnus Jemne, the architect who had designed the Skinner Room and the Savages' home, also constructed the Children's Room. The pecan paneling he used for the room was milled from the trunks of pecan trees that grew on the Savage family's property.

In 1953 Jones announced the opening of the Library Film Bureau, a gift of the Friends of the Saint Paul Public Library. The bureau contained "carefully chosen material on the familiar problems of family relationships and child care, on city redevelopment, conservation of bird and animal life, on native cultures, historic places, people of other lands, problems of government, the country's wealth, and community relationships." No Western or Tarzan films, there.

Puppeteer Fame

AMONG THE EARLY PRODUCERS of shows at the Saint Paul Public Library's puppet theater was Jerry Juhl, a hobby puppeteer in high school. After graduating from college, Juhl went to a Puppeteers of America convention, where he met Jim and Jane Henson and a sixteen-year-old named Frank Oz. The Hensons teamed up with Juhl to form the Muppets and invited Oz, as soon as he graduated from high school, to join them. Oz did and became known to the world as Miss Piggy. Juhl became the principal writer for the Muppets.[156]

Puppeteers Daniell and Stephen Hayes stage a miniature opera on February 17, 1950, in the puppet theater in the Children's Room.

Right: Agatha Klein, in charge of the Film Bureau at the Central Library, checks out a film to a library patron on November 14, 1953.

Below left: The Music Room in the Central Library as it appeared May 15, 1954.

Below right: Mable McCoy at the card catalog in the Music Room, April 25, 1948.

PERSONAL PURSUITS

Jones's interest in the arts wasn't just professional. She herself did watercolors, beginning in the late 1930s on her return from a conference in the state of Washington when she stopped off at Jasper Park in the Canadian Rockies. With a dime-store box of watercolors and a pad, she spent three days sketching and found the experience to be tremendously exhilarating. She continued painting, and her work was later exhibited in the Listening Room of the library.

Reaction to her poetry was not so favorable. Back in April 1930 she submitted six poems to Oscar W. Firkins, professor of English at the University of Minnesota, for critical analysis. Her cover letter stated that she "hoped he will find something of interest if not of value" in her work.[157] The professor replied, "[The poems] are neither boorish or inspired, but they contain no warrant for advising you to adopt poetry as a career or even a sub-career. There is something in you which may be different, or just wishes to be different—on the scant data I cannot say which, but the resulting value is not high."[158]

One of her poems, written in 1920, was titled "A Mood":

> Dusk in a foreign city
> Dull leaden skies and chill
> Sharp winds bringing winter
> Dusk and the coming night.
> Cruel grey flapping winds
> Relentless beating down
> Dusk in a lonely city
> In a noisy, red-roofed town.

While much of her verse was dark, some reflected a sense of humor, as did this 1929 work:

> The peach is sour
> The grape is tough
> The day is cold
> My bed is rough
> And that you'll say
> Is quite enough.[159]

Jones liked to entertain. She planned a party for library staff at the Women's City Club in St. Paul on November 11, 1940, the day on which the memorable Armistice Day storm struck the city around noon. Though she had cake, cookies, and ice cream ordered for fifty people, only three made it to the party—and one of the three, Rodney Loehr, had to leave his car in a downtown lot for five days before it could be dug out from a snowdrift.

Jones herself did not own a car, and throughout her entire career, winter and summer, she walked to work. She later said that decision was a mistake. "If I had it to do over again I'd have had a car. But I always liked to walk. I did a lot of thinking while I walked. If I were driving I knew I couldn't do the thinking."[160]

THE BOOKMOBILE

From the days of William Dawson Johnston's administration, the library had maintained a vehicle that transported books to playgrounds, schools, and library stations. A 1924 headline announced the retirement of "Library Liz," a Ford flivver piloted by driver Bernard J. Mitchell that, over three years, had delivered a million and a half books and traveled 25,000 miles—the limit for a car of that time.[161] By 1935 the library delivery truck was visiting each branch library, daily transporting hundreds of books back and forth. The truck also supplied sixty kindergarten rooms and brought supplementary reading materials to every school

in the city every six weeks. The Central Library was supplying more than a thousand classrooms with books.

The library trucks had names. In 1938 a new truck, called "Flaming Youth," replaced a truck called "Old Blue Mare" that was retired after 76,000 miles of service. The first true Bookmobile, purchased in 1949, was a two-ton, maroon and cream-colored buslike vehicle, twenty-five-feet long, that was stocked with books and staffed with a driver/maintenance man and a librarian. The Bookmobile carried 2,800 books and, in 1953, traveled 4,128 miles and stopped for fifty-two hours a week at schools and housing projects. The librarian, Barbara Brown, became well known to grateful patrons of the Bookmobile.

"One lady always sent her little girl to be at our weekly stop at Como School with a request for five books," Brown reported. "The mother sent my report card back each week with the books—grading me from very good to poor on my selections for her. At Christmas she sent the driver and me delicious Swedish pastry. One old gentleman with a cane came in and said, 'Happy Day. I've waited thirty years for you people to bring the library to me.'"[162]

REVAMPING FRIENDS, BUILDING BRANCHES

In 1945, perhaps unaware that a Friends of the Library had been founded in 1923 only to become inactive, Perrie Jones organized a new Friends of the Saint Paul Public Library to "seek to widen the use of the library by spreading information about its many services to those who are not aware of them, and by accepting gifts or books . . . will expand or create services not covered by the city

budget."[163] The organization was composed of educated, upper-class women volunteers who, by holding teas and book sales, raised several thousand dollars a year to buy books and materials.

Members of the Friends of the Saint Paul Public Library conducted another service called Home Bound Books, a program that may well have been Perrie Jones's idea. The women volunteers took books to people who were homebound, usually by illness. One of the recipients of the books was the bedridden Myrtle Briggs. Myrtle and her husband, internist John Briggs, were friends of Perrie Jones, and, as the months passed, Myrtle received a regular weekly supply of books, delivered to her home by the faithful women of the Friends.

When Myrtle Briggs died in 1972, Dr. Briggs told everyone that his wife's principal joy during the final years of her life were the Home Bound books brought to her by the Friends of the Saint Paul Public Library. When John Briggs died a few months later, he left their entire estate, about $1.6 million, to the Friends. Unequipped to manage a grant of that size, the officers of the Friends went to the First Trust Company for help.

Briggs's attorney had given him good advice. If the Briggses had left their money to the library itself instead of the Friends, it could well have been spent by the city on other needs. Also, governmental bodies are prohibited from investing money in the stock market, except in fixed-income products. Over the long term, the lawyer advised his client, money invested in the market would grow more rapidly. The Briggses' legacy to the Friends organization would have long-term benefits that neither the

Friends organization nor the library itself could foresee.

Like Jennie Jennings before her, Perrie Jones soon found that her ambitions for the library were tempered by world events. Jones's experience in France during World War I may have made her more acutely attuned to the ominous events taking place in Europe than many of her fellow residents of the Midwest. While Twin Citians, the Depression behind them, flocked to the premiere of *The Wizard of Oz,* starring Minnesotan Judy Garland, disturbing events were taking place elsewhere. The Daughters of the American Revolution refused black contralto Marian Anderson permission to sing in Constitution Hall. Britain and France declared war on Germany, which had invaded Poland and Czechoslovakia. As Nazi propaganda leaflets suddenly began appearing in Twin Cities mailboxes, Jones asked citizens to bring them in for

Children attend a puppet show and garden party for dolls on the library terrace on July 29, 1943.

study. By 1942, the Japanese had attacked Pearl Harbor, the United States was in the war, and Germany had invaded Russia. And known only by a few, Enrico Fermi—on the squash court of the University of Chicago—had produced the first controlled nuclear chain reaction. Jones saw fifty-seven of her staff members—one-third of her staff—leave for the service or war-related jobs. Shortages, gas rationing, and the fact that tens of thousands were dislocated by war reduced adult attendance at the Saint Paul

Perrie Jones points out to Mrs. Guy Tomasino, junior clerk stenographer, how library cards are to be recorded, September 14, 1948.

Public Library. Only children's participation went up. "We feel that the public library has a definite opportunity and responsibility to emphasize its work with children at this time when, unavoidably, service to adults will decrease," Jones stated.[164] When World War II ended in 1945, the number of library card holders was at its lowest point since the 1920s.

That would soon change. Servicemen and women returned from the war eager to establish homes and resume the lives they had once known. In 1946 the library issued 2,000 new cards. Circulation increased every year until 1950, when the enormous popularity of television made itself felt. Libraries all over the country reported declining attendance and circulation, blaming the hours people spent watching television. "Competition with the demands and beguilements of the day grows more severe," Jones commented sadly.

The Market House property at Seventh and Wabasha, long owned by the library, was sold in 1946 for $826,000. The money was immediately dedicated to the remodeling of the Saint Anthony Park Library in 1946 and the building of three branch libraries: Rice Street in 1952, Highland in 1954, and Hayden Heights in 1955.

WORK ETHIC

Jones "was not the old-fashioned librarian who hovered over her books and protected them and didn't like to have people handle them and was sorry that they were wearing out from use," remembered Al Heckman of the Norwest and Grotto Foundations. "Perrie was very pleased when books were worn out from use." Ronald M. Hubbs, president of the Saint Paul Company, was impressed by Jones's ability to get things done. "She was a doer. If she said that something needed to be done she would do it. You could always depend on that. She had a lot of friends and she believed in books."

Jones's co-workers found her to be a dedicated librarian with great strength of character. If she believed in something, nothing would stop her until her goal was achieved. Jones was vigorous in rejecting any attempt at censorship beyond that required for "respectability." In 1950 a group pressured her to remove a book by Paul Blanchard titled *American Freedom and Catholic Power* from the library. Jones replied in a letter, "In no case should any material be excluded because of race or nationality or the political or religious views of the writer. That, I believe, expresses clearly the obligation laid upon a librarian, obligations which I, as the Librarian of the Saint Paul Public Library, shall do my best to fulfill. Your request is denied."[165]

Jones was not always successful in communicating her objectivity to all of her staff. A patron came into the library looking for a well-known book on Protestant theology. The reference librarian was surprised that it was not on the shelf. Curious, she began checking and soon found that all of the major works written in the past decade on Protestant theology that had been purchased by the library were missing from the shelves. The librarians began to look for the books and soon found them, stacked in an obscure closet. When the cataloger, an older devout Roman Catholic woman, was confronted about the Protestant books in the closet, she replied that, absolutely, she had put them there. She believed it was her responsibility to protect the public from such nonsense.

Jones was a brisk and demanding administrator who was active in library associa-

tions at all levels, especially those dealing with hospital librarianship. She believed that if an organization invited an individual to serve in an office, it was an honor that one should accept without question. On the whole, Jones's staff found her easy to work for. "When Perrie Jones did things, she did them for the Public Library, for the group, and that made for good morale because everyone felt he was part of a team," former employee Rodney Loehr remembers.

In 1952 sixteen-year-old Don Kelsey went to Mechanic Arts High School and took the St. Paul Civil Service examination for a clerk position with the city. A few days later he received a letter saying there was a vacancy for a library page at the downtown Central Library. When Kelsey reported for work in the government documents section, he was immediately taken to Perrie Jones's office. "She greeted me and took me around and introduced me to the entire staff of over 100 people. She was an amazing woman. You had a sense from the minute you started working there, regardless of the level you

At Perrie Jones's instigation, the Friends of the Saint Paul Public Library gave awards to readers. In a ceremony on October 11, 1949, Jones gave certificates to four patrons of the library. From left: Mrs. Joseph Worscher, unidentified woman, Ernest H. Gustafson, and Edward H. Swain, and Jones. The certificate to Mrs. Worscher read, "In recognition of the sixty-two years you have used the library of this city, the Friends of the Saint Paul Public Library wish at this time to tender you a certificate of appreciation recording your long standing association with this institution. October 11, 1949."

were on, that you were a part of something important and that you mattered."

Jones instilled in the library staff a work ethic of perfectionism and enormous pride in the manner in which they delivered service to the public. Kelsey remembers that at the end of the day in the Reference Room every book had to be back in its place on the shelf. "If you did not finish your shelving before it was time to punch out for the day, it was not the library's fault that you didn't get your work done. You punched out and finished the work on your own time."

One Friday Kelsey had a date and did not get half of a cartload of books shelved. Afraid he would be late, he hid them in the stacks. He remembers that as the worst date of his life because he spent the entire evening worrying that someone would find that cart of books. "I showed up at the library at 6:30 the next morning when the custodian was unlocking the door. I didn't even take my coat off before I ran up there and shelved those books as fast as I could go."

END OF AN ERA

Perrie Jones retired in 1956. During the nineteen years of her stewardship, the Saint Paul Public Library underwent remarkable growth. She was an astute businessperson and superb administrator who added three new branches to the system and instituted the Bookmobile to service the small stations. When she took over in 1937, the budget was $234,479, the library owned 394,377 volumes, and circulation was 1,307,703. In 1956, the year she retired, the budget was $661,439, there were 600,000 volumes on the shelves, and circulation was 1.5 million. Cardholders numbered 89,712, more than at any time in the library's history. The Bookmobile was annually distributing 149,843 volumes. The St. Paul newspaper was publishing a regular column on new books in the library.

Over two decades, Jones had earned the respect of patrons and peers as she deftly choreographed the library's comeback from financial hardship. Not surprisingly, Jones was honored by the University of Minnesota with its Outstanding Achievement Award after her retirement.

George Anderegg reads about butterflies, August 31, 1946.

In a 1957 speech honoring city council-man Frank Marzitelli, Jones revealed something of the library's relationship with the city commissioners:

> When I retired, many said to me, "Well, now, I suppose you'll write a book." And I thought to myself, "There is one book I could write. And the title would be *The Commissioners I Have Known.*" My favorite commissioner was Frank Marzitelli. He came in to the job in June 1950. The site of the St. Francis Hotel had been sold and we had over a half-million dollars in our jeans and we were rolling up our sleeves to have a go at our new branch building program. We had five and we needed five more. For twenty years we had been champing at the bit for lack of funds. And then we were presented with a commissioner ready to urge us on, give us confidence and point the way.
>
> We were lucky. The Rice Street branch went up first and I shall never forget the opening ceremony, the crowd, the commissioner's words that Saturday afternoon in March. But even before the last chair was in place the commissioner was negotiating for two more sites and we were working on two new floor plans. There was hardly a week in those thirty months he was Commissioner of Libraries that he did not drop in to just say "Hello," to see how we were getting along.[166]

Jones died on November 7, 1968, at the age of eighty-two. When the terms of her will were announced a year later, it was learned that she had left nearly a half million dollars to the Saint Paul Public

Five-year-old Elaine Nelleson reads at Como Park Elementary School, site of one of the Saint Paul Public Library's book stations, August 12, 1942.

Library to be administered by the Wilder/Minnesota Foundation. Called the Perrie Jones Fund, its purpose was to provide scholarships and grants for the staff of the Saint Paul Public Library for the improvement and strengthening of public library service. In her will she stated, "First priority shall be given to the need for scholarships and grants for members of the staff of the Saint Paul Public Library whether on full or part time and second priority to the methods or means for improving and strengthening characteristic of Jones that the intent of her will was to provide for the exchange of ideas and enable others to broaden their horizons.[167]

It was also characteristic of Jones to nurture the staff she had so carefully hired. At the end of World War II, she had assembled a group of professionals proud of their role as the public's information service and profoundly knowledgeable in specialized fields. By the end of 1956, reference librarians were answering more than 100,000 questions a year. Patrons wanted to know how long it took for a ship to travel around the world, how to get the odor of skunk out of clothes, where to find a list of Italian tile importers or out-of-town addresses, and how to spell words. A popular request was how to spell the word "camaraderie." When the telephone company began charging for directory assistance, people called the library for phone numbers. The librarians had to tell them they could supply only addresses.

Frederick Curtis reads about corn husk dolls in the Juvenile Department of the Central Library, August 1946.

the Library's services." Having served as librarian for nearly two decades, she was "aware of the many occasions when a small recurring fund outside the city or governmental budget would provide a certain desirable flexibility in the library's administration."

Jones wanted her grant "to enable them [librarians] to widen their horizons and so acquire experience in other public libraries as well as academic training so as to offset the ever-present danger of becoming ingrown." As an example of how the grants might be used, she wrote, "bringing well-known librarians to the Saint Paul Public Library to conduct training courses for the staff." It was

Loyal to their profession, Jones's staff extended that loyalty to the library system for which they worked. Many stayed in the same jobs for forty years or more until they retired. Observes librarian Linda Wilcox: "One of the things we discovered at the library was that people never left. The library was a lifetime career, a way of life. It was a career they loved and they loved the institution."

As a result of Jones's judicious hiring, the staff of the Saint Paul Public Library had become extraordinarily close, an extended family. Jones had made few social distinctions among the levels of library professionals. Clerks and pages received the same courtesy and attention as senior librarians. Librarians of all grades, together with library technicians and clerks, bonded to each other and to the institution to create a culture unique to the city. They knew members of each other's families, celebrated weddings, graduations, and births, socialized together outside of work, and, in some cases, perpetuated social customs beyond their usefulness. If a librarian became ill and ran out of sick leave, for instance, her fellow librarians would be quick to donate their own to help out.

The young Don Kelsey worked for six years as a page at the Central Library before leaving for the University of Minnesota to study—what else?—library

science. Kelsey's future career was determined by his teen years' experience working under the library's demanding professionals.[168]

Perrie Jones's leadership style helped create the sense of community that bound people to the library and to their co-workers. Newcomers, eager to share in the sense of belonging, responded to the nurturing of the old guard, thus perpetuating an intimacy in the work environment that lasted more than fifty years, from the middle to the end of the century—an intimacy that outlasted even the J. Archer Eggen years.

Testimonial dinner for outgoing librarian Perrie Jones on December 1, 1955, in the ballroom of the Lowry Hotel. From left: Charles Kneissel, chair of the Library Advisory Board; Pierce Butler Jr., toastmaster; Perrie Jones; Dean T. C. Dlegen, speaker; Severin A. Mortinson, commissioner; and George Brack, vice chair, board of trustees, Friends of the Saint Paul Public Library. Gifts were a three-piece set of luggage and a watch.

Library director J. Archer Eggen presents pins to retiring librarians on September 25, 1959. From left: Rella Havens, Eleanor Carney, Elsa Ihn, and Grace Peterson.

TEN

Progress, to a Point

TO SUCCEED PERRIE JONES as head librarian of the Saint Paul Public Library, City Commissioner Severin Mortinson named J. Archer Eggen, a native of Virginia, Minnesota. Eggen had studied engineering before switching to library science at the University of Minnesota. He was head librarian of public libraries at Fergus Falls, Minnesota, and at Cedar Rapids, Iowa, before he began his new post in St. Paul on February 15, 1956, at a salary of $805 per month. He was forty years old.

The library that Eggen inherited from Jones was flourishing but showing its age. The new director had both the desire and the expertise to make the necessary improvements. Eggen admitted to having an "edifice complex," being more interested in buildings than in books, and had directed the construction of the Cedar Rapids Public Library. He immediately focused attention on the Central Library's physical plant. The old wooden windows were deteriorating to the point that librarians were afraid to open them for fear they would fall apart. Eggen not only replaced the windows with double-pane, metal-frame windows, he oversaw installation of a climate-control system. He modernized the interiors of the three Carnegie branch libraries while leaving their exteriors intact.

One of Eggen's objectives was to continue the decentralization of the library. His strategy was successful. In 1937, 34 percent of the library's circulation took place in the branches and stations. By 1955, this had increased to 56 percent. In 1958, just two years after Eggen's arrival, the library set a circulation record of 1,840,000, breaking the old record set during the Depression.[169] The Lexington and Sun Ray Branch Libraries also opened during Eggen's tenure, in 1967 and 1970 respectively.

Eggen later took the first steps to bring the library into the electronic age. In 1968 he brought in IBM equipment to maintain records electronically. Tasks once done by hand—recording the acquisition, removal, and duplication of books on the shelves—became largely automated. A year later, Eggen had a microfilm checkout system installed to replace the audio-recording checkout system. Librarians could now photograph the book's information on microfilm rather than record it via a microphone onto a vinyl disc.

Also during his tenure, the libraries of St. Paul and Minneapolis, in cooperation with the counties of Anoka, Carver, Dakota, Hennepin, Ramsey, and Scott, formed in 1969 the Metropolitan Library Services Agency. MELSA became the official coordinating agency for public library services in the metropolitan area. Members benefited from reciprocal borrowing arrangements, joint research projects, and planning for automation.

To his credit, Eggen would claim many accomplishments by the end of his twenty-two years as library director. But his interest in modernizing stopped at devices and buildings. His personal and professional demeanor differed dramatically from what the staff had been accustomed to under Perrie Jones. Eggen clung to the social and cultural

Librarian Mrs. Kuchenbacker checking out materials for a patron in the Science and Industry Room, November 1959. Note the microphone and the audio charging machine used to record materials checked out of the library.

The second-floor Circulation Room of the Central Library, October 1958.

mores of an earlier century. Changes took place in broad areas, such as the mechanics of how books were cataloged into the system, but not in how the staff should dress, which books should be permitted in the Children's Room, and with whom the staff could socialize during and after work.

Eggen's diffident style also affected his relationship with the Friends of the Saint Paul Public Library, which Jones had nurtured since establishing it in 1945. In what became known as the "tea and crumpets" period, Eggen reduced the role of the Friends members to pouring tea for library events rather than assisting with policy or decision-making. In his last decade as library director, Eggen also engaged in a tug of war with the managers of the Perrie Jones Fund, which Jones had left in her will to benefit the library staff. Eggen attempted to control the Perrie Jones Fund, one of the first permanent endowments established for the city of St. Paul and given to the fledgling Minnesota Foundation to manage. According to Jerry Steenberg, Eggen's successor, "Paul Verret [of the Saint Paul Foundation] wanted to elevate the presence of the Friends and Eggen did not want that. Eggen ran the fund out of his office and Paul wanted to do it differently."

CHAUVINISTIC MINDSET

For twenty-two years, the management style of J. Archer Eggen butted heads with the library culture nurtured by and inherited from Perrie Jones. On the surface, Eggen's dominance prevailed. Below the surface, staff cohesiveness formed under Jones remained intact as librarians clung to loyalties and what they considered to be their professional values.

From the staff's perspective, librarians and library work took a back seat to Eggen's focus on buildings. A dictatorial, hierarchical individual, Eggen maintained a distant relationship with his staff. He addressed only the higher-ranking librarians, and his attitude expanded the psychological distance between the various grades of workers in the library into a vast gulf. Eggen seldom spoke to the clerks and lower-ranking librarians during their entire time of employment. Tall, elegant Agatha Klein, the assistant librarian in charge of the Central Library, did the day-to-day work of running the organization.

One staff person remembers, "He would sit in his office in the morning and read the *Wall Street Journal,* the *New York Times,* and the local papers. The door would be open but he was remote. His way of relating to people was artificial and he did not reach out to the people working in the library. I think he was basically very shy." Every day a clerk wheeled into Eggen's office a library cart, called a truck, containing one copy of each new book for adults that had arrived. It was understood that the truck was not to leave until Eggen had made his selections. "It was reading selection time and he had first divvy on the new titles," Steenberg remembers.

The staff was more than 90 percent female and, to the women's annoyance, Eggen had pet names for the senior librarians, whom he called "girls." One woman was referred to as "Little Mother." Others, who had several children, he called "Cheaper-by-the-Dozen" women. If a woman had had a permanent wave, he would say, "Don't worry. In a month or two the frizz will be gone." Every time Eggen encountered

Mary Clare Huberty, head of circulation, who wore her hair short, he would stop by her desk and ask, "Do you know what happens to girls with short hair?" When she would routinely reply, "No, Mr. Eggen," he would say, "Nothing," and walk on.[170]

A formal, if not quaint, dress code prevailed. Male librarians could wear only long-sleeved white shirts with ties firmly knotted at their throats. Female librarians were to be dressed in attractive but not provocative feminine attire. Sleeveless tops were forbidden, as were slacks and trousers. Hose was to be worn winter and summer, despite the lack of air-conditioning, and skirts were to extend below the knee.

Yet following a staff talent show given at the Hamline Library auditorium at the close of work one Friday, Linda Wilcox participated in a singing and dancing line. At the conclusion of the number, Eggen told her that she should have hiked up her skirt a bit. "My knees were

Librarian Agatha Klein with leaders of one of the Great Books discussion clubs. The clubs were started by director Perrie Jones in the 1940s. At one time ten clubs held regular meetings.

Managerial Styles

THE TWO HIGHLY CAPABLE library administrators who worked directly under J. Archer Eggen were Maurine Hoffman, supervisor of the branches, and Agatha Klein, who was in charge of the Central Library. In many ways, Hoffman reflected the management style of Eggen. A woman of commanding presence, she would make unannounced visits to the branches. The branch librarians felt as if they should stand at attention, click their heels, and salute when Hoffman came into their buildings. "She was like a German general," one says. "You did not mess with Maurine."

As soon as Hoffman appeared at one branch, the librarians would be on the phone to the other branches with the message that "Miss Hoffman is making the rounds." Piles of papers and books would be quickly straightened, wastebaskets emptied, and chairs aligned.

Agatha Klein, though she could be formidable, was softer around the edges and more genteel than Hoffman. Every afternoon, at precisely ten minutes before three, before going to the round table for her coffee with Eggen, Klein would walk through the library and greet the librarians. Klein practiced walk-around management long before it came into vogue.

covered and he thought it was too long," she recalls. Wilcox was convinced that Eggen had a fun side to him as well as being "stand-offish. He was not approachable. He thought of himself as a funny person but he did not come off that way. In the lunch room when the administrators sat at the round table, he would throw things at me—a crumpled paper cup or something like that."

Remembers Patricia Ethier: "Mr. Eggen would stop by the desk of women who had just been married and, with a sly look, ask, 'Do you have something to tell

me?' 'Are you pregnant?' is what he wanted to know."[171] Following a job interview with Eggen, twenty-two-year-old Linda Wilcox went across the hall to be interviewed by Agatha Klein and the director of the branches, Maurine Hoffman. "They asked me about my future plans. I was going to be married in the next few weeks and they asked what my husband's position was and if I would be practicing birth control." Eggen was "very much an old boy person," adds Kathleen Flynn. "He never could have gotten away with that behavior today."

Eggen had little time for new ideas offered by freshly minted librarians. In 1969, when she applied for a position with the Saint Paul Public Library, Alice Neve came armed with a master's degree in library science from Case Western Reserve University in Cleveland, Ohio. When she walked into the director's office for her interview, Eggen was sitting with his feet up and his back to her, looking out of his office window onto Rice Park. Eggen never removed his gaze from the window nor did he turn around to face Neve. She remembers, "He said, 'You've come because you think you are going to get a job at the Saint Paul Public Library.' I replied that I hoped so. 'Well,' Eggen said, 'you are probably one of those librarian whipper-snappers who think they can change the world. It's not that easy.'" The interview ended as abruptly as it had begun. Neve cried in the car with her parents all the way back to their home in Wisconsin. But three weeks later she received a letter saying she had been hired.

When Flynn graduated from Pratt with a library degree, she suggested opening up a small branch in the skyway area in Town Square. "I don't think he even read my proposal," she says. "He thought, 'Fresh out of library school and she has all these ideas.' That was 1978. Nothing came of it."[172]

THE ROUND TABLE

A major feature of the Eggen years was a large, round table in the staff break room and the rigid protocol concerning who could sit at it. Librarians at the highest level were expected to appear at the table promptly at 10:00 a.m. and again at 3:00 p.m. for coffee or tea, served by the "coffee ladies," Gertrude Nowan and Ruth Klinkhamer. No librarians under the level of department head ever joined Eggen at the round table, and if one did make a mistake and sit there, she was told the table was reserved for the "Round Table crew." "We all knew our place," Neve says. "The hierarchy was very evident."

Wilcox remembers the round table as the place where only the administrators sat. "I got the feeling it was a command performance. You had to be there to have coffee with J. Archer. It was kind of a joke. Everyone laughed about it. Under Eggen the round table was a fixture."

A library staff member with whom Eggen related well was Gerald Steenberg. Almost as soon as he hired Steenberg in 1961, Eggen began mentoring his new employee to succeed him as head librarian. Every morning, just before ten o'clock in the years when Steenberg was assistant librarian, Eggen would appear in Steenberg's door and jingle the change in his pocket. Steenberg would get up from his work and the two men would go down the hall to have their coffee together at the round table.

Eventually, to counter the fact that Director Eggen had problems developing

rapport with his staff, an outside consultant was brought in to conduct a team-building seminar with the administrators and library department heads. "No one would respond to the seminar leader," Steenberg recalls. "He asked us to suggest something that would improve relations. We all sat there

J. Archer Eggen, director, Saint Paul Public Library System, 1956–1978.

Librarians Kathleen Flynn (left) and Alice Neve at the round table in the Central Library break room. Flynn later became acting library director. Neve became head librarian at the Lexington Branch Library and later the Rondo Community Outreach Library.

like lumps on a log. I didn't know what to say, but finally I said, 'I think, Mr. Eggen, that when you and I go for coffee before work begins in the morning we should sit with other staff, rather than just the two of us sitting there."

Employees who frequented the staff room before 8:00 a.m. were not the librarians but members of the technical staff who worked behind the scenes and did not meet the public.

"They don't care about anything like that," Eggen replied. "Oh, yes, they do," said Steenberg. "Let's try it a couple of times and see how it works." To his credit, Eggen accompanied Steenberg to the break room and, on occasion during his final two years at the library, sat with other employees. But this took place only before work began. After 8:00 a.m. Eggen's rigid social segregation of staff into their levels of employment continued.

Occasionally the staff would stage mini-rebellions. Patricia Ethier remembers that the Skinner family maintained its interest in the Skinner Room for Young Adults, and a Skinner daughter in Illinois would send a sizeable monetary gift every year. As the librarian in charge of the room, Ethier would respond, writing a letter of thanks and appreciation for the gift. "One year Archer decided it was not my place to write that letter. He told me to write it but he would sign it. I replied that I was sorry, but I did not ghost-write."

The library staff was not above some dissembling of its own. During the annual St. Paul Winter Carnival, people hunting the prize medallion would come into the library asking to see the city plat book. Fearing the document would not survive the manhandling of the medal-

lion-seekers, the librarians always told them that they were sorry, but the plat book had just been sent to the bindery.

During the summer the libraries conducted reading programs for children that culminated, in the branches, with outdoor activities and treats. One hot Friday, the staff at Sun Ray Branch Library spent the afternoon outdoors with the children, conducting games and serving ice cream. Because of the library dress code they had not been able to dress appropriately for the activity, and so were especially hot and uncomfortable. At closing time one of the mothers appeared at the door of the library bearing a tray with icy gin and tonics for the six sweaty librarians. They immediately locked the door, pulled down the blinds, and cooled off with the drinks before going home. For the rest of the summer, and into the fall, every Friday someone brought gin and tonics for the staff at the Sun Ray Library.

Then there was the *LSD* episode. Librarian Theora Halstead of the Science and Industry Room wrote an internal newsletter for staff called *Library Staff Doings,* or *LSD.* Librarians chuckled over the acronym's "little bit naughty" allusion to the illegal drug. The newsletter featured tidbits about the staff's families—who had a new grandchild or a child who was graduating—as well as funny things clients had said. "We all loved the *LSD,*" says circulation head Mary Clare Huberty. "We looked forward to it every month. Theora was a clever writer." Linda Wilcox remembers that "when it appeared in the delivery, we would immediately rip it open to see what was being said." Library staff member Jan Hiebert, who was married to newspaper columnist Gareth Hiebert, shared her

Theora Halstead of the Science and Industry Room was the editor of the infamous LSD library staff newsletter.

copy with him and Hiebert commented on it in one of his *Pioneer Press* columns.

When City Commissioner Leonard Levine read Hiebert's column, he was not amused and summoned Theora Halstead to his office in City Hall. Halstead's husband was irate. "Don't you dare go over there without a tape recorder," he told his wife and bought a minirecorder for her. No one now recalls the outcome of her meeting with Commissioner Levine, but the *Library Staff Doings* newsletter was discontinued for about a year. When it started up again, it was a single sheet folded in half and stapled. The outside contained the usual benign notices of staff birthdays, weddings, and news of children. Only on the inside, out of sight, appeared the humorous tidbits the staff had sent in. Alice Neve remembers that they were careful in their quoting of customers and that no names were used. "There was simply the need to laugh and have joy in our work," she says.

THE GOLDEN AGE OF LIBRARY PROGRAMMING

The period between the early 1960s and 1979 saw the flowering of library programming. The branch libraries as well as the Central Library staged puppet shows, contests, quizzes—activities of all kinds for every age of young person. Thousands of children signed up for reading programs.

J. Archer Eggen understood the value of public relations to the library and established a publications office, under the direction of Elaine Wagner, to write news releases, newsletters, and scripts for the library's biweekly broadcast on radio station WMAN. In 1965, when the library received a grant of $104,000 from the Federal Library Services, the publications program expanded and the name

Girl Scouts earned merit badges in bookbinding in the Children's Room, ca. 1960. The backdrop is the puppet theater with the Norse god carved by architect Magnus Jemne.

An adult volunteer helps children fill a piñata with small toys and candy for a Mexican Christmas party in the Children's Room, December 13, 1960.

129

of the office was changed to Community Relations.

The office purchased a van (which the women had to learn to drive), filled it

Librarian Elaine Wagner in costume for a library program, April 7, 1966.

with books and puppets for the puppet shows, and set off to bring the library to the people. Lyndon Johnson was in office and his War on Poverty was in full bloom. As part of the Littlest Listener program, "mothers and their young children were invited to visit the library for an hour," Wagner remembers. "While the children were shown picture books and taught alphabet games, their mothers enjoyed coffee and discussions on child care or parent education and we explained what the library had to offer them. We took the van to the parks and, over the loudspeaker, announced that, 'The puppets are coming, the puppets are coming!' We did the puppet shows out of the back of the van."

Staff members from Wagner's office carried programs and reading lists to community centers, housing projects, and recreation centers, wherever they could find an audience. Before a new program idea could be implemented, Wagner had to submit it for the approval of three administrators: J. Archer Eggen, Agatha Klein, and Maurine Hoffman. Often the three did not agree. Wagner learned to cope with this problem by taking her proposals to Eggen first. When he had approved, she would then go to the other two. If one expressed reservations, Wagner would murmur, "Mr. Eggen liked this," and approval would be quickly forthcoming.

These and other activities for youth burgeoned for almost two decades before ending in 1980, when the library's budget was cut. Then the Community Relations office was closed and the van sold. Programming for library patrons essentially ended until it was later taken over by the Friends of the Saint Paul Public Library. Retired librarians, veterans of decades of service to youth, still pull from their closets folders of artwork, posters, and fliers they designed to entice young people into the world of books.

Children did not complain about the selection of books in the library, but adults often did. Librarians were continually braced to reply to the complaints of patrons who objected to the content of some books. "If people did not like a book they just wanted it out of the library," Wagner says. "I spent a lot of time answering people's concerns about books." One day, after Wagner had carefully explained to a client the library policy on not censoring reading material, the irate woman, unconvinced, told her, "You're going to go to hell."

Wagner herself admits to having committed one act of censorship during her career. The Skinner Room for Young Adults had been converted to the Paperback Book Room. Paperback books were considered "second-class" publications at the time, so much so that the librarians had them "rebound in order to feel good about them," Wagner said. The early paperback books ordered by the library were not salacious bookstore tomes but reprints of classics. When Wagner opened one of these paperbacks she discovered that, inside the front cover, the publisher's publicist had written a lurid description of the book's plot that bore little resemblance to the true content. With some embarrassment Wagner admits that she got a pair of scissors and carefully cut those paragraphs out of the book.

One book the librarians feared would get them into trouble was the popular and notorious *American Psycho,* which related in gruesome and graphic detail

the activities of a serial killer. The 1991 bestseller (which became a 2000 movie) was widely discussed and the *Pioneer Press* checked the Minneapolis and St. Paul libraries to see if they carried it.

Librarian Karen Avaloz was a second performer in the program on April 7, 1966.

Minneapolis turned out to have but one copy, shelved under Reference. St. Paul had thirteen copies, the number the librarians customarily ordered of a popular book. As Wagner explains, "After we read the newspaper story, we wondered what to do. We couldn't take it off the shelf. That was not what we did." To the librarians' relief, despite the publicity given the book's presence in the library by the *Pioneer Press,* no one complained.

BUILDING THE LEXINGTON LIBRARY

One St. Paul area that was conspicuous for its absence of library service was the neighborhood bounded by the Cathedral of St. Paul and Summit, Lexington, and University Avenues. Everyone agreed that this was the district most in need of library facilities, and in 1953 St. Paul voters had passed a united improvement bond issue that allotted $125,000 for a new branch library for this area. That was as far as the agreement went. Neighborhood groups began to argue about where the library should be located. Some wanted it near the middle of the geographic area, while others wanted it near Central High School.

The African American Rondo neighborhood had been decimated and almost destroyed by the construction of the I-94 freeway during the 1950s, and residents believed, with considerable justification, that their interests were being ignored by the city. The Dale-Selby and Dale-University civic organizations both called for libraries in their areas. "The general area to be served . . . includes the city's Negro area where lack of recreational and other facilities were partly blamed this week for the Negro-White brawl after two football games," the press reported.[173]

The arguments over the location of the library allowed city officials to avoid making a decision. Meanwhile, construction costs kept on rising. Before long, the $125,000 that had been appropriated was no longer enough to build a branch library. The project was effectively shelved until 1963, when it appeared that federal aid to build the library would be forthcoming. This pumped new life into the library project, and Commissioner Robert Peterson appointed a committee on site selection that, in turn, hired an out-of-town library consultant. The consultant recommended that the library be built near the intersection of University and Lexington.

Civic and church groups in the neighborhood protested, pointing out that the need for a library was greatest in the Selby-Dale neighborhood, that there was little housing where the library was proposed to be built, and that heavy traffic on University was a threat to the safety of children. Henry Longbehn, secretary of the Uni-Dale Commercial Club, threatened a boycott of the new library if it were built near Lexington and University.[174] Months of discussion followed. It was a full two years later, in 1965, before the press could report that commissioners had voted to buy and remodel the Centre Theater building at 1078 University Avenue. To be known as the Lexington Library, it would become a regional library, second in size only to the Central Library, with some 30,000 to 50,000 volumes, and staffed with "community librarians" who would take books into the neighborhoods.[175]

A final protest meeting that lasted more than two hours ended with officials insisting that changing the site now would risk losing a $100,000 federal grant toward the purchase and remodeling of the building—a project that was expected to cost $270,000. As it turned out, remodeling the Centre Theater cost $443,900. The Lexington Library, the largest and most modern branch of the St. Paul system, opened for business on June 5, 1967. It contained almost 20,000 square feet and, besides the library, housed the Bookmobile fleet, offices for extension services staff, and hospital and Bookmobile personnel. The Lexington Library served a burgeoning clientele for thirty-four years until flooding roof drains in 2001 forced the city to rethink its decision on where it had located the library.

DUMPING BOOKS

The titular head of the library system was the St. Paul city commissioner, who was assigned oversight responsibility. The only time the librarians saw most of their political bosses was at the end of the summer, when they would be called on to give out prizes to winners of the summer reading contests. That was less true when

Commissioner Leonard Levine was head of the libraries between 1970 and 1982. Because a city ordinance prohibited the sale of city property, librarians had for many years hauled worn and outdated books to the city dump. Librarians periodically weeded the collections to make room for new volumes. When Levine heard that books were being thrown away, he went to the media to publicly express his outrage. "It's a crime that these books have been hauled to Hoerner-Waldorf [to be turned into pulp] or buried in the dump,"[176] he said. Instead of dumping the books, Levine proposed a book sale in Rice Park complete with music, artists, puppet shows, popcorn, and the attendance of authors to autograph new books.

From the librarians' perspective, they were being attacked unfairly. Library officials explained that the books had to be thrown out because city regulations did not permit them to dispose of them in any other way. As Elaine Wagner expresses it, "He [Levine] was the savior and we were the bad guys."

Five thousand people turned out to purchase eighteen thousand used books at the library book sale held in Rice Park in September 1971.

A year later, an editorial in the *Pioneer Press* expressed satisfaction over how the problem had been resolved: "The days of book burning seem to be over in St. Paul. Not that there was anything sinister about the destruction. It was just that the library periodically has to clear out a few tons of books and that an idiotic law prevented giving the old books away. Anyway, about 5,000 persons turned out Saturday to buy 18,000 books at bargain prices." The editor confessed to having a "warm feeling about that many people standing in line for a long time at the Civic Center just to thumb through and buy the old volumes."[177]

THE TELEPHONE SYSTEM

A few of the Central Library systems were so antiquated that they were quaint. When Jerry Steenberg went to work in the Central Library building in 1961, the library had advanced, technologically, very little beyond what it had been when it was completed forty-four years before. When Steenberg walked up the front steps and through the main door, he came to a small nook containing a desk where an employee sat to direct library patrons. Behind the desk was a switchboard operated by Mae Boucher, who had been the operator since the day the library opened in 1917. This relic of a switchboard connected each of the libraries with the Central Library and with each other. All of the calls to and from the library buildings went through Boucher, who served as an early warning system for the staff.

When Gerald Steenberg was head librarian at the Highland Park Branch in 1963, for instance, he would get calls from Boucher when she overheard Eggen saying, "I'm going out to High-

Mae Boucher at the library switchboard, 1947.

land." She would call Steenberg and murmur, "Jerry, I don't know if Mr. Eggen said anything about coming your way, but he is."[178] Boucher's successor on the switchboard continued the practice. Librarian Roxanne Aschittino remembers that "one of [Eggen's] things was that the chairs must be pushed in at the tables and kept straight. When we got the call from the switchboard we would rush around, push all of the chairs in, and line the books up on the shelves."

In the evening the switchboard was operated by the pages. During the years he was employed as a page, Don Kelsey often ran the switchboard. He soon learned to yank off his headset when he saw the extension light belonging to Della McGregor light up. As the famed children's librarian had aged, she had become hard of hearing. When Kelsey said, "Operator," she would shout back "Mae?"

"No, this is Don," he would reply.

"How are you, Mae?" McGregor would holler back.

One evening while Kelsey was on duty at the switchboard, Children's Room patron Mrs. Arthur Savage approached him and asked if she could borrow a nickel for the parking meter. "It would be a privilege for me to give you a nickel," Kelsey replied.

"Oh no, I settle my accounts," insisted the generous benefactor.

Among his papers Don Kelsey still has an envelope from the 1950s with a three-cent stamp on it containing the nickel Mrs. Arthur Savage returned to him.

HOMELESS IN THE LIBRARY

Patricia Ethier remembers the many kinds of patrons at the Central Library, from the likes of Mrs. Savage to the homeless. "The literati came in for loads of books, mothers dropped their children off at the library and went shopping, others came in with their children and checked books out for them," she said. One day two children were being disruptive in the Cochran Children's Room and Don Kelsey told them they needed to behave. The librarian on duty got a horror-stricken look on her face and called Kelsey over to her desk.

"Don't you know who those children are?" she asked.

"No, but they are bothering people," Kelsey replied.

Said the librarian, "Those are Mrs. Savage's grandchildren."

A week later Kelsey was summoned to the reference desk. "Someone wants to talk to you," he was told. He went out and there stood Mrs. Savage.

"Are you the young man who spoke to my grandchildren the other day?"

Kelsey admitted that he was.

"Good," she said. "They needed that."

Three or four times a month a man came into the lower level of the library in the evening carrying a duffle bag. He would sit down on the steps, put on a pair of tap shoes, and begin dancing on the marble floor, which resonated with every click of his toes and heels. After a time he would stop. With tears rolling down his face, he would remove his tap shoes and leave. The staff learned that he had been a professional dancer who had been injured in the war and was now unable to remember his old routines. He called himself the "Blue Star."

"The homeless would come into the library in the morning, and when it was time for lunch at Dorothy Day, they would all get up and leave and then all come back," Ethier says. "One day, when it was damp and wet outside, a man dried his socks on the radiator. Some people would go to sleep in the library. Judy Levine was adamant about that. You couldn't sleep in the library."

One man, whose name was Peter, came in every Saturday to check out the limit of ten books. He was dressed in layers of tattered clothes and in the winter had newspapers stuffed into the sides of his galoshes. They could always smell his arrival—one librarian would grab a perfumed handkerchief, hold it to her face, and run back into the stacks when she saw him approaching—yet the staff became fond of Peter. One Saturday, when he failed to appear, a librarian went over to the Union Gospel Mission to inquire about him and learned that Peter had died during the week. Many on the staff felt that, with Peter's death, they had lost a peculiar friend.

Another library patron who may have been homeless loved westerns. He would start at the A's, read to the end of the alphabet, then start over again. His clothes were dirty, he had yellow fingernails that curled over his fingers, and he too smelled. The checkout system in use in the 1960s required the circulation librarians to say and spell the patron's name into a microphone and state his address, along with the book and transaction number, all of which was then recorded onto a vinyl disc. "When I would see him coming to the desk I would take a really deep breath and hope that I could get through the whole thing before I would have to breathe again," Roxanne Aschittino remembers.

"One day when I was checking in his books, I opened them up to take the card out of the back and found there were bugs in the book," Aschittino says. She took the book to her supervisor, Ortha Robbins. "Ortha opened her drawer and handed me a pair of clean white cotton gloves and told me to tear the page out of the book and throw everything into the trash." Then she drew herself up and said, "I will speak to the gentleman now." Adline Carlson remembers Robbins as one who always treated the library's customers with respect. "She listened to what they wanted."

Ortha Dorothea Robbins, a native of Wisconsin, was a St. Paul librarian for forty-one years. Much of that time she was head of circulation before moving on to become supervisor of public services for the Central Library. Robbins was Linda Wilcox's first supervisor when, as a young bride, Wilcox went to work for the Saint Paul Public Library. "I still remember my first day. Ortha let me know right away that the rule was 'On your feet and off your fanny.' Ortha said, 'Never, never point. Get up and take the customer to what he wants. And do not chew gum.'" Robbins subscribed to the hierarchical order that ruled the library in those years. Linda was to be addressed as "Mrs. Wilcox" because she was Robbins's assistant. Lower-ranking library clerks and aides were to be called by their first names. When Robbins died in 1999, she left her entire estate—$1 million—to the Friends of the Saint Paul Public Library.

LIBRARY VANDALISM

Though most people revered the library, some vandalism did take place. "There was a very tall man we called 'Stretch,'" Ethier remembers. "We never knew for sure if he was the one doing it, but we would find pages in books glued together. We had strong feelings he was doing it."

Another patron came in and asked to see a magazine containing a picture of *Gone with the Wind*'s Vivien Leigh. When the patron opened the magazine, he found that the picture of the British actress had been cut out. Investigating further, the library staff discovered that many pictures of Leigh had been cut out of books and periodicals. They notified the police and, when the patron returned and asked to see another magazine with a picture of Leigh, a plainclothes officer was called

Librarian Ortha Robbins.

Library administrators share in Ortha Robbins's "retirement coffee" at the round table in the library break room. From left: Kathleen Flynn, Ortha Robbins, Shirley Brady, Carole Williams, Liz McMonigal, Doug Guthrie, Fran Galt, and Jerry Steenberg.

"This Monstrous Miss Robin"

ORTHA ROBBINS, one of the most customer-oriented of St. Paul's veteran librarians, had an encounter with a playful patron. An undated, unsigned tongue-in-cheek letter sent to the mayor records the incident:

As a tax-paying citizen of the City of Saint Paul I demand immediate action! The pain of having all one's fond memories of the joy and enlightenment of one's youth and the nearly sacred reverence with which one has always regarded the public library utterly, utterly destroyed is inexpressible. I cannot conceive of a credible explanation for the treatment I suffered from what passes these days for 'administrators' of a public institution once so dearly cherished.

Often in the course of girding on the sword of truth I have found myself engaged in battle of a lesser sort. Incompetence, impertinence, indifference, lies, laziness, hostility, harassment, even pure stupidity—yes,—all these have I encountered, against all have I struggled and over all have I triumphed.

My weapons in this fight have been indignation, righteous anger, quick wit and the conviction of the rightness of my cause. My employment of them seldom fails to reduce my opponent to a shuddering speechlessness. In this way are benighted souls chastened and taught the error of their ways. Even the pleasures of philosophy pale beside the joy of combating smallness of mind and spirit.

However, this latest incident is beyond all forbearance or redemption. The fulfillment of my crusade was totally denied in a disturbing encounter with a Miss Eartha Robin [Ortha Robbins]. Fresh from total victory over clerk, librarian and supervisor—each in turn, and with varying degrees of difficulty, at last brought to their knees, quaking and begging for mercy, pleading with me to likewise enlighten their superiors—I relished the opportunity to make my beneficent influence felt by the administration as well.

Imagine my utter frustration when this devious Miss Robin refused to succumb to my instruction. Oh yes, she pretended sympathy and understanding. But I could discern her calculated, underhanded tactics. All this calm, smiling good humor could not in the least be penetrated by my well-honed skills. In the end I was reduced to leaving her office calmly. I even smiled myself. But, the humiliation and degradation of this defeat will not be soon forgotten. This sinister, perhaps Communist-inspired, defection of the public will must be stopped at once. If civil servants are thus able to avoid the consequences of their behavior and tax-paying citizens are deprived of their God-given right to correct and intimidate them, the very moral fiber of our nation is at risk.

This monstrous Miss Robin must at once be removed from contact with an unsuspecting public and further must be stripped of any potential power to influence other public servants with her harmful ways. Perhaps a filing job in a back corner could be found to provide her with useful employment until her retirement.

From the Saint Paul Public Library archives.

to observe him. As he read the article, the patron slowly moved his hand down the page. As he did so, he cut out the article with the razor blade he had taped to his finger and then slipped it into a manila folder he brought with him. The police went to his home, where they found velvet-covered albums filled with photographs of Vivien Leigh. Where Leigh's husband, Laurence Olivier, had appeared in the same picture, the patron had carefully cut it away.

Those who abused their library privileges often later felt guilty about their actions. Amid the library's papers in the Minnesota Historical Society's archives is an undated, handwritten note on lined paper, which reads:

> My name is Michael Liebgatt. This check for $5 is for an item that I stole from the library about five years ago. I had already talked to a man concerning this matter and he told me to send an amount for the item I took that would seem alright to me or whatever it was worth at the time. He told me to send it to Friends of the Library. I hope that the matter is settled between the library and me. Thank you.

The library also became a favorite place to which to donate memorials. Weekly checks, usually of $5 or $10, were sent to the library administration or to the Friends with a note asking that a book be purchased as a memorial to a loved one. Typical is a letter dated September 12, 1978:

> Enclosed is our check for the Friends of the Library in memory of our brother, Judge Albin S. Pearson. During his five years at the Wilder

Infirmary the books from the library were his greatest pleasure. . . . The library was a source of great comfort and help to all of us.

FIRST-RATE LIBRARIANS
St. Paul benefited from the expertise of some extraordinary librarians, Della McGregor among them. Under the direction of McGregor, the Skinner Room for Young Adults was opened in 1939 at the Central Library. McGregor also worked with her friend, Mrs. Arthur Savage, in designing the Cochran Children's Room.

McGregor began her career in 1911 as a children's librarian at Sheboygan, Wisconsin, and was hired by Dr. William Dawson Johnston to come to St. Paul in 1915 while the library was still in the Market House. In her handwritten report on the Children's Room in November 1916, she wrote, "On Monday, October 30 at 4:15 p.m. the old House of Hope church ceased to be a store house of literature for the juvenile population of St. Paul. With the opening of the Children's Room in the new building the juvenile readers received a new impetus and the attendance increased by leaps and bounds. On the day of opening 150 books were issued from the room which has been temporarily assigned . . . awaiting the completion of the building and the arrival of furniture."

In her annual report for 1918, McGregor had noted that the library had been closed for eight days because of the influenza epidemic, but, despite this, the total circulation of children's books was 555,010. Since there were 40,106 children in St. Paul between the ages of six and sixteen, she figured that the average number of books read by each child was 13.8. In her annual report for 1933, McGregor noted that she had compiled a list of books for children to offset the demand for Tarzan stories. She had strong views on what was appropriate children's literature. She did not approve of such popular books as the *Nancy Drew, Hardy Boys,* and *Bobbsey Twins* series. She called them "fluff" and would not purchase them for the library.

McGregor headed the Children's Room and Youth Services at the Central Library for forty-seven years, but she was also known throughout the United States as a premier children's librarian. She chaired the Children's Section of the American Library Association in 1932 and organized the first Newbery Award dinner in Chicago. Over the years she worked closely with the editors and publishers of children's books to promote quality in literature and reviewed books for the *Saturday Review of Literature.* It was a tribute to McGregor's reputation, and a feather in the city's cap, that she could attract authors with national reputations to a small city in the Midwest. When an author was due to arrive, McGregor would send a letter to the principal of one of the elementary schools, asking him to select "one excellent boy and one excellent girl" to meet the author. The children were instructed, through their school principal, that they were not to ask questions of the author, nor to bring books for signatures. They were to sit quietly with their hands in their laps and absorb the experience.

In recognition of her distinguished career and work to promote high standards in children's literature, McGregor was given the Grolier Award in 1961. After she retired from the Saint Paul

St. Paul City Commissioner Severin Mortinson awards a prize of a collegiate dictionary with a specially printed bookplate to thirteen-year-old Nancy Carlson for reading the most books (seventy-two) during the summer vacation of 1960.

Children's librarian Della McGregor with a young reader, May 4, 1961.

Public Library, the University of Minnesota appointed her, at age seventy-six, to be library director of the Minnesota School of Mathematics and Science Center. For many children and their parents, Della McGregor *was* the Saint Paul Public Library.

Years after McGregor had retired and Alice Neve ran the Children's Room, Neve noted an elderly gentleman standing in the doorway and leaning on a cane. When Neve asked if she could help him, he replied, no, that he was just reminiscing about when he used to bring his children downtown on the streetcar to attend the puppet shows in

Librarian Alice Neve reads to a rapt audience in the Children's Room at the Central Library.

the beautiful Children's Room. He peered at Neve more closely, then asked, "You aren't Della McGregor, are you?"

There were many such outstanding librarians. Roxanne Aschittino says that she "worked for really terrific librarians who were smart, had a sense of humor, worked very hard, showed up on time, and never asked us to do something they were not willing to do themselves." Of administrator Kathy Stack she says, "She was brash—you never want to ride in a car with her—and inspired her staff to give 120 percent. We worked extra days because we enjoyed the people we worked with. Kathy inspired that kind of response in people who worked with her."[178]

Former page Don Kelsey remembers that, as he was being taken around to meet the staff, expressions of bemusement would cross librarians' faces when they learned he would be working as a page for Florence Mathis. Mathis's pages, it seemed, did not last very long. When Kelsey started work back in the stacks, he was told that, when a buzzer sounded once, he was to go to the reference desk; two buzzes were to call him to Miss Mathis's desk; and three buzzes were the summons to the desk of Robert Hoag, head of the Reference Department. For the first three months of Kelsey's employment, Florence Mathis was out of the library on medical leave.

One Saturday morning, Kelsey was sitting in the library workroom, reading a book before it was time to begin work, when for the first time he heard two buzzes. "I jumped out of my seat as if it were wired, ran out, and just as I was turning the corner, realized I still had my book in my hand. I put it behind my back." Miss Mathis was sitting at her desk when Kelsey stood before her, breathless. She looked up at him and asked, "And who might you be?"

"I am Don Kelsey, the government publications page."

"And what do you have behind your back?"

"A murder mystery."

"Who wrote it?" she inquired.

"Erle Stanley Gardner."

"Young man," she announced, "I *met* Mr. Gardner."

It turned out that Florence Mathis was a devoted mystery fan. Claims Kelsey, "I learned more from Miss Mathis in the two years I worked for her before she retired than I did from any other single individual I ever worked with."[180]

Eva Smith, a tiny woman, was another member of the reference staff. One year she gave Kelsey a call slip for Dickens's *Pickwick Papers*. When he brought it to her, he casually asked why she was reading the book. She looked at him with astonishment and replied, "Young man, it's Christmas!" When he appeared not to comprehend, she asked, "You *have* read Dickens, haven't you?" When he shrugged, she took him by the hand, led him to the stacks, and, pointing out the Dickens shelf, said, "You will begin here." Under her tutelage, Kelsey read two-thirds of Dickens's novels before she retired. For her farewell party at the library, Kelsey and another page bought her an orchid. Miss Smith cried. No one had ever given her an orchid before.

One of the tasks of the pages was to make the elaborate Christmas cards that each department sent to all the other departments, library branches, and the Bookmobile staff. Roxanne Aschittino remembers that she spent hours working on the cards. "When I started in the sixties this is what I would do Saturdays in addition to putting a crèche on Emma Robbins's desk, not knowing she was Jewish."

Kelsey worked from five to nine every night, and the pages staffed the reference desk in the evening. "There were about a hundred standard reference works at the desk and we were taught how to use each of them. The training was rigorous. When someone called in with a reference question, before we could give the answer, we had to have the reference book open to the page where the answer was and have our finger on the citation. It was marvelous training."

Shelving in the Central Library's children's area is designed for the large format of children's books and incorporates familiar characters. Here the Cat in the Hat reposes at the end of a shelf of books for children.

THE BRANCHES

CENTRAL LIBRARY   FARICY '97

ILLUSTRATIONS BY RICHARD FARICY

The first of the Saint Paul Public Library's twelve branches had modest beginnings. Book repositories, called "stations," materialized in the early twentieth century as a shelf of volumes placed in local stores by the Central Library staff in response to demands from neighborhood residents. The stations were especially convenient for young mothers and factory workers whose obligations made it difficult to travel to the Central Library. But as the city and the demand for stations grew, it became clear that a better system of outreach was needed.

With the help of philanthropist Andrew Carnegie, the Saint Paul Public Library built its first three branches. Carnegie was the son of a self-educated weaver who emigrated from Scotland with his young family in 1848. As a working boy at a cotton factory in Pennsylvania, Andrew was befriended by a man who lent his personal library to poor youth. Carnegie later wrote, "It was from my own early experience that I decided there was no use to which money could be applied so productive of good to boys and girls who have good within them and ability and ambition to develop it as the founding of a public library in a community."

In his later years, the steel and railroad magnate funded more than 3,500 libraries throughout Europe and America. Communities requesting Carnegie grants had to own the site on which the library would be built. To ensure proper care of a completed library, grant recipients had to pay an annual maintenance amount equal to 10 percent of Carnegie's gift. "The community that is not willing to maintain a library had better not possess it," he said.[181]

ST. PAUL'S CARNEGIE LIBRARIES
Carnegie's largesse was not lost on St. Paul officials, who applied for funds to build the Saint Anthony Park, Arlington Hills, and Riverview branches of the Saint Paul Public Library. Each was designed by Charles A. Hausler, St. Paul's first city architect from 1914 to 1923. Born in St. Paul's West Seventh Street neighborhood in 1889, Hausler apprenticed with Louis B. Sullivan in Chicago in his late teens and afterward returned to his hometown, where he formed various partnerships with William Alban, Percy Bentley, and Ernest Hartford. Hausler designed several of St. Paul's schools, fire stations, and park buildings as well as the city's Carnegie libraries.

All three Carnegie branches debuted on October 12, 1917. The Arlington Hills Branch (at 1105 Greenbrier Street), formerly a station at Bodin's Drug Store, opened in a neighborhood populated by Swedish, Irish, Italian, and Mexican immigrants. The Riverview Branch (1 East George Street), once a station at Bastyr Drug Store, commanded a view of the Mississippi River to the north, east, and west. The Saint Anthony Park Branch (2245 Como Avenue), a former station at Fieseler's Drug Store and Wallace and Franke's Grocery, was within walking distance of elementary and high schools, Luther Seminary, and the St. Paul campus of the University of Minnesota.

The Beaux Arts–style branches incorporated ideas from James Bertram's booklet "Notes on Library Bildings" (sic). Carnegie and Bertram believed libraries should have dignity, and so favored monumental entrances, grand staircases, marble floors, and high ceilings and windows. The main floor was to have an adult reading room on one side and a children's area on the other, with the librarian's desk between the two. The front door was to be located in the center, opposite the librarian. The steps leading to the reading rooms was an identifying characteristic of Carnegie libraries. Only the Arlington Hills Branch had a flat roof, which kept the custodian there busy retrieving lost balls.

The three Carnegie branches serve different constituencies. While the Saint Anthony Park neighborhood remains predominantly white, its library is frequented by university and seminary students of Chinese, Korean, Japanese, and African heritage who are attracted to the branch's world language collection. The Arlington Hills Branch serves relatively high concentrations of St. Paul's newest residents: Asian, Latino, and American Indian patrons, many of them teenagers who wait two or more hours for time on the computers. In the late 1980s, Arlington Hills librarian Pat Gerlach established a collection of books and materials to help workers search for jobs and train for careers. The library also installed two computer stations where job-seekers could compose their resumes and fax them, without charge, to prospective employers.

From the start, the Riverview Branch has served primarily Spanish-speaking patrons. Florine Frischkorn, an early head librarian at Riverview, knew the names and borrowing habits of most of her branch's visitors. She would send staff members to area stores to buy recordings of popular Mexican and Spanish music, and she started bilingual story times for neighborhood children. Although many of Riverview's Spanish-speaking patrons have moved to other parts of St. Paul, they still check out the branch's many Spanish-language materials. "We see lots of East Side addresses on library cards presented at Riverview," says Mary Margaret Sullivan, Frischkorn's successor. "It has become a destination." To support the library's outreach effort, Spanish-speaking staff have been assigned to Riverview. A Homework Help Center is staffed by twenty tutors.

In 1981, Riverview was one of three branch libraries that St. Paul officials recommended closing due to declining circulation. Patrons protested via public meetings and petitions, insisting that Riverview should stay. When a closer look at the numbers revealed that, on a per capita basis, the branch had a higher circulation than many others, the library was spared. But it was in need of extensive remodeling, as were the other outdated Carnegie branches.

Realizing that attempts at modernizing the buildings in the 1950s with lower ceilings, fluorescent lighting, and institutional green paint had been misguided, the Carnegie branches were restored to their original glory. In a dramatic design reversal, the librarians' desks were returned to their former positions in front of the door. The false ceilings and fluorescent lights came down. Up went award-winning light fixtures, designed by the engineering firm of Gausman and Moore, that echoed the elegance of the Palladium-arch windows. Bathrooms, elevators, and mechanical and storage rooms were added. Each of the Carnegie branches was placed on the National Register of Historic Places in 1985.

Other changes followed. At Saint Anthony Park, the children's area had become so crowded that

Riverview

St. Anthony Park

patrons had to take turns at the shelves to select books. Under the direction of architect Phillip Broussard, construction began in 1998 on a circular addition to the branch to house the city's largest collection of children's books and materials. Circulation tripled after the expansion, with nearly one-third of the library's patrons coming from Minneapolis and suburban Ramsey County.

The Carnegie branches hold a special place in the hearts of many a library patron. At an anniversary celebration of the Arlington Hills Branch, librarian Karen Smith overheard several older gentlemen reminiscing about the happy hours they had passed at the library as children. To a man their favorite author had been Joseph Alexander Altsheler, a writer of adventure stories for boys. One elderly man, leaning on the arm of his daughter, told Smith that he could remember when the library was built, which streetcar ran by the building, and how much the library meant to him when he had to drop out of school and go to work as a copyboy to support his family after his father's death. He too admitted that his favorite author had been Altsheler.

The man was Fred Heaberlin, and he had been an editor at the *Pioneer Press* for forty years. He lived to be one hundred years old. Near the end of his life, Karen Smith presented Heaberlin a copy of the Altsheler book he had treasured as a boy.

DEPRESSION-ERA CONSTRUCTION

Not until 1930 did the Saint Paul Public Library add two more branches to its system: Merriam Park and Hamline-Midway. Until then, Merriam Park's first "library" was a whitewashed coal bin at Longfellow Elementary School. Hamline-Midway began as a collection of books in Mrs. Hull's Millinery Store, later the site of Florian's Pharmacy. In both communities, the residents raised money for the lots on which to build their libraries and deeded them to the city.

Both branches were built in the Collegiate Gothic style by city architect James C. Niemeyer, a St. Paul native and World War I veteran who studied at the College of St. Thomas and the Royal Academy of Rome. They were small; the larger, Hamline-Midway, was all of sixty by eighty feet. They were first known as the Henry Hale Memorial Libraries, after St. Paul judge and benefactor Henry Hale.

Merriam Park

Hamline-Midway

The Hamline-Midway Branch (1558 West Minnehaha) is the only Saint Paul Public Library with a working fireplace. The building was made handicapped-accessible, with an elevator, in 1985 and upgraded for energy-efficiency in 1990. It focuses on books for children and youth. Every year, thanks to an annual gift from Ethel Ridgway, the branch gives a book to every first-, second-, and third-grader at Hancock Elementary School. With the Friends of the Saint Paul Public Library, Hamline-Midway hosts six book chats and readings a year by St. Paul authors.

The Merriam Park Branch (1831 Marshall Avenue) was originally conceived as a Carnegie Library by William Dawson Johnston, head librarian of the Saint Paul Public Library. More than $3,000 had been raised by women's clubs of the community to fund the site. Plans were shelved for the duration of World War I, but shortly after the war ended, Carnegie libraries were no longer being funded.

The 1930 Merriam Park Branch building might still be standing if it had not started sinking. In the late 1970s, cracks appeared on the walls and the roof began to leak. Librarian Linda Valen remembers that "some nights we had to put big sheets of plastic over the freestanding shelves to protect the books from water coming in." In 1981 the northwest corner of the building was underpinned, but when it continued to settle, and when it was determined that further attempts to save the building would threaten the stability of a neighboring church and houses, plans for a new library were drawn up.

The community chose the Minneapolis architectural firm of Meyer, Scherer, and Rockcastle for the project. Jeffrey Scherer's design called for a handsome copper-topped brick exterior that featured artifacts from the old building: limestone panels from above the front door and windows, carved pilaster heads, sill pieces, and decorative floral designs. A stone carving of the building's original name— "Henry Hale Memorial Library – Merriam Park Branch"— was installed over the new entrance. A Longfellow quotation ("The love of learning, the sequestered nook, and all the sweet serenity of books") is carved into the stone of an exterior wall.

"The building is not just a building," noted Scherer at the building's 1993 dedication. "It is part of the

Rice Street

Highland

literacy of the community." The Reverend John Marcus Cox, pastor of Olivet Congregational Church next door, expressed similar sentiments in a letter to St. Paul mayor James Scheibel: "I have watched with pride as the building has gone up. . . . The result is an edifice of grace and charm, full of light, truthful to its purpose, welcoming to its public, humane in its proportions, and declaring that this city holds the love of learning and the seeking of truth to be of far more importance than the 'bottom line.'"

Neighbors have held long connections with the Merriam Park Branch. For years a group of elderly women called the Study Club held their monthly meetings in its basement, complete with refreshments served on good china, table linens, and silverware. The Twin City Bungalow Club donated its vast collection of books, magazines, and other materials to the library and updates it every year. Because the branch is located across the street from Charles Thompson Hall, a metro-area deaf social club, it works with the deaf and hard-of-hearing community—one of the few libraries in the nation to do so. The branch has a TTY

telecommunications machine, a DEAF/Hard-of-Hearing Collection, story times with a deaf story-teller, and American Sign Language interpreters for summer reading programs.

Some neighbors have had a hands-on affiliation with the library. Early one morning in 2003, custodian Jay Morrisey noticed a woman painting something on the front door. When he asked what she was doing, she replied, "I'm sealing the teak wood around the front door with linseed oil."

"Who said you could do that?" Morrisey asked in amazement.

"No one," she replied. "I figured you all were too busy, and I had the time to do it."

She dipped her brush in the oil and continued her work. Morrisey watched her for a moment, then, realizing that she was too short to reach the top of the door, took the brush and helped her finish the job.

THE MIDCENTURY BOOM

During the 1950s, the Saint Paul Public Library

Hayden Heights

Lexington

found the resources to build three more branches: Rice Street, Highland Park, and Hayden Heights. Each has been replaced or remodeled.

The first Rice Street Branch (1011 Rice Street) was built in 1952 as a small, flat-roofed structure with a partially excavated, dirt-floor basement. The building had a small vestibule, recalls librarian Ginny Stavn. "In the children's area, everything was down low so youngsters could reach, and there were long benches, ten or eleven feet long, where they could sit and look at books," she says. "The shelving was low, which allowed us to put out plants and little displays."

In 2002, fifty years to the day the first Rice Street Branch debuted, a new one opened, thanks to the energetic lobbying of community members. Excited children spent a day helping librarians move books from one location to the other, forming a line and passing books hand to hand from the old branch to the new. Community volunteers finished the job the next day. When the move was completed in March, the old site became a parking lot for the new library.

The Highland Park Branch (1974 Ford Parkway) originated as the St. Clair Branch Public Library. Housed in a portable classroom at Cleveland Elementary School, it was run entirely by volunteers who had started agitating for a library shortly after the three Carnegie libraries were completed in 1917. When Cleveland School closed for the summer, the library books would be moved to the Hermann Miller Shoe Store at 2044 St. Clair until classes resumed in the fall and the books were moved back into the school. The Ford Parkway building was constructed at last in 1954, dubbed by one *St. Paul Dispatch* writer as a "drive-in public library" for its twelve parking spaces and freestanding street-level stacks.

In 1972 Ellerbe Architects was hired to more than double the size of the Highland Park Branch, from 4,550 square feet to 11,850. In 1995 architect Bill Anderson, who had designed the adjoining Hillcrest Recreation Center, melded the two structures, adding 1,500 square feet to the library as well as seven parking spaces. The branch is the busiest within the Saint Paul Public Library system, with a collection of 132,138 books. Somali cab drivers

Sun Ray

West Seventh

regularly check their E-mail at the library, while Russian immigrants ask for advanced calculus, chemistry, and physics textbooks in their language.

Built in 1955, the first Hayden Heights Branch (1456 White Bear Avenue) was a small, yellow brick building that was replaced less than two decades later. In 1979 a white brick structure designed by Gene Flynn and Gene Freerks went up across the street from the original. It features a central skylight and windows on all sides and contains an expansive 12,295 square feet on a single level. In 1998 the ceiling was replaced and its lighting was upgraded. The Saint Paul Public Library's main automotive collection is housed at the Hayden Heights Branch, including shop manuals for American cars manufactured between 1938 and 2000. The library also maintains an automotive repair database as well as a workstation for job searches.

URBAN-RENEWAL BRANCHES

The national urban-renewal movement of the 1960s and 1970s led to the addition of two more branches within the Saint Paul Public Library system: the Lexington Avenue Branch and the Sun Ray Branch.

The West Seventh Branch followed in the mid-1980s. The Lexington Avenue Library (1078 Lexington Avenue), which was added in 1967, was housed in a remodeled theater. The community had been deeply divided over its location, admonishing the mayor and City Council in letters to the editor and guest editorials, saying that the chosen site was not even remotely near the center of the African American community it was intended to serve. But library director J. Archer Eggen held to his vision of where the new branch should be built and what it should look like, right down to the chairs and art: low-slung leather Barcelonas and Charles Beck prints. Eggen also commissioned Beck to create doors for the conference room that later housed the Homework Help Center. The Lexington Avenue Branch was the first of the branch libraries to be air-conditioned.

By the late 1980s, the Lexington Avenue Branch's Young Reader Program was serving a Hmong population as well as an African American clientele. The program was established in response to a request from area childcare workers. "We don't know how to read to children," they admitted. "We

Rondo

Dayton's Bluff

don't know how to do a successful story time, we don't know where to get the books, and we want to be taught." One day a group of women who were Hmong childcare workers came for their first lesson, accompanied by a Hmong gentleman who was there to make sure the library was a safe and appropriate place for the women to be. At the end of the class, the librarians served food to the child-care workers. When the workers returned for their next session, they brought food to share with the librarians. As librarian Alice Neve remembers, "It was an example of when you eat with someone, you communicate on a different level. It was wonderful."

The Lexington Avenue Branch reopened in 2006 as the Rondo Community Outreach Library (461 North Dale Street). The complex houses an 18,718-square-foot library with sixty underground parking spaces, plus ninety apartments and six townhouses. Reflecting the community it serves, the branch contains original Rondo Oral History records, a South-east Asian history and culture area, and more than five hundred titles in Spanish. The Homework Center and Business Resource Center also were expanded, the latter with electronic and print resources to assist persons with small-business startups. The Book-mobile is housed at the Rondo Branch.

The Sun Ray Branch (2105 Wilson Avenue), built in 1970, was designed by city architect Robert L. Ames in consultation with the firm of Freerks, Sperl, and Flynn. The building featured concrete slabs, cement block, and brick in what was believed to be the latest in construction techniques. It is remembered by librarians not only for the throngs of children who came to story hours, but also for the roof that leaked and the dozens of buckets they placed to catch the drips. The Sun Ray Branch was remodeled in 1985 and again in 2000, when, in conjunction with the remodeling of the Central Library, an addition was planned to house the materials management operation of the library system.

The Sun Ray Branch serves Southeast Asians, Hispanics, and African Americans, and other residents of Washington and Ramsey Counties. The library is working to more closely align its collection with the neighborhood's changing character. Books on tape, CDs, DVDs, and videos all are in demand. The Homework Help Center opened in 2003. The library also hosts a toddler storytime, a "Baby Lapsit" storytime, and "Read 'n' Play" on a weekly basis.

The West Seventh Branch (265 Oneida Street) began as a pilot project called the "popular library." Financed by the Friends of the Saint Paul Public Library and the Northwest Area Foundation, it opened in 1984 in the West Seventh Community Center. The library stocks six thousand paperbacks, hardcovers, magazines, and newspapers. The smallest of the branches, its primary goal is the provision of books for recreational readers as well as weekly story-times and a summer reading program.

INTO THE TWENTY-FIRST CENTURY

The most recent of the Saint Paul Public Library's branches—Dayton's Bluff Branch Library (645 East Seventh Street)—opened in 2005 in a brick and glass structure shared with Metropolitan State University's library. The collections of the Dayton's Bluff Branch are independent of the college library collections, but the staff collaborate in training, programming, and purchasing decisions. A reciprocal agreement allows responsible cardholders thirteen or older to check out books from either library. Dayton's Bluff, which is the only public library in Minnesota to operate in such a shared arrangement, was designed by the Meyer, Scherer, and Rockcastle firm of library architects.

Approximately 70 percent of the material in the Dayton's Bluff Branch is for children and teens. The branch depends on the Metropolitan State University Library to provide the adult and academic materials for its patrons. The library serves a diverse neighborhood population of approximately eighteen thousand, as well as students from across the Twin Cities who take classes at Metropolitan State University. The area is popular with new immigrants. Patrons of the library include recent Hmong immigrants, refugees from Burma, and many from Latin America.

Richard (Dick) Faricy

FOR MORE THAN THIRTY-FIVE YEARS, St. Paul architect Dick Faricy has specialized in preserving historic buildings. As cofounder of Winsor/Faricy Architects, he brought new life to such St. Paul icons as the Landmark Center, Como Park Conservatory, and Bandana Square, the one-time home of the Northern Pacific Railroad. His firm also restored International Market Square in Minneapolis.

Some years ago, Faricy was giving a talk as a member of St. Paul's Heritage Preservation Commission when he attracted the attention of Jeanne Fischer of the Friends of the Saint Paul Public Library. Before Faricy realized what was happening, he had been named to the board of the Friends. He served as its chair from 1992 to 1994.

One day, while looking at photographs of branch libraries with Peter Pearson, executive director of the Friends, Faricy commented that the images were "really terrible." Pearson countered with the request that he draw better pictures of the buildings. A couple of months later, Faricy had more than a dozen color sketches to show for his efforts. The sketches were used to make notecards, which were sold to benefit the library, and the original drawings hang in the Friends office.

In honor of the library's 100th anniversary, Mayor George Latimer proclaimed "Saint Paul Public Library Day" on September 19, 1982. From left: Mayor Latimer, library director Gerald Steenberg, Friends of the Library president Truman Porter, and honorary anniversary chair Garrison Keillor.

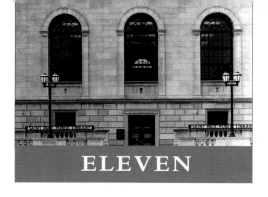

ELEVEN

Long-Term Planning

J. ARCHER EGGEN RETIRED in 1978 and died in 1999 in Green Valley, Arizona, having outlived each of his three wives. As anticipated, St. Paul mayor George Latimer appointed long-time library employee Gerald (Jerry) Steenberg to succeed Eggen. Steenberg was a St. Paul native and a graduate of the University of Minnesota library science school who had begun working in 1961 as a library assistant.

Steenberg had climbed the career ladder rapidly, becoming head librarian in 1962 at Highland, at that time St. Paul's largest branch library. After seven years at Highland he moved to the new Sun Ray Branch Library. Remembers Steenberg: "Archer said to me, 'I'm going to give you a shell. I will approve things but you arrange the shelves and the collection.' It was a wonderful opportunity. I could select my staff." In 1972 Eggen named Steenberg supervisor of the branches, and in 1974 moved Steenberg to the Central Library as assistant director. Members of the library staff expected Steenberg to be named library director when Eggen retired. As Kathleen Flynn remarks, "Everyone liked Jerry."

Steenberg's appointment transformed the psychological atmosphere of the library. "The tone needed changing very badly," he remembers. "The steps between the plateaus in the library were a mile high by then. People were concerned about their authority. I thought it was time for us administrators to use our first names, like the rest of the staff."

"Jerry made the library more human," Mary Clare Huberty remembers. "He tried to get rid of the caste system, tried to break through that and make everybody feel that they were part of a great big team. He succeeded. That was needed." Adds Linda Wilcox: "Jerry was a real people person who loves gathering people together and telling stories. He was very welcoming. For Eggen there was a real pecking order from the top down and you did not cross the line on whom you talked with. Jerry talked to everybody; he knew them and asked about their families."

"There was a big change in mood when Jerry came in," agrees Pat Ethier. "He had worked with all of us. We were on a first-name basis. You would never have done that with Archer or Agatha [Klein], for that matter, though she was a lot easier to deal with than he was." Kathleen Flynn agrees. "Jerry was very good with customers and he modeled that for the rest of us. The best thing Jerry did was make this place a more comfortable place to work. Things just suddenly became friendlier, warmer. He drastically changed the work environment here." Steenberg's concern for the staff was genuine. A library clerk had very bad teeth and "the story went around that Jerry paid to have her teeth worked on," Ethier said.

One of the first changes Steenberg made was to allow women to wear trousers. Every woman who was working at the library at the time remembers the day the policy changed. There were still some restrictions, however. The trousers

Librarians at the famous round table in the library break room. From left: Ginny Lufkin, Karen Kol Peterson, Jerry Steenberg, Carole Williams, Carolyn Sorensen, Sue Ellingwood, and Adline Carlson.

had to be part of a matched suit, and there was much debate about what, exactly, constituted a "pants suit." Denim and low necklines were prohibited. Turtlenecks were preferred.

Steenberg also happily watched as the Friends of the Saint Paul Public Library took charge of their organization once again. "As Eggen drove out of the driveway [for the last time], Paul and Nancy Harris carried the files of the Friends in boxes out of Eggen's office into the Friends' office at the [Saint Paul] Foundation," Steenberg recalls. "Paul had said, 'We can make this [the Friends] a real organization.'"

Steenberg was acutely aware of the power vested in the city commissioners under the form of government then in operation and was careful never to give offense to anyone in City Hall. He tiptoed around the politics swirling about the courthouse and accommodated the demands of those over him in the city. This occasionally got him into trouble

with his staff, even before he became library director.

Commissioner Leonard Levine was elected in April 1970 and served until 1982. The first two years of his term, before the new city charter was adopted in 1972, he was commissioner of libraries, auditoriums, and civic buildings. One day during this period Mary Clare Huberty, in charge of circulation, received a call from Jerry Steenberg telling her to clear out the library fines (approximately $20) owed by Levine's wife. Huberty refused. "I said, 'No, if you want that done you have to come down here and do it yourself. It's not right and I don't want to be a part of it.' And he did."[182]

From the late 1970s on, the library's budget had failed to keep pace with operating costs. This forced severe reductions in expenditures for books and cut staffing and hours of service. Other libraries in Minnesota had increased spending for materials by 117.8 percent between 1976 and 1980; St. Paul had increased its spending by only 10 percent. For the entire United States, spending on books for libraries had gone up a whopping 294.2 percent in the same period.[183]

St. Paul's library management had been spending its time on "housekeeping" concerns, dealing with the crisis-of-the-day instead of focusing on long-range planning and setting a direction for the institution. Without a credible plan into which budgeting requests could be fit, the library was at a disadvantage when competing with parks, police, and other city services for funding. Some officials even began to wonder if the urban public library *was* a vital resource and if the public should continue to pay for its services.

TASK FORCE ADVICE
In July 1979, St. Paul's activist mayor George Latimer, with financial support from the Saint Paul Foundation, the Perrie Jones Fund, and the Friends of the Library, appointed a citizens task force to produce a five-year plan for the library. It would be the first time in the city's history that an extensive study of the library was undertaken. Heading the task force was Humphrey Doermann, president of the Bush Foundation. Other members were Robert S. Davis, retired vice president of the Saint Paul Companies; Reatha Clark King, president of Metropolitan State University; Frank D. Marzitelli, executive director of the St. Paul–Ramsey Arts and Science Council; Erma McGuire, assistant superintendent of the St. Paul Public Schools; Richard A. Moore, an attorney with Moore, Costello and Hart; Truman W. Porter, vice president of Midway National Bank; Peter P. Stumpf, Minnesota state senator; and Fred B. Williams, director of the Martin Luther King Center. Library director Jerry Steenberg was an ex-officio member and Nancy Harris, of the Saint Paul Foundation, staffed the organization and kept it moving forward. The group hired the library consulting firm of HBW Associates, out of Dallas, Texas, and awaited the consultants' report.

The task force received the final report in February 1981. The report was filled with recommendations, many of which the library acted upon immediately. The Central Library became more of a reference center, administration was reorganized and simplified, and the budget for materials was increased. As the report stated, "Books, tapes, films, periodicals are the basic tools of library service. The funding in St. Paul has been inadequate over the years to keep this city current."[184] Some branches (Highland Park, Sun Ray, Lexington) were designated "area libraries" and assigned larger collections and more staff. The others became "community libraries." As Kathleen Flynn explains, "It all had to do with the staff we had, the budget we had to work with. It all came down to money."

The task force noted that St. Paul was the only major U.S. city to restrict its choice of library administrative personnel to a "promotion only" basis. The report observed that, "The management of a $3 million a year enterprise requires highly specialized skills," and St. Paul paid high enough salaries to be competitive nationally. As Dr. William Dawson Johnston had done back in 1915, the task force urged the library to recruit top management on a nationwide basis.[185]

The consultants surveyed the community and learned that worry about getting materials back on time was a major deterrent to the public's using the library. At the time, only the Central Library had a twenty-four-hour book-return facility. Soon, book-return boxes sprouted at all of the branch libraries.

A major change that the library made in response to the task force report was the establishment of a single checkout and entrance point in the Central Library. Instead of three entrances to the building, there would be only one: at the street level on Fourth Street, through the former entrance to the Cochran Children's Room and Skinner Room. Instead of seven points at which patrons could check out books, there would be just one. To draw attention to the new main entrance to the library, architect Bruce Cavin proposed the erection of an aluminum and glass canopy over the door. When a drawing of the awning appeared in the paper, it provoked a storm of protest.

Russell Fridley, director of the Minnesota Historical Society, wrote Steenberg that the canopy "is ill-advised in the extreme by introducing a visual intrusion that is out of character with this handsome and historic structure."[186] Beverly Vavoulis, wife of former St. Paul mayor George Vavoulis, called the canopy a "tepee." The *Pioneer Press* weighed in opposing it as well, writing that the canopy "would be as destructive as graffiti on a clean wall. The library would do the cause of historic preservation a favor by finding an empty shelf for the canopy plan—one hard to reach, quickly covered by a layer of dust."[187] Even the City Council, not known for its sensitivity to architectural aesthetics, was prepared to enter the canopy controversy.

Jerry Steenberg, trying to please everyone involved, said, "I don't think the canopy is definitive. There may be other ways to deal with the entrance." The canopy problem was resolved when he received a phone call from Mayor George Latimer. "I hope," said Latimer, "that the crash I just heard is the canopy plummeting into the Mississippi River." "Yes, Mr. Mayor," Steenberg replied. "It is."

BAR-CODING THE LIBRARY

Another task force recommendation was that the library embrace technology. During the late 1970s and early 1980s, St. Paul's neighboring libraries had modernized their systems by bar-coding all books and materials to enable them to keep track of circulation by computer.

St. Paul was six to seven years behind, and MELSA, the regional library association to which St. Paul belonged, indicated that, to more fully participate, St. Paul needed to conform to the new bar-code standard. Steenberg organized a committee of senior librarians to determine what should be done. After several meetings Roxanne Aschittino spoke up and volunteered that she and circulation head Mary Clare Huberty could take on the entire job of bar-coding the library systemwide. Aschittino pointed out that she and Huberty worked well together, having just completed the major project of putting theft detection strips into all of the books. Steenberg agreed.

The job was enormous. More than 700,000 books as well as phonograph records, audio and video tapes, films, magazines, folders—anything that could be checked out—had to be given a bar code, the code typed into the computer and linked to the material bearing the code. Aschittino and Huberty organized their crew and started with the Hayden Heights Branch. They closed the library and for ten days the staff, with help from the other branches, bar-coded all the books. They brought in casseroles, cakes, and pies to keep them going. Kathleen Flynn remembers, "We had food all over the place. It was a good accompaniment to that job because we had a deadline, a lot of work to do, and we were doing it as a tightly knit group, like a family." Aschittino says they considered writing a *Bar-Code Cookbook* when the job was finished, but never did.

When one branch was bar-coded, the team moved on to the next. With each branch they became faster. The Central Library, the last to be tackled, was closed the longest. An unanticipated benefit to the five months of bar-coding was that the barriers that had been built up during the J. Archer Eggen years, separating people at the various levels of library work, broke down. Supervisors and technicians, senior librarians and clerks all worked side by side to bar-code the materials. The gulf that had once seemed unbridgeable largely disappeared, and workers at all levels cooperated to get a difficult job done.

THE FRIENDS COME INTO THEIR OWN

An unexpected but highly beneficial outcome of the citizens task force effort was the impetus it gave to the continued emergence of the Friends of the Saint Paul Public Library as a major player in the affairs of the library system. The Friends' stature had been elevated in the early 1970s through the foresight of Perrie Jones and John and Myrtle Briggs, who left sizeable trusts in their wills to the Friends. The Jones Fund was to be used for the benefit of the library staff while the Briggs Trust allowed for material purchases. As a power struggle over the purpose of the Jones Fund emerged between the Friends and library director J. Archer Eggen, the Friends became a barely functioning organization that had dwindled to about thirty members who rarely met. But when regulations dictated by the Tax Reform Act of 1969 were enacted by the IRS, the Friends had to get involved to avoid having the Briggs Trust, then handled by the First Trust Company, pay penalties and fines if reporting was not handled correctly.

As Paul Verret, president emeritus of the Saint Paul Foundation, puts it, the Friends organization had "an enormous amount of money, but it didn't have a

way to spend it and didn't have a way to account for it." If improvements were not made quickly, the Briggs Trust would no longer be able to grant funds to the Friends. Warren Burger, an attorney with Moore, Costello, and Hart and the administrator of the Briggs Trust before

Photographer, author, and former St. Paulite Gordon Parks signs books at the Lexington Avenue Branch Library, 1981.

Author and University of Minnesota professor Patricia Hampl signs her book **A Romantic Education** *at a Central Library book fair, 1981.*

Jeanne Fischer was a popular book reviewer and a longtime board member of the Friends of the Saint Paul Public Library.

Library director Jerry Steenberg, Truman Porter of the Friends of the Library, librarian Kathy Stack, and city councilman Vic Tedesco cut the ribbon to inaugurate the new, single entrance to the Central Library.

being appointed to the Supreme Court, urged his former law partner, Richard A. Moore, then chair of the Saint Paul Foundation, to offer help to the Friends with its recordkeeping and reporting duties. He did, and the Friends reorganized, enlarged its board, elected Truman Porter president, and asked the Saint Paul Foundation to manage the fund. Verret arranged for the foundation to provide the Friends organization with staffing, accounting, and reporting services. He assigned Nancy Harris, who was already staffing the Perrie Jones Fund, to staff the Friends organization as well. Besides Porter, the new board of the Friends included Jeanne Fischer, vice president; Cynthia Gardner, assistant secretary; Paul A. Verret, treasurer; and members Mildred Bakken, William Queenan, Kathey Sonnen, Fred A. Waterous Jr., and Jean West.

The newly energized Friends sent out a newsletter. In its first issue it reported on the new board and stated its purpose: "If ever the library needed an active, working Friends organization, now is the time." It pointed out that the library's publications office had been discontinued in 1979, the staff reduced from 169 to 152, and operating hours cut. The budget had remained the same while the cost of books had doubled. "There are no villains in this situation," the newsletter asserted. "Nevertheless public libraries tend to be low-profile 'safe' places to make budget cuts. To make the most of what is potentially available *the library needs strong advocates*"[188] (emphasis in the original). On the back of the two-sheet newsletter was a coupon for citizens to clip to join the Friends. An annual membership cost $2.

THE FIRST CAPITAL CAMPAIGN

In 1982, library director Jerry Steenberg approached Friends' treasurer Paul Verret with a request for $25,000 to $50,000 for improvements to the library as a way to observe and celebrate its 100th anniversary that year. Verret suggested that, since the needs of the library had been well documented in the citizens task force study, and since they far exceeded $50,000, Steenberg should think bigger—a lot bigger. "Let's organize a campaign to raise enough money to really make a difference for the library," Verret urged.

Steenberg and a committee of the Friends added up the cost of the improvements to the library that had been identified in the study. The Saint Paul Foundation and the McKnight Foundation each offered to match every dollar raised during the campaign. Garrison Keillor not only agreed to be honorary chair of the fund drive, but he attended most of the meetings and supplied ideas.

St. Paul celebrated the 100th birthday of the library with a parade that marched from Mears Park to Rice Park, as well as band performances, book signings by Minnesota authors, games, theatrical productions in the park and in the Municipal Auditorium, and a display that illustrated a century of the library's history. The evening ended with the Butch Thompson Trio playing for a dance in the library's Social Science Room. An estimated 8,000 to 10,000 people celebrated the centenary of the Saint Paul Public Library.

The campaign to celebrate the library's 100th anniversary raised almost $2.5 million. The drive not only paid for

Paul Verret was president of the Saint Paul Foundation from 1975 to 2003. During his tenure the foundation worked with various organizations to revitalize the community, including the Friends of the Saint Paul Public Library, the Mississippi Riverfront Corporation, the Children's Museum, the Science Museum of Minnesota, and the Minnesota History Center. Verret's leadership helped make the Saint Paul Foundation one of the largest and most active community foundations in the country.

The Great Library Book Sale was held in Rice Park on the occasion of the Saint Paul Public Library's 100th anniversary, September 1982.

many of the improvements to the library recommended by the consultants' report, it marked the growing maturity of the Friends of the Saint Paul Public Library. When Nancy Harris, who had been staffing the Friends, left the Saint Paul Foundation to join the Peace Corps, Edie Meissner took over her position, devoting half of her time to the Perrie

Jones Fund and the Friends organization and half of her time to the foundation as program officer. It soon became apparent to Jean Hart, programs vice president of the Saint Paul Foundation, that the growing Friends organization needed a full-time executive. Verret agreed, and in late fall of 1991, Hart hired Peter Pearson as the organization's president.

PETER PEARSON AND THE FRIENDS

Before he became president of the Friends, Peter Pearson had had an unconventional career. The Chicago native followed an older brother to St. Mary's College in Winona, Minnesota, earned a master's degree in educational psychology at Iowa State University, then earned an elementary school teaching certificate and a second master's degree in educational administration at the University of Minnesota. Pearson taught sixth grade for four years, worked as an autopsy assistant at Minneapolis's Mount Sinai Hospital and then as a bartender at the hotel where the Vikings football team spent its pre-season, served as principal of a parochial school in Robbinsdale, and, at the time Hart hired him as head of the Friends, Pearson was the executive director of the Learning Disabilities Association.

By now the assets of the Friends had grown to $4 million. Most of the board, chaired by Richard Faricy, had served for fifteen years; one had been a member for twenty-five years. "That first year I kind of tiptoed around, trying to push board members into appropriate roles for a maturing organization," Pearson recalls. Member Jeanne Fischer agreed with his changes, but said, "I miss some of the things we used to do on the board—such as blowing up balloons for the celebrations."

When library staff members learned that Pearson planned to become active in fund-raising for the library, they became a touch apprehensive, not knowing in what direction he was planning to go. Pearson assured them that the Friends' policy would be to raise private money for materials not already financed by the city and not to pay staff salaries, which, the Friends maintained, was the city's responsibility. He eased librarians' fears by spending six months doing little more than visiting the branches and talking with staff, finding out what they needed and what their priorities were. He found that they needed operational support and money for materials, and learned that they wanted to keep the libraries open evening hours, which none did at that time.

Friends chair Dick Faricy, whose sensibility to the competition between St. Paul and Minneapolis was fine-tuned, explained to Pearson that he had one rule for the Friends' operation. Since the organization purchased needed services through contracts for tasks, such as writing the Friends newsletter, conducting author programs at the branch libraries, and composing the annual report, he told Pearson, "I want to be very clear about one thing with you: All contractual money will be spent on *this* side of the river."

Faricy and Pearson had differing visions for the role of the Friends. According to Pearson, "Dick did not want to ruffle feathers—did not want to upset the [Saint Paul] Foundation or City Hall." When Pearson wanted to lobby the city for more money for the library, Faricy advised him to go easy and not to push. "He knew that we were flying in the face of the mayor, working against what the mayor proposed in his budget."

THE FRIENDS BEGIN TO ADVOCATE

This changed when Faricy asked board member Carol Ryan to chair the Friends Advocacy Committee. Ryan, like Pearson, had no qualms about getting in the face of St. Paul mayor James Scheibel when he proposed cuts to the library budget. Ryan called the first Friends Advocacy Committee meeting in the winter of 1992 after the mayor released his budget showing a proposed $100,000 cut to the library budget. The cuts would have eliminated the library's membership in the Metropolitan Library Service Agency (MELSA), closed libraries on Saturdays for a year, and cut the equivalent of twenty-two full-time staff positions. Advocacy Committee members called on City Council members to tell them that the library could no longer take cuts like this and that the Friends organization would be rallying behind the library to give it support.

Peter Pearson, president of the Friends of the Saint Paul Public Library since 1992, is active in regional and national library agencies and heads the Friends' library consulting service.

Library director Jerry Steenberg turned up at work on his fiftieth birthday to find his office decorated with balloons.

Friends of the Library chair Richard (Dick) Faricy, a member of the organization's board for fifteen years, passes the gavel to new Friends chair Carol Ryan in 1995. Ryan had previously served as the first chair of the Friends Advocacy Committee.

The Friends regrouped and planned strategy. Their first step was to send out a news release about the library's need for funds. To their delight the story was given major coverage in the *Minneapolis Tribune* and *Pioneer Press*. The second step was to participate in an exercise called "Public Testimony." Near the end of October 1994 anyone in St. Paul could come to a City Council meeting at 5:00 p.m. and speak for two minutes on any item in the proposed city budget before the budget was finalized. Members of the Friends made up more than 90 percent of the audience, and every one signed up to speak for two minutes in favor of additional funds for the library.

Council chair Dave Thune stopped the testimony to ask if anyone else present was waiting to speak on an issue other than the library. One woman raised her hand and said, "I want to talk about parks." When she had spoken for her allotted two minutes she added, "If I had known that the Friends of the Library were going to be here, I would have been with them too because our libraries are so important." The result of the "Public Testimony" was that the City Council changed the mayor's budget and funded everything the library had requested.

To the committee's surprise, City Council members were supportive. The council had never heard a unified voice come forward in support of the library and explain to them what the library needed. After listening to members of Ryan's Advocacy Committee, the City Council overrode the mayor and restored the proposed $100,000 library cutback.

In the Friends' second year as an independent organization, Peter Pearson and Carol Ryan started their campaign for the library a few months earlier. They met with library director Jerry Steenberg, who brought them his list of the library's needs—principally money for books and funds to keep the libraries open more hours in the week. The Friends took the request to Mayor Scheibel who again told them there was no additional money in the city budget for the library.

In the third year of Friends' lobbying, Pearson and Ryan again went to Mayor Scheibel and asked him to put money in the budget to fund one extra open night for the branch libraries. The branch libraries were open two evenings a week, and the Friends wanted the budget increased so the branches could be open three evenings a week. It was a modest request in light of those made the previous two years. Scheibel laughingly replied, "I know what is going to happen. If I don't do it, you will go to the City Council and get it anyway. So I am going to give it to you now and get the credit for it."

The Advocacy Committee went to the City Council with the message that all the council had to do was support the mayor's budget. By then council members were so enamored of the libraries that, on their own, they added funding for opening the libraries a fourth night in the week.

The Friends' early activist successes put the library staff on their side. They saw that the Friends were not going to force any personal pet programs on them. Instead, the Friends asked the library staff what it needed and promised to try to get it for them. For Pearson, advocacy and fund-raising go together. "If you are going to raise funds for a publicly supported institution," he says, "it is critical that you add the lobbying component to be sure that the city continues its strong support. Since 1992 the city has added funding for the library every year."

Another area that the Friends took over from the library was adult programming. Budget cuts in the early 1980s had ended programming for adults. In 1986 the Friends became one of the few Friends organizations in the entire country to make library programming a significant part of its mission. By 1987 St. Paul had the second highest per capita circulation of library books in the country. Only Seattle ranked higher. St. Paul circulated 8.29 items per person while Seattle sent out 8.96. Circulation had increased 24 percent since 1979.[189]

By then, the Friends of the Saint Paul Public Library organization was feeling its oats. Pearson and Jean Hart realized

that the Friends needed to move out of the Saint Paul Foundation offices and establish an independent identity. Paul Verret concurred and helped the Friends secure a grant to purchase office equipment and furniture. In January 1994, the Friends moved into two rooms and a reception area in the Norwest Center in downtown St. Paul, taking the first steps toward becoming a financially stable, independent nonprofit organization. Pearson gives Verret and the Saint Paul Foundation "100 percent credit for what the Friends is today. I cannot say enough about what Paul and the foundation did for this organization."

ARRIVAL OF THE HMONG

More was happening in the libraries than an increase in circulation and funding. The patrons were changing. In the late 1970s and early 1980s refugees from the conflict in Southeast Asia began arriving in St. Paul. Immigrants from Vietnam, Cambodia, and Laos found their way to Minnesota, and by 1990 St. Paul was home to the largest urban Hmong community in the country. The 1990 census revealed a 612 percent increase in the number of Asians in the city over the past decade.[190]

The Hmong quickly realized that education and libraries were the tickets to their children's future. Responding to the need, the librarians, especially those in the branches, rushed to provide specialized services for the newcomers. The first problem they encountered was how to issue library cards for the Hmong. Patrons of the library were identified on their library cards with a first and last name and date of birth. As Mary Clare Huberty, head of circulation, explains it, "You might have a lot of Bob Johnsons, but only one who was born on February 10, 1962."

Garrison Keillor autographs copies of his Lake Wobegon Days *at a 1985 book-signing at the Central Library.*

When the Hmong came in to register for library cards, the librarians discovered that a great many of them had the same last name (only twenty or so clan names are used in the Hmong community) and many first names were also the same. For a date of birth, it seemed to her that they all listed January 1! When Huberty found that she had a great many people with the same names and birthdate in the database, she knew the system had to change. She switched to using Social Security numbers, and library cards proliferated in the Hmong community.

With the arrival of the Southeast Asians, the librarians' role changed. As Kathleen Flynn recalls, "When I became a librarian . . . we did a form of outreach where we would go into schools, but it was relatively tame. We had our programs that we decided we were going to give with not a lot of information on what the community might need. Our population

was predominantly white and the library was a much more genteel, middle-class institution. As our population changed, we had to start changing, learn how to deal with customers from different cultures, with social problems. It was a whole new learning curve."

The staff immediately went on a search for materials in languages other than English and formed a World Languages Committee, with community participation to help them. Materials in Spanish were readily available, but it was hard to find books in Russian. City policies restricted the library from ordering materials directly from publishers outside the United States or Canada. While they were able to find popular Vietnamese novels to add to the collection, works in Hmong presented a greater problem. Because the Hmong did not have a formal written language until the 1950s, there were few published materials.

Charles Johnson, a professor at Macalester College, translated many Hmong folktales into ESL (English as a Second Language) booklets, and these formed the basis of the early Hmong collection. In 1991 the library hired Ma La, a Hmong management trainee, to help Hmong immigrants learn how to use the library. Elaine Wagner remembers that children who did not speak English would come into the Central Library. "I would bring them into the Children's Room and improvise, do a lot of pantomime. We did puppet shows and showed them picture books that told universal stories."

Many Hmong and other immigrant families got their books from the Bookmobile when it made stops at public housing communities. Often more than 150 children would be waiting for the Bookmobile to pull up at McDonough Homes near downtown St. Paul. A Hmong mother told a librarian, "We have no books at home. The only books my children read are from the Bookmobile." Another child who won a paperback in the Summer Reading Program said, "I have never had a book of my own before."[191] The Bookmobile was the "only link to the library system for many residents of public housing projects, senior high-rises, and those blind spots of neighborhoods not within walking distance of a permanent branch," according to Bookmobile librarian Mary Jo Datko. More than 60 percent of Bookmobile users were under fourteen years of age, a reversal of the percentages at the regular library.[192]

Jerry Steenberg ended thirty-four years of service with the Saint Paul Public Library in 1995. He had held the gamut of positions throughout the system, from entry-level librarian to head of a branch library, to supervisor of branch libraries, to assistant library director, and then, for twenty-seven years, to head librarian. The West Seventh Branch Library was built under his watch. Steenberg lists as one of his major accomplishments the hiring of Carole Williams. "I couldn't wait to get her on the staff," he said, "and was hoping she would succeed me."

The Bookmobile is, in many ways, the children's library. Children are its largest constituency and its arrival is always greeted with enthusiasm. This Bookmobile was a gift from the Friends of the Saint Paul Public Library in 2002.

Bookmobile Redux

THE FIRST SAINT PAUL PUBLIC LIBRARY Bookmobile was purchased in 1917. Since that time, the library has owned six vehicles, the most current having been purchased in 2005 with funding provided by the *Pioneer Press*. The Bookmobile, which is now housed at the Rondo Community Outreach Library, provides biweekly service to nearly fifty sites within St. Paul, including high-rises, apartment complexes, parks, and child-care centers. The library on wheels carries more than 5,000 items, including books in several languages, as well as magazines, videos, DVDs, and recorded books. Large-print books are provided on long-term loan to more than a dozen short- and long-term health-care facilities. The Bookmobile, which is staffed by one part-time and three full-time employees, circulates 50,000 to 60,000 items per year.

Driver Bernard Mitchell with the Saint Paul Public Library truck at the Merriam Park Branch Library, September 1931.

Library assistant Robin Madsen with the 1980 Bookmobile.

Bookmobile driver Bernard Mitchell and librarian Maurine Hoffman assisting Bookmobile patrons, 1950.

Children crowd the interior of the Saint Paul Public Library's Bookmobile, ca. 1980s.

The F. Scott Fitzgerald alcove on the third floor of the restored Central Library.

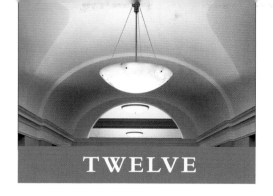

TWELVE

Central Library's Restoration

CAROLE WILLIAMS, a native of Omaha, Nebraska, had planned to pursue an elementary teaching career in the Des Moines Public Schools when she won a scholarship to study librarianship. Intrigued by libraries, she went on to earn a master's degree in library science at the University of Michigan and worked in libraries in Wisconsin and Iowa before coming to the Saint Paul Public Library in 1974.

In July 1997, Mayor Norm Coleman named fifty-six-year-old Carole Williams director of the Saint Paul Public Library, making permanent a job she had held temporarily since Jerry Steenberg retired eighteen months before. Coleman called the library director post one of the city's most critical positions.

Williams's fellow staff members thought of her as a "wonderful person—one of the finest people who ever worked for the library." To Linda Wilcox, Williams was "determined, strong, and every inch a lady." Another said, "Williams was a very reserved person, private. She expected a lot and therefore got it." She believed in strong management and liked order. She urged the librarians to adopt a "cockpit" approach to their desks and keep them in better order. Elaine Wagner remembers, "She came to us at midcareer—started at the Hamline Branch and rose up through the ranks with us. She was in Community Relations and then became head of the branches."

During her administration, Williams's office door was always open. Wilcox remembers that "if I had a joke to tell her or something had happened, I would wave in the doorway and she would say 'Come on in.' I always felt she had time to listen. She collected paperweights and loved reading sleazy romance novels. That was her way to relax and escape." When faced with problems she would say to her staff, "We will work on this together and get through this." For Wilcox, when Williams was at the library, it was the best work situation she was ever in. "If I came back in another life, I would do it all over again. I loved the library. A day did not go by that I did not learn something."

TRAUMATIC REORGANIZATION

Soon after taking over the library, Carole Williams recognized the need to reorganize its departments. Since its beginning, the library had been organized under subject headings: Art and Music, Business and Science, Social Science and Literature, and so on, with experts in the field running the departments. Everything was specialized. The problem was that some departments were underused by the public while others were mobbed. As Kathleen Flynn explains, "The only way we could manage that kind of disparity was to have the staff trained so every librarian could handle any department and any subject."

Williams believed that the library of the future would feature seamless service where a customer would go to one location to have all of his needs met. To do that, the specialized departments would have to be disbanded. A customer would go to the reference desk with his question and the librarian

Carole Williams was named library director in 1997 and served throughout the renovation of the Central Library. She retired in 2002, one week following completion of the project. Among her many accomplishments was the initiation and oversight of the reorganization of Central Library services to provide for an information commons and a remodeling of the branch libraries to make them handicapped-accessible.

there would take, not send, him from place to place to find his materials.

For the librarians, the change was huge and catastrophic. As Wilcox explained, "Librarians were identified by their specialty or their topic. . . . This is what they had their degrees in and had worked on all these many years. They would lose their identity if they had to answer questions on a topic they did not know much about—help somebody find a car repair manual and advise them on what carburetor they needed. There was a feeling among the staff that they were losing their worth, their way of life, and that they would not be able to serve the public as well, to give good service. It was truly a time of loss. It almost felt like there had been a divorce."

Working with the heads of the departments, Williams reorganized them out of existence, leaving only Reference and Circulation. J. Archer Eggen had never shared decision-making with a committee, while Jerry Steenberg had had "committees all over the place." According to Flynn, "People had gotten used to a lot of conversation and discussion as we moved forward." Williams and her administration moved with dispatch to bring about the reorganization. Collections were broken up and books discarded because of a lack of space as the library became more of a generalist institution. Painfully aware of the trauma her changes were causing, Williams brought in speakers to talk with the staff about how to adapt to loss and change, and worked to counter the rumors that "the administration is taking over." Despite her efforts to make the transition smooth, it was difficult.

Looking back, Wilcox calls the reorganization of the library Williams's greatest

achievement. "Carole saw that the library was going to have to change. It could not stay the same. She knew what she was about and brought this vision forth, which, at the time, people did not appreciate. Despite the fact so many people were angry and shed tears, she got us ready for the twenty-first century. The Saint Paul Library is positioned much better today than it would have been if she had not made the changes she did."

THE GREAT TECHNOLOGY CHANGE

For Williams, the Saint Paul Public Library was the "people's university," a phrase she repeated at every opportunity. When she took over as director, the library consisted of thirteen buildings and a Bookmobile, all operated by a staff of approximately 230 part-time and full-time employees with a budget of $8.8 million. "The library has the ability to level the playing field to make sure all people have the information they need," she said. "It [the library] must be a leader in nurturing literacy and the value of reason." Technology, she realized, would revolutionize how libraries served their clients, and she promised to connect every Saint Paul Public Library to the Internet. Like William Dawson Johnston, Williams was determined to get the library books out of the stacks and into the community.

Technology was bringing about a seismic change in the way the library was arranged and how librarians gave service. "We were accustomed to our card catalog drawers that we used to pull out," Wilcox remembers. "First we got the microfiche, and then we got the computers and began putting things on-line. It was a huge change for everybody. Everyone had to learn to work with computers; they didn't have any choice.

We had training up the kazoo, classes at the Science Museum, classes given by the city, electronic training workshops, motivational things. We started calling ourselves 'navigators.' We would not just cough up an answer or pull a book from the shelves the way we might have done before. We would help people navigate their own way through the library."

In a stunning reversal of the years when the library budget was the first one to be cut, Mayor Norm Coleman, in 1997, promised to spend $200,000, double the amount of the previous year, on new materials for the library. The Friends of the Saint Paul Public Library added another $50,000 in private donations,

and budget director Joe Reid noted that the library was one of the few city departments that would not be asked to trim its operations for the coming year. Council member Mike Harris predicted that, as in previous years, the council was likely to raise the mayor's proposed library budget.[193]

Another of Williams's innovations was the organization of the Labor Management Committee. The library was the only agency in the city with such a committee that worked on the budget, Wilcox says. "Every year when it came time to work on the budget, administration sat down with the union representatives and we hammered things out. It was always

Library staff on the steps of the Central Library, October 2000.

Sandy Kiernat and Toni Carter (below) cochaired the Citizen Advisory Committee for the Library Strategic Planning Process from 1995 to 1996. The plan, developed by the committee, was instrumental in gaining the enthusiastic support of Mayor Norm Coleman for the remodeling of the Central Library.

with the understanding that if we came to gridlock, Carole would have the final say. As far as I know, we never came to that point and always reached consensus. It turned out to be such a benefit."

THE CENTRAL LIBRARY RENOVATION

Beginning around 1980, Williams and the heads of the branch libraries began to meet regularly to discuss what to do about the Central Library. All of the librarians knew that it was not what it should be. Only 29 percent of the Central Library's floor space was accessible to the public. Items never dreamed of when the library was built in 1917—compact discs, microfilm, videocassettes, and computers—now overflowed every available space. Fluorescent lights and tangles of wires hung from the hand-painted ceilings dimmed by decades of coal smoke and grime. Old metal shelving blocked light and views from the high arched windows. The volume of books alone was up 400 percent from the day when the library had opened.

The discussion of what to do about the stately but dysfunctional Central Library continued for years under the guidance of a formally organized committee, which elicited advice from facilitators and an architect. Most of the discussion revolved around plans to make the building larger by adding a wing, but the Heritage Preservation Commission was opposed to that idea. During the administration of Mayor James Scheibel, the library committee, after much deliberation, completed a formal proposal to remodel and update the Central Library. The librarians presented their document to the mayor with the expectation that he would pass it on to St. Paul's delega-

tion to the state legislature with a request for funding. To the committee's dismay, Scheibel refused to do so.

For a time, disappointment on the part of library staffers was profound. Before much time had passed, however, they realized that they had dodged a bullet. Their plan had been developed at the beginning of the computer revolution, when few could envision the profound changes about to take place. The remodeling project the library staff had worked on for almost a decade had not included provision for computers in a remodeled Central Library.

Despite the setback, Carole Williams did not let the prospect of remodeling the Central Library fade. "The Central Library is the architectural gem of downtown," she insisted. "If we can't make it bigger, we have to make it more serviceable." She found her opportunity in 1994, when St. Paul mayor Norm Coleman began a major library-planning project. The goal of the project was to develop a comprehensive plan for library service that would meet the needs of everyone in the city. The Friends provided the funds to hire Nancy Homans, staff member in the Department of Planning and Economic Development, to serve as a part-time facilitator for the project.

Thus began a year-long community-wide effort, initiated by the library administration, to find out what St. Paul citizens wanted from their public library. Sandy Kiernat and Willetha (Toni) Carter cochaired the committee, which conducted dozens of community workshops and focus groups. They met with communities of color, people with disabilities, librarians, young people, the elderly, immigrant groups, teachers, and members of the Friends. Everyone recognized that the city was changing. Whole neighborhoods were made up of new immigrant groups; dozens of languages were spoken in the schools; some classes of residents had never set foot in the library, which, to them, had the image of a white, middle-class institution. Everything was discussed, from acquiring materials in non-English languages to opening the libraries at night, to eliminating fines for the late return of children's materials.

The community meetings also brought out the librarians' concerns about everything from relationships with the new communities developing around them to the use of technology. Williams and her core group of administrators knew that librarians must get out from behind their desks, become emissaries to diverse groups, and form partnerships with other institutions. Some librarians found this new role hard to accept, as it differed so dramatically from their traditional library training. But it was the emphasis on technology that Carole Williams used to illustrate the plight of the Central Library. Technology at the library was so primitive, she said, that it was the equivalent of a computer from the 1970s running the entire library system in the 1990s.

The *Plan for Libraries* that was presented to Mayor Norm Coleman at the end of a year's study in 1995 described the era as one characterized "by an abundance of information and . . . by the isolation of too large a segment of the community from the tools necessary to tap the power of this new key economic and societal resource." The report maintained that "securing St. Paul's future as a healthy community will require more than improving service for those who

already use libraries. The challenges of the future . . . compel the Saint Paul Public Library to seek out relationships with all its citizens."[194]

When the recommendations made in the plan were added up, they came to $20 million worth of improvements. The biggest expense, $15 million, was the cost of remodeling the Central Library and turning it into a center for new computer technology. The remaining $5 million was needed for new materials for the collection, for the outreach program, and other, "softer" items.

"We told the mayor that the Friends would endeavor to raise $5 million if the city would come up with $15 million," Pearson said. "The mayor agreed. No other mayor had ever made that kind of commitment to the library." The only way the city could raise that kind of money was by selling bonds. Because the amount was so large, the bond sales would have to be spread over four years. In practical terms, this meant that the remodeling of the Central Library also would be spread over four years. Initial plans were to keep the library open during

After spending seventeen years in the Minnesota state attorney general's office, Norm Coleman was elected mayor of St. Paul in 1993. He won a second term as mayor in 1997 and, after narrowly losing a race for governor, won election to the U.S. Senate in 2002.

Creative Cooking

CUSTOMER REQUESTS for information not only keep librarians on their toes, the requests often tax their imaginations. A customer called librarian Linda Wilcox at the Sun Ray Branch Library with a request for a recipe for a marinade. Wilcox looked one up in a Betty Crocker cookbook. The recipe called for red wine. The customer replied that she did not have any red wine in the house, but she did have some white. "Could I just add some food coloring?" she asked.

In 2000 Dick and Nancy Nicholson created a million-dollar endowment to support the purchase of books, materials, and services for the Nicholson Information Commons on the second floor of the Central Library. Dick Nicholson, a lifelong collector of rare books and works on Minnesota, served nine years on the board of the Friends of the Saint Paul Public Library.

the reconstruction and remodel it in chunks. One section would be closed for six months for remodeling and then another. In Pearson's opinion, "it would have been horrible. And it would have added huge additional costs."

THE FRIENDS' GUARANTEE OF THE BONDS

It was at this point that the Friends of the Saint Paul Public Library stepped up and did what Pearson says is "one of the best things we have ever done." The Friends' endowment fund, at that time, was about $10 million. Pearson proposed using the fund as a guarantee for the city's bonds so all of them could be sold at one time. Once the money was in hand, the construction on the library could continue without interruption. By closing the Central Library for eighteen months and doing all the construction work at the same time, the city would save about $1.5 million.

Pearson took the idea to his board of directors. One said, "This is not an appropriate role for an outside group. The city should be taking this on itself." That was true enough, but the fact was the city could not. Others raised the specter of the city defaulting on the bonds, in which case the Friends would lose its $10 million endowment. Banker Andy Boss, the Friends' chair at the time, answered their objections.

"If this [remodeling of the Central Library] is ever going to happen," Boss said, "the Friends will have to take the responsibility and the leadership because there is no other group out there championing the library. We have the resources to do it. If the city were to default on these bonds, imagine what a dire condition this city would be in. We probably would not have a library, and if

we did not have a library, we would not need the Friends of the Library. So what are we really risking here? We would not even exist if the city got to that point."

Boss convinced the Friends board to use the endowment to guarantee the city's $15 million in bonds.

The bond sale of $15 million, the largest capital improvement bond project undertaken by St. Paul, was approved. In addition to providing the guarantee, the Friends also paid for all of the legal and administrative work, plus filing fees—totaling about $300,000—for the sale.

The Friends' $5 million capital campaign, headed by Tom Swain, was going well, eventually raising almost $6 million. The Saint Paul, Mardag, and Bigelow Foundations all contributed. A gift by Dick and Nancy Nicholson, another $1 million, provided an endowment fund for the Nicholson Information Commons—the largest and most beautiful room in the renovated library.

THE NICHOLSON INFORMATION COMMONS

The Nicholson gift came about, in part, because Dick Nicholson and Peter Pearson were both members of the St. Paul Rotary Club. Pearson found himself sitting next to Nicholson at a meeting and said to him, "You know, Dick, you and Nancy should have a room named after you at the Central Library because of your love of books." Pearson says that Nicholson laughed and that was the end of it. At their next Rotary meeting Pearson repeated his suggestion. Again Nicholson dismissed the idea with a laugh.

"I think it was a couple of months later," Pearson says, "that I was with him again

A view of the renovated Nicholson Information Commons, the largest room and the architectural highlight of the reno-vated Central Library. Paintings on the ceiling beams depict publisher marks (ca. 1910) and the acronym of the Saint Paul Public Library. The stairway in the middle of the picture leads to the mezzanine, added during the restoration, that houses the Saint Paul Collection. With the exception of the computers, the room looks now as it did when it was built, including such details as the design of the light fixtures and the cork floor.

and I thought I would needle him one more time. I did and he looked at me and asked, 'What would it cost?'" Caught by surprise, Pearson blurted out, "A million dollars." "Would you take a multi-year pledge?" Nicholson asked.

PACKING UP CENTRAL LIBRARY

Early on in the planning for the remodeling, the city had determined that it could not afford to set up a temporary Central Library. Instead, Carole Williams and her library staff would have to pack up every single book, magazine, folder, piece of paper, and recording in the library and find someplace else to put it during the eighteen months that the Central Library interior would be restored and updated.

The most frequently used and needed materials were sent to the meeting rooms of the branches, where they could be accessed by librarians and customers. Car repair manuals, which were in constant demand, went to the Hayden Heights Branch Library. Highland Branch Library received much of the literature and Russian-language materials. Children's books and materials on grant-writing and foundations went to the Saint Anthony Park Branch Library. Materials of a more archival nature were to be packed up and placed in storage in the Ramsey County Building on Kellogg Avenue.

Emptying out the Central Library was a monumental task involving what may have been close to a million items. Mary Clare Huberty was key to the success of the project, measuring shelves and figuring how many boxes they would need. The work was hot and dusty. One said it "felt like slave labor, like chaos and bedlam." Librarians came to work in their jeans, brought treats to share, and bonded over the task. "There was a lot of fun, good spirits among the staff." Williams was collegial in her administration. Senior librarians Sue Ellingwood, Linda Wilcox, and Kathleen Flynn were the three administrators who made up the director's "cabinet"—the "four musketeers" who planned and executed the complicated move.

The architectural firm of Meyer, Scherer, and Rockcastle of Minneapolis, internationally known library specialists, took on the task of remodeling the Central Library. Everyone who had looked at the library had bemoaned the fact the building was too small. When architects Jack Pohling and Jeff Scherer toured the building, they immediately asked, "Why are you doing technical services here in this beautiful building? You are wasting 10,000 square feet." Technical services included the ground floor receiving area where books came into the library and the fourth-floor area where they were cataloged. The architects built a million-dollar addition on to the Sun Ray Branch Library and moved technical services there. The space gained in the Central Library became the expanded children's area.

Thanks to the excellent work of the architectural firm and contractors, the renovation of Central Library came in under budget and ahead of schedule. In Pearson's estimation, it was "the best bargain that ever came into the city." Architecture critic Larry Millet approved, writing in the *Pioneer Press,* "Repainted, buffed up and shining with new life, the building's signature spaces—the main reading room, the old reference room and the lobby with its grand staircase—look simply wonderful. The reading room, or

A New Children's Wing for Saint Anthony Park

THE CONSTRUCTION OF the new children's wing of the Saint Anthony Park Branch Library was a project that engaged the entire community. Of all of the neighborhoods in St. Paul, St. Anthony Park was the only one to have had an ongoing local library association, continuously active since the library was founded. Though the addition of the children's wing had near-unanimous community support, residents blanched when the construction crew knocked a huge hole in the back of their beloved community gathering place. Construction also took out the library's bathrooms and, for a time, Porta Potties were set up on the library's lawn for the half-dozen librarians working in the building. Eventually, to complete the construction, the library had to be closed. The Bookmobile was called on to temporarily fill readers' requests for books and the library's storytelling program was moved to the St. Anthony Park Elementary School. Management assigned Saint Anthony Park's librarians to other buildings.

The dedication of the new children's wing in a reopened Saint Anthony Park Branch Library in April 2002 was a joyous occasion for the entire community, celebrated with punch and cookies, flowers and welcoming speeches. Saint Anthony Park branch manager Rose Ann Foreman and library director Carole Williams (top photo) welcomed the community into its restored library. Among the other speakers were Warren Gore, a long-time resident of Saint Anthony Park and a former president of the Park Library Association, and Andy Boss (at right), who at the time was the board chair of the Friends of the Saint Paul Public Library.

information commons, is particularly fine with its ornate ceilings restored to their original lively colors."[195]

The hand-painted ceilings had been carefully cleaned by a firm from Michigan that used Wonder Bread and Ivory Soap to clean the paintings; apparently something in the bread pulled the grime out of the paint. When the building opened on October 5, 2002, patrons found that the public browsing areas had increased by 14,000 square feet, the Youth Services area had doubled in size, and the eight levels of cast iron stacks that had blocked the riverfront windows were gone, replaced by almost nine miles of new shelving. Dozens of computer desks, each topped

A banner proclaiming "Shout It Out!" the motto for the reopening of the Central Library, hangs on the building façade.

The Highland Park High School band plays for the reopening of the Central Library on October 5, 2002.

Musicians perform outside the entrance to the Central Library in September 2005 at the dedication of the library's new Bookmobile, sponsored by the **St. Paul Pioneer Press.** *The old Bookmobile was donated to (and driven to) Manzanillo, Mexico, a sister city of St. Paul.*

View of the Mississippi Room on the third floor of the Central Library. Located across the stair lobby from the Greenleaf Clark Room, the Mississippi Room has vaulted ceilings and houses some of the most-used materials in the library, including DVDs and popular fiction.

The nonfiction room on the library's second floor, across from the Nicholson Information Commons, features large arched windows and, on the south side, a semicircular alcove framed by tall columns. Lee Woodward Zeigler, one-time director of the School of Art at the St. Paul Institute of Arts and Letters, painted the medallions and monograms on the ceiling.

The Remodeled Rice Street Branch Reopens

WHEN PATRONS TURNED OUT to participate in the opening of the new Rice Street Branch Library, few were nostalgic for the old building. They remembered how the front door, which had been next to the circulation desk, let in a blast of cold air every time someone entered the building. The old furnace had stood on the main floor and a heating pipe snaked around the magazine section. In the summer the building had been blazingly hot.

Neighborhood activists led by Harold Hebl, chair of the Rice Street Library Action Committee, had lobbied for five years for a new building. The committee won the support of Mayor Randy Kelly when members gave him a tour of the old library, showing him the partially excavated dirt basement. After Hebl's librarian wife, Agatha, testified before the mayor's budget committee he moved the timetable for the construction of a new Rice Street Branch to 2002, putting its dedication a few months ahead of that of the renovated Central Library.

On March 4, 2002, fifty years to the day from the opening of its predecessor, neighbors lined up to enter their new Rice Street Library (top photo). When all were gathered inside, Mayor Kelly and City Council members Janice Retman and Jim Reiter, assisted by a young library patron (at left), cut the ceremonial ribbon, formally opening the renovated branch, with its new study rooms and Internet-accessible computer area. The northeast corner of the library, with its easy chairs, coffee tables, and floor-to-ceiling windows, was to become the living room—the communitiy front porch—of the neighborhood.

with a shiny new machine, filled the central area of the Nicholson Information Commons. Williams's co-workers give her major credit for the successful completion of the project. Flynn calls her a "dynamite lady. . . . When it comes to picking a project and pushing through with it, she's just superior."

Carole Williams planned to end her twenty-eight years with the Saint Paul Public Library by retiring on November 1, 2002, less than a month after the opening of the Central Library. Four weeks before the library's completion, however, Williams learned that the breast cancer she had had years before had metastasized into stage four ovarian cancer. Days after the library opening Williams had surgery, but the cancer was too far advanced. She never returned to the library following her surgery, but in the winter of 2003 the Friends honored her with a special event at the Town and County Club of St. Paul.

Both Carole Williams and her husband, Bill, twenty years her senior, were cared for at the same time at Sholom Hospice Care facility, across from the Fairgrounds in St. Paul. Bill, who also had been ill for some time, died in April 2004 and Carole in October. Until the end, Carole's brother kept a jar of Manhattans, a cocktail she greatly enjoyed, mixed in her room. He and Peter Pearson would join her for cocktails, one of them holding the paper cup as she sipped through a straw. "I think it helped her more than the morphine," Pearson observes. He later gave the eulogy for Williams at her memorial service, and he keeps a picture of her prominently displayed on his desk.

"Until the Fat Lady Dances"

THOUGH SHE DID a great deal of it for the capital campaign to remodel the Central Library, public speaking did not come easily to library director Carole Williams. At times she would mix up her words. Librarian Linda Wilcox began to keep a list of the malapropisms. "Carole never realized she was saying these things," Wilcox says. "We loved her for these little word mix-ups." A few months after Williams's death, Wilcox circulated some of the phrases to fellow librarians, writing, "Every time I read these, I laugh like I was hearing them for the first time. I want you to do the same. Carole would be delighted to know that she is very much alive with us in the gift of laughter."

Among Williams's mixed-up phrases were:

"Writing on the handwall."

"Until the fat lady dances."

"Until the next foot drops."

"Shoot yourself in the hole."

"We'll just clobber something together and see if it passes mustard."

"Going like hot guns."

"Somehow we will mangle through this."

"Running by the seat of their pants."

"Best thing since sliced liver."

"Put the wheel to the rubber."

"Talking out of both sides of their tongue."

"Being willing to put our eggs into what we will fight for."

Puppet Popularity

MOVING THE PUPPET THEATER proved to be the most wrenching, for the public, of all the moves made during the restoration of the Central Library. Many patrons objected strenuously. They remembered bringing their children downtown on the streetcar to watch the puppet shows. To them, the puppet stage was almost a shrine. Workmen took special care to dissemble, put in mothballs, and then reinstall the puppet theater in a special place in the new Children's Room.

The Children's Room features the puppet theater and a ceiling that, with the touch of a switch, can be turned into a star-lit sky. The round cushions are for children to use during storytelling sessions.

The Dayton's Bluff Library, built in conjunction with Metropolitan State University, serves both the community and college students. It is operated jointly by the Saint Paul Public Library and the university. Completed in the spring of 2004, the $21 million building contains 82,000 square feet.

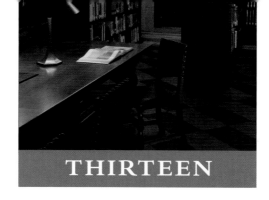

THIRTEEN

Becoming Learning Centers

THE *PLAN FOR LIBRARIES* report and the growing understanding of the needs of St. Paul's new immigrants changed librarians' perceptions of themselves. As Kathleen Flynn explains, "It used to be that librarians did not see themselves as teachers or social workers. We were not educators. The idea of the formal educational system and the library were totally separate." Shirley Brady, successor to Della McGregor as head of the Children's Room, had been adamant that "we do not do homework in the public library." Alice Neve recalls, "The philosophy I was taught was that you should help a child a little bit to find the materials but, heavenly days, you shouldn't help him do the assignment." That concept underwent a major change with the advent of the Homework Help Centers. Says Neve, "It was not about doing the homework for a student but giving him the tools." She considers the development of the Homework Help Centers "the most meaningful, hugest change" in libraries of her entire career.

HOMEWORK HELP CENTERS

It all started at the Lexington Branch Library in 1999, when Dr. Celeste Raspanti, who was a member of the board of the Friends of the Saint Paul Public Library and an avid patron, called on Alice Neve to explain her idea. Raspanti had observed young people in the Lexington Avenue Branch Library, many of them children of immigrants, who obviously needed some assistance but couldn't get it because the librarians were overwhelmingly busy. What they needed, Raspanti thought, was the kind of help that could be provided by an educated vol-

unteer with a good heart who would be willing to explain things. What would happen, she wondered, if the library staffed a table labeled "Homework Help" with some volunteers for a couple of hours in the afternoon? Raspanti offered to spend her summer recruiting volunteers.

On the one hand Neve said, "Hurrah!" On the other she wondered, "What will the librarians say? We were not trained for this." Nevertheless, in the fall of 2000, two volunteers began sitting for a few hours in the afternoon at a table in the middle of the Lexington Branch Library under a sign similar to the Charlie Brown cartoon "Doctor Is In" banner, waiting to offer their help. Immediately they had clients. The volunteers had expected to be helping elementary and junior high school children, but people of all ages came to the table for assistance.

The librarians quickly realized that the program should be expanded. With financial assistance from the Friends of the Library and the Mardag and Bigelow Foundations, the Lexington Library hired Marika Staloch of Volunteers in Service to America, to organize the project. The help center could be housed in the library's conference room, but furniture and materials were needed. The library also needed a system for recruiting and training volunteers. By January 2, 2001, the Lexington Library formally opened its Homework Help Center.

The branch had received a grant for the center on the basis that they would be serving elementary

St. Paul mayor James Scheibel reads to children at the Lexington Branch Library, early 1990s.

and junior high level children. By the end of the third day, it was being flooded with high school students and adults as well. Concerned, Neve phoned Peter Pearson, president of the Friends of the Saint Paul Public Library, to ask him what to do. "Forget it," he replied.

Initially the center was open three days a week from 3:00 to 5:00 p.m. Soon, the hours were extended into the evening and more days were added. Twenty-five to thirty students showed up every evening. Adult learners from the nearby Ronald M. Hubbs Center, a program of the St. Paul Public Schools' community education department, and from St. Paul's Technical-Vocational Institute (now St. Paul College) joined the younger students, as did immigrants studying for citizenship exams.

From the beginning, the students have helped each other at the center. Younger people help adults struggling to learn English. Neve observed a Somali woman being taught by a young Hmong student

Young patrons and their parents at the Lexington Branch Library.

and a young man whose first language was Vietnamese helping a native English speaker with his math homework. Except for the VISTA personnel who manage the center, everyone who works at the center is a volunteer. Many have told Neve that working there is the "single most rewarding volunteer experience they have ever had."

The success of the Lexington Homework Help Center did not go unnoticed. Soon, with funds from the Friends and foundation grants, centers were installed at the Riverview, Sun Ray, and Rice Street Branch Libraries. With four centers humming, the number of student visits for assistance approached 18,000 annually.

THE DAYTON'S BLUFF-METROPOLITAN STATE PARTNERSHIP

As Homework Help Centers blossomed throughout the city, the East Side neighborhood of St. Paul was still lobbying the city for public library service after more than fifteen years. Beginning in the

John McKay shows off his first library card, August 2001.

Patrons of the old Lexington Library at work on the twelve computers that provided Internet access to the neighborhood. The waiting list always had the names of fifteen to twenty individuals who were awaiting access to a computer.

early 1990s, State Senator Randy Kelly took up the cause for the East Side and also for Metropolitan State University, an East Side institution that lacked a library. To the best of everyone's recollection, it was Dr. Susan Cole, then president of Metropolitan State University, who suggested that the two libraries be combined. Why not build a jointly owned and managed library to serve the needs of university students and the East Side community? The Metropolitan State–Dayton's Bluff Library was born—at least on paper.

While Senator Kelly and the St. Paul delegation lobbied the state legislature for funds to help build the library, the Metropolitan State Foundation, under the leadership of Andy Boss and Nancy McKillips, began raising money. Metro State purchased the site of the Nobles Company on East Seventh street, formerly a munitions factory, on which to build the new library, fully aware of the symbolism of the purchase—books and students would occupy the place where weapons had once been made. Hopes were high when the legislature met in 2000, only to be dashed when lawmakers turned down the request for construction money. The project was not defeated, insisted a determined Senator Kelly, only delayed. In 2002 a request for $17.4 million went back to the legislature, and this time it was approved.

Architects of Meyer, Scherer, and Rockcastle had already drawn plans for the building, and ground was broken in the spring of 2002. A joint committee of university and public library officials managed the project. At first, library director Carole Williams worried that the public library half of the endeavor would be swallowed up by Metro State,

that the new library would become little more than a delivery stop for students coming to pick up their books. "Carole was adamant that we were going to remain unique, a branch of the Saint Paul Public Library that happened to be located near the Metropolitan University campus," Linda Wilcox remembers. "We would cooperate, but we would not be swallowed up."

After a few tentative meetings, which included Wilson Bradshaw, the new president of Metropolitan State University, good working relationships were established. "As soon as we started working collaboratively and felt we were being heard—doing the dance together—things started to roll," Wilcox says. A committee composed of Dean David Barton and Associate V.P. Dan Kirk, plus Nancy McKillips from the university's foundation, and Carole Williams and Linda Wilcox from the Saint Paul Library, did much of the planning. "We worked with the architectural firm, made the day-to-day decisions, and wrote grants to raise money from local corporations and foundations," Wilcox recalls.

The concept of cooperation between two public entities was popular with funders. The committee named rooms in the building after major donors, such as Cargill and the 3M Company. Plans for the new library included a large Homework Help Center equipped with half a dozen computers, a children's reading room, and community meeting rooms. Thorny problems such as whether to share a circulation desk with Metro State University were hammered out. The new community-university library, while built on university-owned land, stood apart from the main campus. A skyway that planners hoped would create a gateway landmark to the East Side stretched across busy Seventh Street to provide safe access to the library from the university's main buildings.

In the spring of 2004, the $21 million Metropolitan State University Library and Learning Center and Saint Paul Public Library–Dayton's Bluff—certainly one of the longest names in library history—opened its doors. The Dayton's Bluff Library has its own space within the building and is autonomous with its own staff, budget, and operating hours. Yet patrons of the public library have full access to Metropolitan State University library resources and Metro State students likewise use public library materials.

Originally Dayton's Bluff Library was open only thirty hours a week, but after the first year, when the library had proved to be popular, hours were extended, and it is now open six days a week. The university library is open seven days a week and has extended night hours. "We came up with a shared list of procedures and concerns," reports David Barton, Metro State dean of library information services. "Management has not been a problem."

THE EVER-CHANGING ROLE OF THE FRIENDS

The librarians were not the only ones who were forging a new understanding of their mission and role. The Friends of the Saint Paul Public Library were also looking at how they could be more effective, sparked by a strategic retreat Peter Pearson organized in 1999. For a day and a half the Friends' board, staff, and a baker's dozen of representative citizens from St. Paul talked about nothing but the library and how to give the institution more effective support.

Wilson G. Bradshaw, president of Metropolitan State University, became chairman of the board of the Friends of the Saint Paul Public Library in 2006. Bradshaw came to St. Paul in 2000 from Bloomsburg University in Pennsylvania and holds a doctorate in psychobiology from the University of Pittsburgh.

Pearson pointed out that the library's budget came out of the city's general fund, along with parks, police, firefighters, and public works, and was such a tiny slice—around 1 percent—that it was barely noticed during the budgeting process. Pearson wondered what would happen if the library had its own budget, with its own line item on the property tax statement. That way, if the city needed more money for police or firefighters, they would not be able to raid the library's budget as easily as it had in the past.

Pearson appointed a task force, chaired by former St. Paul mayor George Latimer, to investigate the idea. The task force spent the year 2000 examining the funding structures of public libraries around the country, trying to find the best fit for St. Paul. In the end they recommended that a separate budget be established for the library and that the members of the City Council be designated as the official board of the Saint Paul Public Library.

City Council member Pat Harris, who also was on the task force, took the plan to his fellow council members. By the end of 2001 they had turned it into a council-supported piece of state legislation and were ready to act on it. Because the proposed switch in library funding would also change the property tax statement, however, they first had to get enabling legislation approved by both the Minnesota House and Senate Tax Committees. Jesse Ventura was Minnesota's governor, the legislature was fractious, but this bit of legislation sailed through. Representative Matt Entenza, a member of the Friends board, saw to its passage.

The only one opposed to what was happening was St. Paul's mayor Randy Kelly. Though he was a strong supporter of libraries—Kelly had championed the Dayton's Bluff Library and would soon give strong support to the Rondo Community Outreach Branch—he believed the proposal would weaken St. Paul's vaunted, strong-mayor form of government. Over Kelly's objections, the City Council unanimously passed the bill, effective January 1, 2004, to create the new library agency that would be funded through a dedicated levy of property tax and local government aid.

Mayor Kelly had ten days in which to veto the ordinance if he chose to. Knowing that his veto would be overridden, he took another tack. He quietly went back to the two legislative tax committees and, telling them it was no longer needed, asked them to rescind the previously passed enabling legislation. The tax committee chairs, believing that it was a noncontroversial piece of business, agreed.

The first Pat Harris learned of this was when lobbyist Joe Bagnoli, who was attending a hearing of the House Tax Committee, noted the item on the printed agenda. Thinking that was strange, he called Harris, who phoned Peter Pearson, explained what was happening, and told him, "Get up to the Capitol right now." Pearson raced to the House Tax Committee hearing and told its chair, Ron Abrams, that whenever he scheduled a vote to rescind the previous enabling action, Pearson "would have one hundred people there to testify in support of it."

The Senate Tax Committee was meeting the same afternoon, so Pearson, now joined by Friends' board chair Sue Haig, rushed off to that meeting. The measure was heard almost as soon as they walked in. Haig and Pearson seated themselves next to Mayor Kelly at the witness table and each expressed an opinion. When the vote came, both tax committees refused to tack on the amendment Kelly had proposed.

Two weeks later, Harris, Pearson, and Kelly held a news conference. At Kelly's request, they stated, the City Council had altered some minor points in the legislation and all were now in agreement. Now, every year, the mayor of St. Paul puts together a separate budget for the library. It goes to the City Council, sitting as the board of the public library, which makes whatever changes it wishes. A separate levy is assigned to the library budget, and it appears on the property tax statement. As far as anyone knows, this structure—having the City Council serve as the board of the public library—is unique. The citizens of St. Paul appear to like the arrangement. In response to a survey, 72 percent of them said they would rather raise their own taxes than cut service to their public libraries.

A NATIONAL AWARD

In the fall of 2002, Gina La Force had been hired to replace Carole Williams. La Force had been the chief executive of the library system in Markham, a Toronto suburb, and was a past president of the Canadian Library Association. Less then three years later, however, in the spring of 2005, La Force resigned, saying she wished to return to her native Canada.

Kathleen Flynn, one of La Force's top assistants and a thirty-three-year veteran of the system, filled in as library director until Melanie Huggins was hired in June 2006. In the year under Flynn's direction, the Saint Paul Public Library was one of three U.S. libraries to receive the 2005 National Award for Museum and Library Service. The award is the highest honor the nation confers on a library for its outstanding contribution to its community and long-term commitment to public service through innovative programs and community partnerships.

Three members of the library staff—director Kathleen Flynn, administration services manager Debbie Willms, and librarian master's degree student Regina Harris—traveled to Washington, D.C., to receive the award, presented to them by First Lady Laura Bush. The description of the award-winning libraries calls them "centers of excellence. They connect people to information and ideas—and to each other. . . . They go beyond expected levels of service to assure that their institutions are accessible and responsive to a wide range of community lifelong learning needs."

The citation for St. Paul called the partnership between the Dayton's Bluff Public Library and Metropolitan State University "a model of community innovation."

Library director Kathleen Flynn and Urban Library program participant Regina Harris were among the St. Paul delegates who traveled to Washington, D.C., in 2005 to accept the National Award for Museum and Library Service given to the Saint Paul Public Library. From left: Mary Chute, acting director, Institute of Museum and Library Services; Flynn and Harris; and First Lady Laura Bush.

Library director Gina La Force holds the 2003 John Cotton Dana award given jointly to the Saint Paul Public Library and the Friends of the Saint Paul Public Library for excellence in public relations. With La Force, from left: Steven Nelson, manager of the library's public information office; Peter Pearson, president of the Friends; and John Larson, librarian.

Cutting the ribbon to mark the reopening of the Lexington Branch Library on September 4, 2001, are Celeste Raspanti, member of the Friends of the Saint Paul Public Library board and originator of the Homework Help Centers; Delores Henderson, St. Paul Public Schools; Carole Williams, library director; librarian Ginny Brodeen; and Jerry Blakey, St. Paul City Council member.

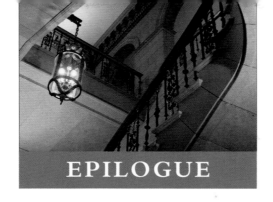

The Flood

WHEN LIBRARIAN GINNY BRODEEN opened the Lexington Branch Library on the first Saturday in April 2001, she couldn't believe what she saw. Water was spilling down the plastered walls and pooling on the carpeted floor. During a downpour the night before, roof drains had failed to function and rainwater had cascaded into the building. The Lexington Branch Library building, which had been going slowly downhill over three decades, had taken a sudden turn for the worse.

Between four thousand and five thousand books were destroyed, including autographed copies of Caldecott Award books treasured by Alice Neve, director of the Lexington Branch Library. Neve, who was out of town when the flooding occurred, had been a member of the Caldecott Award Committee, and her notes from those meetings were among the soaked books. Brodeen and fellow librarian Judy Hoffman took the collection home, where they dried out the books and carefully ironed the notes dry.

The rest of the cleanup took a little longer. For six months the Lexington Branch library was closed for repairs, but Neve found the silver lining. The flooding was a "terrible thing that happened to us that resulted in something good," she said. "We were able to do the community outreach that we wanted to do and that the neighborhood needed without being encumbered by a building."

As Friends' president Peter Pearson explains, "Alice Neve made it her hallmark in this library system to make the Lexington library all about outreach. She reaches out to underserved communities and makes them feel that the library is their home, that they are welcome there. She sees her role as librarian almost as a social worker in the community. . . . After all, if people come from East Africa, they may not know what a library is. Alice loves that role, and she pulled a staff together that is all about the same things."

When the Lexington Library reopened in September 2001, the librarians had reorganized the interior to better serve their clients. Materials for English-language learners were moved closer to the entrance and books in languages other than English were prominently displayed. Despite the improvements, the building was as crowded and inadequate as ever. Patrons sat on the floor because there was no more space at the tables. Neve talked with anyone who would listen about the need to replace the Lexington Branch Library, knowing at the same time that every cent of construction money was being used for the restoration of the Central Library. Lex was on hold.

On hold, that is, until Mayor Randy Kelly once again rallied to the cause. The city owned land on the southwest corner of University Avenue and Dale Street that, for decades, had been an embarrassment to St. Paul—the site of the infamous Faust Adult Theater that attracted traffic in drugs and prostitution. The city had finally purchased the business and demolished the building, but had had no immediate plan for redevelopment. As a temporary

Archie Givens and his Legacy Management and Development Corporation were major partners with the city of St. Paul in the construction of the Rondo Community Outreach Branch Library. Givens is president of the Givens Foundation for African American Literature, an extensive collection housed at the University of Minnesota. Among the boards he sits on are the H.B. Fuller Foundation, Weisman Art Museum, Western Bank, and the Guthrie Theater. Givens is a former president of the National Mental Health Association, for which he chaired the first committee to address issues of mental health care for minorities and the disadvantaged.

measure, the city had given the space at no charge to the Neighborhood Development Corporation of Aurora St. Anthony to see if they could make use of it. The corporation had put a market on the corner, but the market had never taken off.

Archie Givens, head of Legacy Management and Development Corporation, began talking with neighborhood groups about what they would like to see on the corner. Ideas ran the gamut from a jazz club to an ethnic restaurant, to a new home for the Penumbra Theatre. Givens was discussing the situation with City Council member Jerry Blakey and Mayor Kelly one day when Kelly pointed out that the city had this library half a mile away that was in an unstable, outdated building it had outgrown. Why not put a new library on that corner? And why not combine the library with housing? That no one in the country had built a library with housing above it before did not deter the mayor. Kelly had been elected on a platform of building more housing in St. Paul.

Mayor Kelly put the Department of Planning and Economic Development to work addressing basic questions: What kind of housing did the neighborhood want? Should the housing be townhouses or condominiums? What number of units made sense economically? That a light-rail line was slated to go down University Avenue allowed one more story to the complex as mass transit allowed for more building density.

A public-private partnership began to form between the city of St. Paul and Givens's Legacy Management and Development Corporation. Legacy, in turn, formed partnerships with neighborhood groups to keep them involved. The

key players and partners that pieced the project together were the Frogtown Community Development Corporation, the Aurora St. Anthony Neighborhood Development Corporation, Model Cities, the Selby Avenue Community Development Corporation, and the Western Initiatives Development Corporation.

The big question was where to get the money. Funds for civic buildings came from the sale of capital improvement bonds (CIBs), a process governed by regulations and managed by a committee. Because the city had already spent $15 million in capital improvement bonds to restore the Central Library, the Lexington Library was low on the priorities list for bonding approval. But two things happened to change the Lexington Library's prospects. First, Mayor Kelly announced that the old Lexington Library would be demolished and a new library to replace it would be built on the Dale-University site. Then, because the mayor and City Council can do what they want with capital improvement bonds, Kelly moved the Lexington Library from the bottom to the top of the list.

Kelly's actions created a furor. If the Lexington Library remained at the top of the list, the CIB Committee argued, it would chop off $9 million in funding from other worthwhile projects. Then City Council member Pat Harris and budget director Greg Blees came up with a novel idea. Because of the new mechanism the city had just adopted for funding the library as a separate budget entity, the library could issue its *own* $9 million in bonds. The funds would not have to come out of the CIB pot after all.

The library budget would have to be increased by a few hundred thousand dollars a year to pay the interest on the bonds, but it was a solution. "Once we had that established and the City Council voted unanimously for it, we knew we had a beginning," Givens remembers. "That was our footing that allowed the rest of it to come together." Only the Saint Paul Public Library director at that time, Gina La Force, was nervous about the plans for the new library. She was new to her job, new to the politics of St. Paul, and new to a project of this size and complexity.

As a public institution within a private development, the new Lexington Library *was* a challenging endeavor. Legacy had to buy the air rights above the library to construct the housing above it. There was much discussion on the location of that invisible line between the library and the housing. The library owned the building up to its ceiling, where parking for residents would begin. Above the parking level would be 100 units of housing. It took months for the lawyers to figure out to everyone's satisfaction where that invisible line started and stopped.

The problems inherent in the unusual situation affected the people who were selling the bonds to finance the project. Bond salesmen had to explain to their investors what it all meant, and more lawyers got involved. Then the insurance people wanted to know who would be liable if there were a leak in the second-floor garage that ran into the library below. "It was a very frustrating and complicated process," Givens remembers. "Everybody wanted to protect himself. It was amazing how many lawyers and opinions there were about this. But the city stuck with us and supported us. The City Council and library staff—Alice Neve and the facilities man at

the library, Lee Williamson—were 100 percent supportive."

According to Tom Sanchez of St. Paul's Department of Planning and Economic Development, if the building had been a housing project, it would have been completed a year earlier, in 2005. He believes that the key to the success of the project was the neighborhood input. "We had a developer who had good experience not just in putting up a project and working out the details, but had a feel for how you work with a neighborhood."

The five-story building with ninety-eight rental apartments and six town-homes cost $25 million, $9 million of which went for the library. The work of five local artists adorns the building. St. Paul artists Seitu Jones and Mary Hart worked together on a large tree-shaped wood sculpture with kitelike "leaves" in the children's area, Susan Warner made custom tiles for a fireplace and hearth, and Harriet Bart etched poetry on the glass of the security gates. Donald Walker's painting of an African American boy reading the *St. Paul Pioneer Press* hangs at the library's entrance.

Minneapolis artist Susan Warner designed the cheery fireplace in the new Rondo Community Outreach Library. Images of books by writers past and present are displayed on the sides while a pencil stretches across the hearth.

A series of colored concrete pavement inserts decorate the sidewalks on Dale Street and University Avenue outside the Rondo Library. Several contain designs—a Hmong musician playing an instrument, a Somali chair—while others contain messages in many languages. In a reference to the lost Rondo neighborhood, one message reads:

"One day the decision was made that a road (I-94) was more valuable than the homes, memories, and communities that would be ravaged by its construction. Rondo Avenue was demolished and our community shattered. The spirit of Rondo lives on in the minds of the old and in the imagination of the young."

Another paver contains a quotation, in English and Spanish, from Cesar Chavez: "True wealth is not measured in money or status or power. It is measured in the

legacy we leave behind for those we love and those we inspire."

Another bears the words of former St. Paulite Gordon Parks: "In my youth, violence, poverty, and racism became my enemies. Photography, writing, music and film were the weapons I used against them."

Others in Hmong, Laotian, and Somali read:

"Without education there is no light."

"From yesterday we learn for tomorrow."

"Many hands made labor lighter. Many ideas open the path bright."

That last message could have been the motto of the project's contractors, who exceeded the city's goals on minority hiring and on buying from minority- and women-owned business suppliers. Handicapped workers labored side by side, at union wages, with union workers.

A GRAND OPENING

A cold wind from the north swirled prematurely into St. Paul the morning of September 9, 2006. Undeterred by the chilly temperatures, a crowd of three thousand lined up on the Dale Street sidewalk and around the corner onto University Avenue to participate in the 10:00 a.m. ribbon cutting for the new Lexington Library, renamed the Rondo Community Outreach Library to honor the African American neighborhood demolished when Interstate 94 was constructed. Hmong, Thai, Laotian, Cambodian, African American, Somali, and European-descended children, along with their parents, stood patiently waiting, peering hopefully through the windows into the library.

Patrons wait outside Rondo Library to enter the new facility on the day of its grand opening.

In his remarks to an enthusiastic crowd, St. Paul mayor Chris Coleman recognized the role former mayor Randy Kelly played in the building of the new Rondo Library and praised community leader Archie Givens for his work in uniting neighborhood groups behind the project.

The doors opened promptly at ten, eliciting a cheer that echoed down the line. Volunteers handed out literature to visitors as they stepped across the threshold. Chairs in the auditorium, set up for hundreds, were quickly filled, yet the line of eager patrons still extended around the block. Organizers urged children forward to sit on the floor of the stage. Long after ten o'clock, visitors continued to file into the building until every corner was filled, every wall was lined, every aisle was packed. Hundreds listened to the program from the crowded entryway.

St. Paul mayor Chris Coleman addressed the crowd to a chorus of cheers and applause as he acknowledged the efforts of his predecessor, Randy Kelly, in building the library. Those who had played major roles in making the library possible took turns speaking, including City Council members, Archie Givens of Legacy Management and Development Corporation, and Wilson Bradshaw of Metropolitan State University and the Friends of the Saint Paul Public Library.

The energy in the room seemed to increase with each speech. Driving it was the audience itself, as multihued as the world. Old-stock residents of St. Paul looked about and wondered what city they were in as hundreds of children representing a dozen nations tumbled together on the stage like puppies. To close the program, the audience sang "Happy Birthday" to the branch before surging past the ends of the severed blue ribbon into their new Rondo Community Outreach Library.

Librarians handed out free books to every adult and child. Patrons of the old

Lexington Library found that the Black History Collection had been expanded, as was the Southeast Asian History and Culture area. Among the new recordings was the largest selection of Somali music in the region. The Homework Help Center had it own space and equipment. Rows of new computers stood ready for use as did assistive technology for sight- and hearing-impaired patrons. Librarians handed out red rubber wristbands bearing the words, "Be smart, read." For Alice Neve, standing in the center of the excited throng like a rock in a tumultuous mountain stream, the Rondo library was her vision come to life.

Schaenzer had been students at the nearby Area Learning Community School when Jones issued a call for workers. The two responded, never dreaming they would participate in the building of a work of art for a library. Now they stood amid a throng of admirers, a little awed themselves over the public response to what they had done.

NEW BEGINNINGS

Melanie Huggins, observing her ninety-first day in St. Paul as the city's library director, had led the audience in singing "Happy Birthday" to the new library. Huggins, the thirty-six-year-old director of youth and outreach services for the

The Bookmobile and Rondo Library staff at the end of a day in August 2006, that had been spent putting books and materials on the shelves of the new library. Alice Neve is circled.

The community celebrated throughout the day. Hmong peace dancers performed, as did a Native American dancer and Los Alegres Bailadores, a Mexican folk dance troupe. Jugglers and a youth jazz ensemble entertained, while storytellers told tales in multiple languages. Everyone ate cookies, tried out the cozy chairs, admired the fireplace, and stroked the treelike sculpture in the children's area. They also took note of two shy young men standing quietly by, who had built the tree designed by Jones and Hart. Andre Atlas and David

twenty-four-branch public library of Charlotte and Mecklenburg County, North Carolina, was hired in June 2006. Huggins was familiar with the Saint Paul Public Library as she had earlier served as a consultant to the system.

When Huggins, who managed a $50 million budget in North Carolina, agreed to come to St. Paul, she was, as she explained, "at a point in my career where I had finished a major project. I was at the top of where I was and there was no place else that I could go. So I

Opening day of the Rondo Community Outreach Library was filled with activities. Clockwise from top left: Hmong Peace Dancers, many of them from the neighborhood, performed; Danielle Daniels told stories to children; library supporters from all over the city joined in the celebration; and Los Alegres Bailadores performed Latino folk dances.

Melanie Huggins was hired in June 2006 to head the Saint Paul Public Library System. She came from Charlotte-Mecklenburg County, North Carolina, where she had managed a $50 million budget and directed the youth services for a twenty-four-branch library system.

was looking for a library directorship. I was fortunate to have been a consultant at St. Paul because I knew the strengths, the weaknesses, the barriers, and the challenges—more about this library system than any other. I would go in knowing what the challenges would be. And the problems were not insurmountable."

Huggins had taken a roundabout route to her library career. She was a studio arts major at Winthrop University in South Carolina, where she received her bachelor's degree in painting, ceramics, and photography. After graduation she worked at art camps for children and waited tables in restaurants. When a friend suggested she try Colorado, she took off for a horse ranch at Peaceful Valley, nine thousand feet up in the Rockies near Estes Park, where she again waited tables.

At the end of the summer, Huggins returned to South Carolina and went to the Employment Security Commission to look through job listings. The agency

told her about an opening at the public library, reading stories to children. "I never in a million years thought that I would work in a library," she says, but applied for the job and two weeks later was hired. It was a pivotal decision.

"I was a paraprofessional assistant in the children's room, reading stories, doing craft programs for only a short time, when I realized that this was everything I loved—music, dance, literature, the arts, kids—all in one job." Huggins started work as a library assistant at the Richland County Public Library of South Carolina in March 1994, and by January 1995 she was in graduate school studying library science. She earned her master's degree on a scholarship from the library, continued working part-time in the library, and met and married her husband—all in that one year.

After graduation from the University of South Carolina at Columbia in December of 1995, she began her first professional job as a librarian in the Charlotte, North Carolina, Public Library, where she worked for ten years before coming to St. Paul.

Looking back, Huggins says that she should have known that libraries would have been the career for her. "We moved around a lot when I was young, and the first thing my mother did when we went to a new community was take me to the library and get my library card. Like most families, we moved in the summer after school was out. As a result, I did not have a lot of friends, didn't know people, so I spent my time reading in the library. Even when I was in Colorado, I spent my one day off a week in the Boulder Library, reading and researching careers I might want to try. People who knew me earlier in my life cannot believe that I am a librarian."

CELEBRATING 125 YEARS

The ghosts of librarians past must surely have been hovering over the Rondo celebration on that chill September day. It had been exactly 125 years and four days since the City Council had voted to establish a free public library in St. Paul. If, indeed, those early library leaders were present, Helen McCaine must have been startled at the exuberance of the patrons. (Weren't people supposed to display gravitas in a library?) Dr. William Dawson Johnston would have sung along with the "Happy Birthday" chorus, while Jennie Jennings would have been astonished at the level of support St. Paul's political leadership now gave to the library. Della McGregor, while approving of the space the library devoted to serving youth, would have been a trifle perturbed at the children's spontaneity, while Perrie Jones and Carole Williams would have applauded the new Rondo and the vision of their fellow librarians.

The librarians of the past would surely be in agreement with Director Huggins when she says that libraries are in the "quality-of-life business. It is no longer enough for librarians to say, 'We have the information you need. We are the keepers of it. We will let you borrow it and then you bring it back.' . . . Information is no longer something only the elite have access to. We librarians have had to change our culture and not only say that we have it and you can get it, but we will help you navigate the resources that exist, because they are overwhelming."

Huggins believes that every neighborhood in St. Paul deserves to have a library that reflects its community. As she looks to the future, she hopes to make St. Paul's libraries more attractive, more welcoming, more engaging.

"There needs to be some serendipity about libraries," she says. "But at the end of the day, it will not be about the facilities. It will be about the people. We must be willing to try new things. If we never touch any of those facilities [in St. Paul] and they all remain exactly the same, I want what goes on in them to be different. And I want the staff to be empowered. We all have to be risk-takers."

In its 125 years of existence, the Saint Paul Public Library has reflected both its times and the character and personalities of its leaders. Originating in an era when libraries were charged with the role of protecting public morals, they evolved to become the informal educators of the public. Generations of children reading their first books, immigrants studying for citizenship exams, researchers and housewives and the homeless—all have sat, elbow to elbow, at the long tables in the library.

Though the tables now hold ranks of computers and copy machines whir in the background, the librarians continue to locate reference books, provide technical help, and offer a warm, human response to an inquiry. Through fire and flood, war and depression, official indifference and dramatic public support, St. Paul's librarians have been unswerving in their devotion to their mission. Libraries, they insist, as they read stories to preschoolers, help teens with homework, and translate materials into Hmong and Somali, are for everyone. Libraries are the neighborhood's pride and meeting place, the single resource that meets the needs of young and old, rich and poor, citizen and immigrant, educated and unschooled. Public libraries are the people's primary school and their university— an open door that welcomes everyone to the wide world of knowledge.

Notes

PROLOGUE

1. Paul R. Gold, "Rats, Politicians, Librarians: The Untold Stories of the Old Saint Francis Hotel and the Rich Historical Legacy of Seventh Place," *Ramsey County History* 31, no. 4 (1997): 4.

2. *Saint Paul Public Library Annual Report* (1895).

3. *St. Paul Pioneer Press,* May 2, 1915.

4. *St. Paul Pioneer Press,* June 16, 1918.

5. *Saint Paul Public Library Annual Report* (1915), 1.

6. *St. Paul Pioneer Press,* January 19, 1917.

7. *Minneapolis Tribune,* April 29, 1915.

8. *St. Paul News,* April 30, 1915.

9. *St. Paul News,* April 30, 1915.

10. Gold, "Rats, Politicians, Librarians," 7.

11. *St. Paul Pioneer Press,* May 2, 1915.

CHAPTER 1

12. William Dawson Johnston, *Notes on the History of the Saint Paul Public Library,* vol. 2 (typescript, Minnesota Historical Society Library, Jan. 1, 1914–Nov. 7, 1921).

13. Patricia Merwin Krezowski, "Saint Paul Public Library, 1882–1931: Origins and Early Librarians" (master's thesis, University of Minnesota, 1984), 1.

14. Larry Brian Hlavsa, "A Brief History of Public Libraries in Minneapolis/St. Paul, 1849–1900" (master's thesis, University of Minnesota, 1978).

15. WPA Papers (Minnesota Historical Society, Division of Archives and Manuscripts, *Chronicle and Register,* February 23, 1850).

16. H. Fletcher Williams, *History of Ramsey County and the City of St. Paul* (Minneapolis: North Star Publishing Company, 1881), 355.

17. Krezowski, "Saint Paul Public Library," 4.

18. Sidney Ditzion, *Arsenals of a Democratic Culture* (Chicago: American Library Association, 1947), 103.

19. Dee Garrison, *Apostles of Culture* (New York: The Free Press, a Division of Macmillan Publishing Company, 1979), 34.

20. Billie Young and Nancy Ankeny, *Minnesota Women in Politics* (St. Cloud, Minnesota: North Star Press, 2000), 64.

21. Krezowski, "Saint Paul Public Library," 9.

22. Joseph Nathan Kane, *Famous First Facts* (New York: H. W. Wilson Company, 1964), 343. Also *New York Times,* June 11, 2006, business section, 5.

23. *Daily Pioneer and Democrat,* December 19, 1858.

24. Reading Room regulations of the St. Paul Mercantile Library Association, adopted September 1858, revised January 1859, incorporated 1859 under the General Act of the Legislature, St. Paul, 1859.

25. *Daily Pioneer and Democrat,* December 1, 1859.

26. John Paul Ostendorf, "History of the Public Library Movement in Minnesota from 1849 to 1916" (thesis, University of Minnesota, 1984), 86.

27. *St. Paul Daily Press,* April 23, 1861.

28. *St. Paul Daily Press,* December 28, 1861.

29. *St. Paul Daily Press,* December 28, 1861.

30. Williams, *History of Ramsey County and the City of St. Paul,* 426.

31. Johnston, *Notes on the History of the Saint Paul Public Library.*

32. WPA Papers (*St. Paul Daily Pioneer,* January 22, 1864).

33. WPA Papers (*St. Paul Daily Pioneer,* June 14, 1866).

34. Hlavsa, "A Brief History of Public Libraries in Minneapolis/St. Paul," 17.

35. *Minneapolis Tribune,* March 20, 1873.

36. Hlavsa, "A Brief History of Public Libraries in Minneapolis/St. Paul," 18.

37. *Minneapolis Tribune,* October 16, 1884.

38. WPA Papers (*St. Paul Daily Pioneer,* January 22, 1864).

39. Ossian E. Dodge, *Fifth Annual Report of the Saint Paul Chamber of Commerce* (1871).

40. *St. Paul Dispatch,* May 15, 1872.

41. *St. Paul Pioneer Press,* May 15, 1878.

CHAPTER 2

42. James A. Rawley, "Edward Eggleston: Historian," *Indiana Magazine of History* XL, no. 4 (1944): 341.

43. William Pierce Randel, *Edward Eggleston* (Morningside Heights, New York: King's Crown Press, 1946), 34.

44. John T. Flanagan, "The Hoosier Schoolmaster in Minnesota," *Minnesota History* 18, no. 4 (1937), 349.

45. Flanagan, "The Hoosier Schoolmaster in Minnesota," 350.

46. Ibid., 350.

47. Randel, *Edward Eggleston,* 74.

48. Ibid., 76.

49. Flanagan, 361.

50. Ibid., 348.

51. Ibid., 363.

52. *Pioneer Press,* December 11, 1863.

CHAPTER 3

53. William Dawson Johnston, *Notes on the History of the Saint Paul Public Library with Historical Introduction and Some Later Additions by Mrs. Jennie T. Jennings* (vol. 2, typescript, Minnesota Historical Society, Jan.1, 1914–Nov. 7, 1921), 35.

54. Johnston, *Notes on the History of the Saint Paul Public Library,* 44.

55. Charles J. Ingles to Jennie Jennings, September 23, 1932, in *Record of the Fiftieth Anniversary Celebration of the Saint Paul Public Library* (Saint Paul Public Library Collection, 1932).

56. Krezowski, "Saint Paul Public Library," 31.

57. Garrison, *Apostles of Culture,* 4.

58. Krezowski, "Saint Paul Public Library," 34.

59. Ibid., 35.

60. Johnston, *Notes on the History of the Saint Paul Public Library,* 4.

61. Ingles to Jennings, *op. cit.*

62. Ingles to Jennings, *op. cit.*

63. *Annual Report of the Saint Paul Chamber of Commerce* (1884).

64. Johnston, *Notes on the History of the Saint Paul Public Library,* 64.

65. Ingles to Jennings, *op. cit.*

66. *Ibid.*

67. *Ibid.*

68. *Annual Report of the Chamber of Commerce* (1888).

69. Krezowski, "Saint Paul Public Library," 50.

CHAPTER 4

70. *St. Paul Pioneer Press,* June 16, 1918.

71. *Saint Paul Public Library Annual Report* (1884), 12.

72. Garrison, *Apostles of Culture,* 183.

73. Jane R. DeCamp to Jennie Jennings, October 5, 1932. Fiftieth Anniversary Celebration of the Saint Paul Public Library (Saint Paul Public Library Collection, October 3–17, 1932).

74. *St. Paul Pioneer Press,* June 16, 1918.

75. Gary Phelps, "The Saint Paul Public Library and Its First 100 Years," *Ramsey County History* 18, no. 1 (1982): 12.

76. *St. Paul Pioneer Press,* June 16, 1918.

77. *St. Paul Pioneer Press,* April 1, 1922.

CHAPTER 5

78. Henry A. Castle, *History of St. Paul and Vicinity,* 3 vols. (Chicago: Lewis Publishing Company, 1912), 179.

79. *St. Paul Pioneer Press,* March 28, 1948.

80. Edward D. Neill to James J. Hill, October 22, 1887, and July 10, 1888 (General Correspondence, James J. Hill Papers, James J. Hill Reference Library, St. Paul, Minnesota). Also *St. Paul Pioneer Press,* July 12, 1888.

81. Edward D. Neill to James J. Hill, July 30, 1888 (James J. Hill Papers, Hill Reference Library, St. Paul, Minnesota).

82. James Michael Reardon, *The Catholic Church in the Diocese of St. Paul* (St. Paul: North Central Publishing Company, 1952), 309.

83. James J. Hill to Edward Feldhauser, August 13, 1898 (James J. Hill Papers, James J. Hill Reference Library, St. Paul, Minnesota).

84. Sources differ on the cost of the remodeling. Patricia Merwin Krezowski in "Saint Paul Public Library, Origins and Early Librarians, 1882–1931" states that the Market House was remodeled for the library at a cost of $15,000. Gary Phelps in "The Saint Paul Public Library and Its First 100 Years" states that $98,359 was spent on remodeling.

85. Garrison, *Apostles of Culture,* 224. Also *The Minnesota Voter* 57, no. 1 (July–August 1978).

86. Phelps, "The Saint Paul Public Library and Its First 100 Years," 10.

87. James Bertram to Edwin S. Chittenden, February 20, 1903 (Cass Gilbert Papers, Minnesota Historical Society, Division of Archives and Manuscripts, St. Paul).

88. Edwin S. Chittenden to Cass Gilbert, September 23, 1903 (Cass Gilbert Papers, Minnesota Historical Society Division of Archives and Manuscripts, St. Paul).

89. R. Clipston Sturgis, "The James J. Hill Reference Library and the Saint Paul Public Library, St. Paul, Minnesota," *The Architectural Record,* Vol XLVII, no. 1 (January 1920): 3.

90. *St. Paul Dispatch,* March 5, 1912, p. 1.

91. *St. Paul Dispatch,* March 15, 1912, p. 1.

92. www.nycarchitecture.com, Carrere and Hastings.

93. Charles C. Soule to James J. Hill, October 22, 1912, James J. Hill Papers, James J. Hill Reference Library, St. Paul, Minnesota.

94. *St. Paul Dispatch,* January 16, 1913, p. 1.

95. *St. Paul News,* April 29, 1915.

96. Electus D. Litchfield to Jennie Jennings, September 30, 1932, *op. cit.*

97. *St. Paul Dispatch,* June 17, 1915.

98. *St. Paul Pioneer Press,* November 4, 1917.

CHAPTER 6

99. *St. Paul Pioneer Press,* February 21, 1915.

100. *St. Paul Pioneer Press,* February 21, 1915.

101. *St. Paul Pioneer Press,* July 29, 1917.

102. *St. Paul Pioneer Press,* March 22, 1920.

103. *Public Library Annual Report* (1918), p. 6.

104. W. Dawson Johnston, "The New Saint Paul Public Library," *Western Magazine* 11, no. 2: 42.

105. *Saint Paul Public Library Annual Report* (1914).

106. *St. Paul Dispatch,* October 26, 1915.

107. *St. Paul News,* April 30, 1915.

108. *Public Library Annual Report* (1919).

109. Hella R. Havens, "Development of the Saint Paul Public Library" (paper prepared for Division of Library Instruction, University of Minnesota, 1930).

110. "Farewell Reception at Saint Paul for Dr. Johnston," *Library Journal* 46 (November 15, 1921): 941.

CHAPTER 7

111. *St. Paul Daily News,* January 4, 1922.

112. *St. Paul Pioneer Press,* January 14, 1932.

113. *St. Paul Pioneer Press,* January 10, 1932.

114. *St. Paul Dispatch,* February 13, 1922.

115. *St. Paul Dispatch,* February 18, 1922.

116. *St. Paul Dispatch,* February 18, 1922.

117. *Saint Paul Public Library Annual Report* (1923), 6.

118. *Saint Paul Public Library Annual Report* (1920 and 1927).

119. *Saint Paul Public Library Annual Report* (1924), 1.

120. *Saint Paul Public Library Annual Report* (1928), 34.

121. Krezowski, "Saint Paul Public Library," 99.

122. *St. Paul Dispatch,* January 30, 1924, 1.

123. *Saint Paul Public Library Annual Report* (1926).

124. A. E. Bostwick and Carl Vitz, *Survey of the Saint Paul Public Library* (1929).

125. Flier in folder, Saint Paul Public Library, Central Library.

126. *St. Paul Dispatch,* March 5, 1930.

CHAPTER 8

127. *St. Paul News,* February 5, 1929.

128. *Library Advisory Board Reports* (1914–1937).

129. *Library Advisory Reports* (1914–1937). Officers of the 1929 Library Advisory Board were John A. Pearson, John Seeger, Julian Kirby, Anita Furness, Mrs. E. J. Stiefel, Charles L. Sommers, Sidney Horsley, and E. P. Davis. Ex-officio were S. G. Hartwell, superintendent of schools, and the principals of Central, Humboldt, Johnson, and Mechanic Arts High Schools and Hill School.

130. *Encyclopedia of Library and Information Science,* vol. 26 (New York: Marcel Dekker, 1979), 284.

131. "What Does St. Paul Want?" Library budget (1933).

132. Ibid.

133. *Library Beacon,* Saint Paul Public Library (December 1932).

134. *Library Advisory Reports,* 1914–1937.

135. *St. Paul Daily News,* August 18, 1935.

136. *St. Paul Pioneer Press,* September 8, 1935.

137. Library budget (1934).

138. *St. Paul Pioneer Press,* February 28, 1932.

139. "Keeping the Library Doors Open," letter attached to the library budget request for 1934.

140. Library budget (1935).

141. *The Library Beacon,* Saint Paul Public Library, vol. 1 (1929).

142. Mena C. Dyste, "Gratia Alta Countryman, Librarian" (thesis, University of Minnesota, 1965), 34.

143. *St. Paul Dispatch,* February 17, 1939.

CHAPTER 9

144. *St. Paul Dispatch,* January 8, 1937.

145. *St. Paul News,* August 19, 1937.

146. *St. Paul News,* August 19, 1937.

147. *St. Paul Dispatch,* September 1, 1937.

148. *St. Paul News,* September 8, 1937.

149. May P. Jesseph, "Perrie Jones: Librarian and Humanitarian" (research project, University of Minnesota, 1976), 3.

150. Jesseph, "Perrie Jones," 10.

151. *St. Paul Pioneer Press,* July 18, 1921, 10.

152. Perrie Jones papers, Minnesota Historical Society, Box 7.

153. Jesseph, "Perrie Jones," 12.

154. Perrie Jones, *One Thousand Books for Hospital Libraries* (Minneapolis: University of Minnesota Press, 1944).

155. *St. Paul Pioneer Press,* December 16, 1936.

156. Interview with Don Kelsey, June 14, 2006.

157. Perrie Jones to Oscar W. Firkins, April 8, 1930.

158. Oscar W. Firkins to Perrie Jones, April 15, 1930.

159. Perrie Jones papers, Minnesota Historical Society, Box 1.

160. *St. Paul Dispatch,* August 25, 1965.

161. *St. Paul Pioneer Press,* November 3, 1924.

162. *St. Paul Pioneer Press,* October 24, 1954.

163. *St. Paul Dispatch,* October 25, 1945.

164. Phelps, "The Saint Paul Public Library and Its First

100 Years," 18.

165. *St. Paul Pioneer Press,* October 28, 1985.

166. Perrie Jones papers, Minnesota Historical Society, Box 1.

167. Jesseph, "Perrie Jones," 35.

168. Interview with Don Kelsey, June 14, 2006.

CHAPTER 10

169. Phelps, Gary, "The Saint Paul Public Library and Its First 100 Years," 19.

170. Interview with Kathleen Flynn and Mary Clare Huberty, June 21, 2006.

171. Interview with Patricia Ethier, June 1, 2006.

172. Interview with Kathleen Flynn, May 22, 2006.

173. *St. Paul Dispatch,* September 13, 1963.

174. *St. Paul Dispatch,* March 2, 1964.

175. *Minneapolis Star,* July 23, 1965.

176. *St. Paul Dispatch,* December 18, 1970.

177. *St. Paul Pioneer Press,* September 14, 1971.

178. Interview with Jerry Steenberg, May 25, 2006.

179. Interview with Roxanne Aschittino, June 19, 2006.

180. Interview with Don Kelsey, June 14, 2006.

THE BRANCHES

181. Bobinski, George S., *Carnegie Libraries: Their History and Impact on American Public Library Development* (Chicago: American Library Association, 1969), 47.

CHAPTER 11

182. Interview with Mary Clare Huberty, June 21, 2006.

183. *The Citizens Task Force for the Library, Report to the Mayor and the City Council of the City of St. Paul* (June 1981), 171.

184. *The Citizens Task Force for the Library,* 8.

185. Library employees, including the director, were hired under Civil Service rules. Under the administration of Mayor Norm Coleman, this was changed to exempt the library director. Gina La Force, hired in 2002, was the first non–Civil Service director to head the library.

186. *St. Paul Dispatch,* August 2, 1984.

187. *St. Paul Pioneer Press,* August 6, 1984.

188. *Newsletter of the Friends of the Saint Paul Public Library,* no. 1 (February 1979),

189. Also *Annual Report* (1988).

190. St. Paul 1990 Census Report, no. 1, City of St. Paul Department of Planning and Economic Development, 5.

191. Annette Salo, "Ethnic Diversity in a Northern Climate." The Acquisitions Librarian 5, no. 9–10: 267–74.

192. "Friends of the Library's 50 Years," *Ramsey County History* 30, no. 2 (1995): 16–17.

CHAPTER 12

193. *St. Paul Pioneer Press,* July 1, 1997.

194. "A Plan For Libraries," Community Discussion Draft (October 4, 1994), 1.

195. *St. Paul Pioneer Press,* September 29, 2002.

Illustration Credits

AFTON PRESS, Afton, Minnesota
p. 34, from *The Mystery of Metropolisville* by Edward
Eggleston, 1873.

**AMHERST H. WILDER FOUNDATION, St. Paul,
Minnesota**
p. 172, Sandy Kiernat.

CHICAGO HISTORY MUSEUM, Chicago, Illinois
p. 48, William F. Poole.

FORBES LIBRARY, Northampton, Massachusetts
p. 49, Charles Ammi Cutter, oil painting by William
Henry Warren Bicknell, date unknown.

**FRIENDS OF THE SAINT PAUL PUBLIC
LIBRARY, St. Paul, Minnesota**
p. 142, Central Library by Richard Faricy; p. 144,
Riverview and St. Anthony Park branches by Richard
Faricy; p. 145, Merriam Park and Hamline-Midway
branches by Richard Faricy; p. 146, Rice Street and
Highland branches by Richard Faricy; p. 147, Hayden
Heights and Lexington branches by Richard Faricy; p.
148, Sunray and West Seventh branches by Richard
Faricy; p. 149, Rondo and Dayton's Bluff branches by
Richard Faricy; p. 151, Richard Faricy, date unknown; p.
161, Peter Pearson, date unknown; p. 162, Richard Faricy
and Carol Ryan, 1995; p. 165, new bookmobile; p. 170,
Carole Williams, date unknown; p. 197, Rondo fireplace,
2006; p. 198, Rondo opening day, 2006; p. 199, Chris
Coleman, 2006; p. 200, Rondo and Bookmobile staff,
2006; p. 201 Rondo opening day (all images), 2006.

**INSTITUTE OF MUSEUM AND LIBRARY
SERVICES, Washington, D.C.**
p. 193, service award presentation, photographer Steven
E. Purcell, 2005.

**LEGACY MANAGEMENT AND DEVELOP-
MENT CORPORATION, St. Paul, Minnesota**
p. 196, Archie Givens.

**LIBRARY OF CONGRESS, PRINTS AND PHO-
TOGRAPHS DIVISION, Washington, D.C.**
p. 33, Edward Eggleston; p. 48, Justin Winsor; p. 63, J. P.
Morgan library, date unknown.

**METROPOLITAN STATE UNIVERSITY,
St. Paul, Minnesota**
p. 191, Wilson Bradshaw; p. 186, Dayton's Bluff.

MEYER, SCHERER & ROCKCASTLE, ARCHITECTS
Cover, photo by Farshid Assassi of Assassi Productions; p.
2, Central library staircase, photo by Farshid Assassi of
Assassi Productions; p. 4, Central Library lobby, photo by
Pete Sieger; p. 69, Greenleaf Clark Reference Room ceil-
ing detail, photo by Farshid Assassi of Assassi Productions;
p. 110, puppet theater, photo by Farshid Assassi of Assassi
Productions; p. 175, Nicholson Information Commons,
photo by Farshid Assassi of Assassi Productions; p. 180,
Mississippi Room, photo by Farshid Assassi of Assassi
Productions; p. 181, nonfiction room, photo by Farshid
Assassi of Assassi Productions; p. 184, Children's Room

entrance, photo by Farshid Assassi of Assassi Productions;
p. 185 (bottom), Children's Room, photo by Farshid
Assassi of Assassi Productions.

**MINNEAPOLIS PUBLIC LIBRARY, Minneapolis,
Minnesota**
p. 53, library, ca. 1890s.

**MINNESOTA HISTORICAL SOCIETY, St. Paul,
Minnesota**
p. 14, Market House, postcard on paper, ca. 1908; p. 18,
House of Hope Presbyterian Church, 1886; p. 20, *Little
Crow's Village* by Klein Rabendorf, lithographer Henry
Lewis, 1854; p. 21, Harriet Bishop, oil painting by
Andrew Falkenshield, ca. 1880; p. 22, William R.
Marshall, photo by Charles A. Zimmerman, 1864; p. 23,
Hamline University, Red Wing, ca. 1865; p. 24, LeDuc
and Rohrer Book Store, daguerreotype, ca. 1853; p. 26,
Charles E. Mayo, photograph by Charles A. Zimmerman,
date unknown; p. 27, Daniel W. Ingersoll, photo by J.
Gurney & Son, Carte-de-Visite, ca. 1872; p. 28, Ingersoll
Block, ca. 1885; p. 30, Thomas B. Walker, photo by Sweet
Studios, ca. 1915; p. 31, Christopher C. Andrews, photo
by D. B. Spooner & Co., ca. 1862; p. 35, *Treaty of Traverse
des Sioux,* oil by Frank Blackwell Mayer, 1885; p. 40,
Central Library circulation desk, 1910; p. 42, Alexander
Ramsey, photo by W. Cogswell, postcard ca. 1882; p. 43,
Maurice Auerbach, engraving, ca. 1885; p. 45, Ramsey
County Courthouse, 1887; p. 49, Gratia Alta
Countryman, photo by Lee Brothers, 1917; p. 54, Neill
family, stereograph, ca. 1860; p. 55, Edward Duffield Neill,
pastel by Floyd W. Horton, ca. 1900; p. 59, David C.
Shepard, ca. 1900; p. 60, James J. Hill, oil by Henry Caro-
Delvaille, 1913; p. 61, Greenleaf Clark, engraving, ca.
1900; p. 64, Central Library cornerstone ceremonies,
1914; p. 85, Hotel St. Francis, postcard, ca. 1935.

**OFFICE OF SENATOR NORM COLEMAN,
St. Paul, Minnesota**
p. 173, Norm Coleman.

**DICK AND NANCY NICHOLSON, St. Paul,
Minnesota**
p. 174.

**RAMSEY COUNTY COMMISSIONERS
OFFICE, St. Paul, Minnesota**
p. 172, Toni Carter, 2005.

**RAMSEY COUNTY HISTORICAL SOCIETY,
St. Paul, Minnesota**
p. 37, Market Street Methodist Church, ca. 1850s; p. 61,
Lucius Pond Ordway.

SAINT PAUL FOUNDATION, St. Paul, Minnesota
p. 159 (top), Paul Verret, date unknown.

SAINT PAUL PUBLIC LIBRARY, St. Paul, Minnesota
p. 17 (top and bottom), Market House fire, 1915; p. 19,
library staff, 1915; p. 44, floor plan; p. 46, Helen McCaine;
p. 52, Central Library architect's drawing; p. 57, Market
House; p. 57, Reference Room, ca. 1910; p. 62, Electus D.
Litchfield and architect's drawing; p. 64 (top), Central

Library construction, 1913; p. 65, Central Library construction, 1915; p. 65, Reading Room, 1916; p. 66,
Central Library, 1916; p. 68, elevator doors; p. 69 (bottom), Greenleaf Clark Reference Room, 1921; p. 70,
William Dawson Johnston, artist and date unknown; p.
73, audiovisual presentation, ca. 1920s; p. 73, schoolchildren on tour, ca. 1920s; p. 74, Riverview branch, 1930; p.
75, library staff, ca. 1924; p. 77, bookmobile, 1915; p. 79,
staff, ca. 1920s; p. 80, Central Library and Rice Park,
1930; p. 83, Webster Wheelock, date unknown; p. 86,
Ruth Tews, 1930; p. 88, Jennie T. Jennings, 1932; p. 90,
Children's Room model ship, date unknown; p. 91, Jennie
T. Jennings, date unknown; p. 92, library patrons, 1933; p.
93 (top and bottom), Classroom Department, 1933; p. 95,
Buell and Christmas, ca. 1935; p. 96 (top), staff, 1933; p.
96, Greenleaf Clark Reference Room patrons, ca. 1931;
p. 97, staff, 1932; p. 98, staff at fiftieth anniversary, 1932; p.
99, fiftieth-anniversary patrons, 1932; p. 100, Della
McGregor, 1943; p. 102, puppet play, 1937; p. 104, pedi-
atric patient, 1943; p. 104, Lucille Francis, 1944; p. 105,
Lucille Francis and Lydia Rosander, 1944; p. 106, race
exhibit, 1945; p. 106, Phyllis Sands, 1946; p. 107, Haas and
Hultgren, 1937; p. 108, Burnett and Landreville, 1945; p.
108, West and Sohlberg, 1947; p. 109, Skinner Room
inauguration (1939) and tulip planting (1948); p. 111,
puppeteers, 1950; p. 112, Agatha Klein, 1953; p. 112,
Music Room, 1954; p. 112, Mable McCoy, 1948; p. 115,
puppet show, 1943; p. 116, Perrie Jones, 1948; p. 117,
Perrie Jones with readers, 1949; p. 118, George Anderegg,
1946; p. 119, Elaine Nelleson, 1942; p. 120, Frederick
Curtis, 1946, p. 121, Perrie Jones' retirement, 1955; p.
122, J. Archer Eggen and staff, 1959; p. 124, Mrs.
Kuchenbacher, 1959; p. 124, Circulation Room, 1958; p.
125, Agatha Klein, 1961; p. 127, J. Archer Eggen and
Kathleen Flynn and Alice Neve, dates unknown; p. 128,
Theora Halstead, 1974; p. 129, Girl Scouts, 1960; p. 129,
Children's Room, 1960; p. 130, Elaine Wagner, 1966; p.
131, Karen Avaloz, 1966; p. 133, book sale, 1971; p. 134,
Mae Boucher, 1947; p. 136, Ortha Robbins, date
unknown; p. 136, Steenberg and staff, date unknown; p.
139, Severin Mortinson, 1960; p. 139, Della McGregor,
1961; p. 140, Alice Neve, ca. 2002; p. 141, children's area,
date unknown; p. 152, George Latimer, 1982; p. 154,
Steenberg and staff, 1982; p. 157, Gordon Parks and Patricia
Hampl, 1981; p. 158, Jeanne Fischer, photo by Brad Stauffer,
date unknown; p. 158, ribbon cutting, date unknown; p.
159, book sale, 1982; p. 161, Jerry Steenberg, date
unknown; p. 164, Garrison Keillor, 1985; p. 166, bookmobile, 1931 and 1980; p. 167, bookmobile, 1950; p. 167 (bottom) bookmobile, date unknown; p. 171, library staff, 2000;
p. 168, F. Scott Fitzgerald alcoves; p. 177, St. Anthony Park
reopening, 2002; p. 178, Central Library reopening, 2002; p.
179, Bookmobile, 2005; p. 182, Rice Street reopening,
2002; p. 185 (top), renovations, 2001; p. 188, James Scheibel
(ca. early 1990s) and Lexington Branch (date unknown); p.
189, John McKay (2001) and Lexington Branch (date
unknown); p. 193, Gina La Force, et al., 2003; p. 194,
Lexington Branch reopening, 2001; p. 202, Melanie
Huggins, 2006.

**WEISMAN ART MUSEUM, Minneapolis,
Minnesota**
p. 32, *Minnesota Prairie,* oil on canvas by Thomas Rossiter, 1865.

Index

Abrams, Ron, 192
Adams, John Walker, 43
Ahern, Mary, 47
Alban, William, 143
American Expeditionary Force, 78
American Library Association, 47–49, 71, 77, 86, 91, 106
Ames, Robert L., 150
Anderegg, George, *118*
Andersen, Elmer L., 160
Anderson, Bill, 148
Anderson, Marian, 115
Andrews, Christopher Columbus, 30, *31*
Anthony, Susan B., 30
Apfeld, Adelaide, *19*
Area Learning Community School, 200
Arnold, Mrs. W. J., 29
Aschittino, Roxanne, 134, 136, 140–41, 156
Association of Commerce, 61
Astor Library, 25. See also New York Public Library.
Atlas, Andre, 200
Athenaeum Library, 29–30
Aurora St. Anthony Neighborhood Development
    Corporation, 196
Auerbach, Maurice, 42, *43*
Avaloz, Karen, *131*

Bagnoli, Joe, 192
Baker, Elsie L., *97*
Bakken, Mildred, 158
Baldwin School. *See* Macalester College.
Bandana Square, 151
Barden, Bertha, *19*
Barton, David, 190
Bastyr Drug Store, 50, 143
Beck, Charles, 149
Beecher, Henry Ward, 30
Ben Bolt steamer, 33
Benson, Helga C., *19, 97*
Bentley, Percy, 143
Bertram, James, 58–59, 143
Bigelow Foundation, 174, 187
Billings, J. S., 56, 58
Bishop, Harriet E., 21
Bishop, Herber R., 16
Blakey, Jerry, *194,* 196
Blees, Greg, 196
Bodin's Drug Store, 50, 143
Boe's Millinery, 15
Boeckmann, Rachel Hill, 67
Bosalis and Papas Confectionary, 15–16, *17*
Boss, Andy, 174, 177, *177,* 190
Boston Athenaeum, 48
Boston Public Library, 22, 24–25, 48
Boston YMCA, 23
Bostwick, Arthur E., 86
Boucher, Mae, *134,* 134
Brack, George, 121
Bradshaw, Wilson, 190, *191,* 199
Brady, Shirley, *136,* 187
Briggs, John, 114, 157
Briggs, Myrtle, 114, 157
Briggs Trust, 157
Brodeen, Ginny, *194*

Brooks, Cyrus, 39
Broussard, Phillip, 145
Brown, Barbara, 114
Bruckner, Ethel, *75*
Bryan, Clara, *19*
Bryan, William Jennings, 15
Buehrer, Bertha, *19*
Buell, Myra, *19, 75, 95, 97*
Burbank, James C., 28
Burger, Warren, 157
Burnett, Edah F., *19, 108*
Burton, Marion L., 67
Bush, Laura, 193, *193*
Bush Foundation, 155
Butch Thompson Trio, 159
Butler, Pierce, 51
Butler, Pierce Jr., *121*

Campbell, J. Charlotte, *97*
Cargill, 190
Carlson, Adline, 136, *154*
Carlson, Nancy, 139
Carnegie, Andrew, 56, 58–59, 143
Carnegie libraries, 56, 58, 143
Carney, Eleanor, *122*
Carter, Willetha (Toni), 172, *172*
Carver, Henry L., 43
Cathcart, J. W., 25, 27
Cavin, Bruce, 156
Central Clothing Store, 15
Central High School, 132
Central Police Station, 59
Centre Theater, 132–33
Chicago Public Library, 48
Chittenden, Edwin, 56, 59
Christ Child Society's Home, 72
Christmas, Jean M., *95*
Church of the Good Shepherd, 61
Chute, Elizabeth W., *97*
Chute, Mary, *193*
Cincinnati Public Library, 48
Civic Center, 134
Civil War, 26, 41–42
Clark, Greenleaf, 60, *61,* 67
Clark's Restaurant, 15
Clarke, Eric K.
Clemans, F. J., 59
Cleveland, Grover T., 98
Clute, Elizabeth, *19*
Cochran, Emilie Belden, 111. *See also* Central Library,
    Cochran Children's Room.
Cochran, Thomas, 111. *See also* Central Library, Cochran
    Children's Room.
Cole, Susan, 190
Coleman, Chris, 199, *199*
Coleman, Norm, 169, 171–73, *173*
College of St. Thomas, 22, 145
Community Food Center, 72
Como Park Conservatory, 151
Como School, 114
Conway, John, 16–17
Conway, Thomas, *99*
Corridan, E. C., *99*

Costello, John, 16
Countryman, Gratia, *49,* 49, 71, 84, 97
Courteau, Stella, *19*
Craidone, Sam, 16
Creek, Maggie, 41
Creek, Mary S., 41, 43, 47
Cromwell, R. F., 26, 28
Cox, John Marcus, 147
Curtis, Frederick, *120*
Cutter, Charles, 48, *49,* 71

Dame, Katherine, 77, *97*
Daniels, Danielle, *201*
Datko, Mary Jo, 165
Daughters of the American Revolution, 115
Davis, Edward P., 85, 89
Davis, John B., 160
Davis, Robert S., 155
Dean, W. B., 28
DeCamp, Mrs. Janes Randall, 98
Detroit Public Library, 77
Dewey, Melvil, 47–48
    and nation's first library school, 48
Dewey decimal system, 49
Dlegen, Dean T. C., *121*
Doermann, Humphrey, 155
Dolan, Mrs., *96*
Donnelly, Ignatius, 30
Dorothy Day, 135
Douglas, Carole Nelson, 160
Douglass, Frederick, 30
Drake, Carl B. Jr., 160

Edmunds, Della, *19*
Edwards, Evan E., 39, 41
Eggen, J. Archer, 121–30, *122, 127,* 134, 149, 153–54,
    156, 170
    and Cedar Rapids Public Library, 123
    and Fergus Falls Public Library, 123
    and the University of Minnesota, 123
Eggleston, Edward, 28, 33–39
    and American Historical Association, 39
    and "Chicken Little" stories, 39
    and Economic Soap, 37
    and *The Hoosier Schoolmaster,* 39
    and *The Little Corporal,* 39
    and marriage to Lizzie Snider, 36
    and Methodist Church at Winona, 39
    and *The Mystery of Metropolisville,* 33–34, *34, 36*
    and private library at Cornell University, 39
Eggleston, George, 34
Ellerbe Architects, 148
Ellingwood, Sue, 154, 176
Emerson, Ralph Waldo, 29–30
Entenza, Matt, 192
Ethier, Patricia, 126, 128, 135–36, 153

Fairbanks, Frank, 67
Fairbanks, Mrs. Frank, 68
Fallon, William H., *109*
Fallon, Mrs. William H., *109*
Faricy, Richard (Dick), *151,* 151, 160–62, *162*
Faust Adult Theater, 195

Federal Library Services, 129
Federation of Grade Teachers, 60
Federation of Women's Clubs, 60
Feldhauser, Edward, 55–56
Feldman, John C., *109*
Ferguson, Lee R. S., 78, 81, 91
Fermi, Enrico, 116
Fettinger, Adelbert, *109*
Fieseler's Drug Store, 50, 143
Fifield, Grace, *19*
Finley, John, 101–03, 107
Firkins, Oscar W., 113
First Trust Company, 114, 157
Fischer, Jeanne, 151, *158,* 158, 160
Fitzgerald, F. Scott, 160
Fitzgerald, Zelda, 160
Flint, S. W., 15
Florian's Pharmacy, 145
Flynn, Gene, 149
Flynn, Kathleen, 126, *127, 136,* 153, 155–156, 169–170,
    176, 183, 187, 193, *193*
Fogg, F. A., 68
Foreman, Rose Ann, 177, *177*
Francis, Lucille, *104–105*
Franklin, Benjamin, 25
Freerks, Gene, 149
Freerks, Sperl, and Flynn, 150
Fridley, Russell, 156, 160
Friends of the Library. *See* Friends of the Saint Paul
    Public Library *and* Saint Paul Library Association.
Friends of the Saint Paul Public Library, 89, 90, 111,
    114–15, 124, 130, 136, 138, 146, 150–51, 154–55, 157,
    159–163, 171–74, 177, 183, 187–89, 191–92, 195, 199
    and Friends Advocacy Committee, 161–63
Frischkorn, Florine, 144
Frogtown Community Development Corporation, 196
Fuch's Drug Store, 50

Galt, Fran, *136*
Gardner, Cynthia, 158
Garland, Judy, 115
Gausman and Moore, 144
Gebhard, Miss, *96*
Gehan, Mark, 101
Gerlach, Pat, 143
Gerould, J. T., 18
Gilbert, Cass, 56, 58–59, 61
Givens, Archie, 196–97, *196,* 199
    and Legacy Management and Development
        Corporation, 196–97
Goodrich, H. F., 107
Gordon, Charles W., 61
Gordon and Ferguson Company, 59–60
Gore, Warren, 177, *177*
Gray, Helen J. *See* Helen McCaine.
Great Depression, 84, 91–94, 97, 101, 103, 115
Great Northern Railway, 54, 61, 72
Greeley, Horace, 30
Greenleaf's Jewelry Store, 26
Griffin, Jeanne, 77
Griggs, Theodore, 61
Grote's Tivoli, 98
Grotto Foundation, 101, 116, 160
Guenzel, Elizabeth Skinner, 160
Guerin, Vital, 15
Gustafson, Ernest H., *117*
Guthrie, Doug, *136*

Haas, Peggy, *107*
Haig, Sue, 192
Hale, Henry, 58–59, 84, 95, 145
Hale, Mary, 58
Hale, Robert, 68
Hale Memorial Fund, 89, 95
Hale Memorial Libraries, 84, 89, 95, 145–46
Hall's Millinery Store, 50
Hall, Charles Thompson, 147
Halstead, Theora, *128,* 128–29
    and *LSD* newsletter, 128–29
Hamline University, 22, *23,* 37, 81
    Red Wing Building, *23*
Hampl, Patricia, *157*
Hancock Elementary School, 146
Handy, W. C., 68
Hardenbergh, W. A., 76
Harris, Mike, 171
Harris, Nancy, 154–55, 158, 160
Harris, Pat, 191–92, 196
Harris, Paul, 154
Harris, Regina, 193, *193*
Hart, Jean, 160, 163
Hart, Mary, 197, 200
Hartford, Ernest, 143
Harte, Bret, 30
Harvard University library, 48
Hausler, Charles A., 68, 74, 143
Havens, Rella, *122*
Hayes, Daniell, *111*
Hayes, Stephen, *111*
HBW Associates, 155
Heaberlin, Fred, 145
Hebl, Agatha, 182
Hebl, Harold, 182
Heckman, Al A., 101, 116, 160
Henderson, Delores, *194*
Henson, Jane, 111
Henson, Jim, 111
Herber R. Bishop (Jade) Collection, 16
Herrmann, Eleanor, 111
Hermann Miller Shoe Store, 148
Hess, Julia, *19*
Hiebert, Gareth, 129
Hiebert, Jan, 128–129
Highland Park High School band, *178*
Hill, James J., 51, 53–55, 59–63, *60,* 67, 85
    Reference Library, 51, 54, 60, 67–68
Hill, Louis W., 67
Hill, Louis W. Jr., 160
Hillcrest Creation Center, 148
Hoag, Robert, 140
Hoerner-Waldorf, 133
Hoffman, Judy, 195
Hoffman, Maurine, 126, 130, *167*
Hohenstein, Mr. 76
Homans, Nancy, 172
Hotel St. Francis, 19, 85, *85,* 119
House of Hope Presbyterian Church, 18, *18–19,* 68, 75
Hubbard, Stanley, 160
Hubbs, Ronald M., 116, 160
Huberty, Mary Clare, 125, 128, 153–54, 156, 163–64, 176
Huggins, Melanie, 193, 200, *202,* 202–203
Hultgren, Emily, *107*
Hunt, Ruby, 160
Hurt, W. T., 15

Iglehart, Harwood, 25
Ihn, Elsa, *122*
Ingalls, Mrs. Clara, *99*
Ingersoll, Daniel W., *27,* 27–28, 44
Ingersoll Building, 26, 41, 43–45, 48, 98
Ingersoll Hall, 38, 44
Ingles, Charles J., 42–44
International Market Square, 151
Investigations and Studies in Jade, 16
Ireland, John, 22
Irvin, Vivian, 67
Irving, Washington, 26

Jackson, Ethel, *19*
Jackson Street Methodist Church, 38
James J. Hill Reference Library, 51, 54, 60, 67, 68
Jemne, Magnus, 108, 111
Jennings, Jennie T., 68, 77–78, *88,* 90–93, *91,* 95, *97,* 99,
    101–03, 115, 203
Jennings, Thomas Brownfield, 91
Jensen, Ethel, *19*
Johnson, Charles, 165
Johnson, Lieutenant, 22
Johnson, Lyndon, 130
Johnston, William Dawson, 18–19, 28, 68–79, *70, 79,* 81,
    83, 90, 104, 113, 138, 146, 155, 170, 203
    and *A History of University Libraries,* 18, 75
    and *History of the Library of Congress,* Volume 1, 71
Johnston-Gordon, William. *See* William Dawson
    Johnston.
Jones, Perrie, 101–04, 106–08, *109,* 113–15, *116–117,*
    117–121, *121,* 123–24, 157, 203
    and *One Thousand Books for Hospital Libraries,* 107
    and Perrie Jones Fund, 119, 124
    and University of Minnesota, 103, 113, 118
    and University of Minnesota school of medicine, 106
    and Wabasha Public Library, 104
Jones, Seitu, 197, 200
Juds, Elsa E., *97*
Juhl, Jerry, 111
Junior League of St. Paul, 106

Kane, Martin, 16
Kane, Mary Alice, 102
Kay, Isabelle, *19*
Keillor, Garrison, *152,* 159–60, *164*
Kelley, William H., 43
Kelly, Josephine, 41
Kelly, Randy, 182, *182,* 190, 192, 195–96, 199
Kelsey, Don, 117–18, 120, 134–35, 140–41
Kiefer, Andrew R., 45
Kiernat, Sandy, 172, *172*
King, Reatha Clark, 155, 160
Kirk, Dennis, 190
Klein, Agatha, *112, 125,* 125–26, 130, 153
Klinkhamer, Ruth, 127
Kneissel, Charles, *121*
Knox, H. M., 28
Kuchenbacker, Mrs., *124*
Kunz, Virginia Brainard, 101, 160

La, Ma, 165
La Force, Gina, 193, *193,* 197
Lambert, Marion, *75*
Landmark Center, 151
Landreville, Mrs. Henry, *108*
Larson, John, *193*

Latimer, George, *152,* 153, 155–56, 160, 191
Lawler, David W., 59–60
League of Women Voters, 160
Legacy Management and Development Corporation, 196–97
Leigh, Vivien, 136
Levine, Judy, 135
Levine, Leonard, 129, 133, 154
Library Committee of the Fourth District, 78
library law of Minnesota, 42
Library of Congress, 25
Liebgatt, Michael, 138
Lindeke, A. W., 59–61
Lindley, Clara Hill, 67
Litchfield, Electus D., 61–63, *62,* 68
Litchfield, William B., 61
Little Crow, 21
Loehr, Rodney, 113, 117
Logue, W. J., *99*
Logue, Mrs. W. J., *99*
Longbehn, Henry, 132
Longfellow Elementary School, 145
Los Alegres Bailadores, 200, *201*
Los Angeles Public Library, 99
Lufkin, Ginny, *154*
Luther Seminary, 143

Macalester College, 22, 42, 54, 81, 160, 165
Madsen, Robin, 166
Maloney, Thomas, 16
Mann, Josephine, *19*
Mardag Foundation, 174, 187
Market House, *14,* 15–19, *17,* 51, 55–56, *57,* 59–60, 85, 116
Market Street Methodist Church, 36–37, *37*
Marshall, William Rainey, *22,* 22
Martin Luther King Center, 155
Marzitelli, Frank D., 119, 155
Mathis, Florence, 140–41
Mayer, Frank B.
   and *Treaty of Traverse des Sioux,* 35
Mayo, Charles Edwin, *26,* 26, 28
McCaine, Helen J., 43, *46,* 47–51, 53, 62, 69, 71, 81, 98, 203
   and *Selected Books on Gardens and Gardening,* 48
   and *Select List of Books for Sunday School,* 48
   and *Select List on Fungi and Mushrooms,* 48
McCaine, William, 47
McCloskey, Mary, 44
McCoy, Mable, 112
McDonough Homes, 165
McGraw, Thomas, 36
McGregor, Della, *97, 100,* 129, 134, 138–140, *139,* 187, 203
   and American Library Association, 139
   and Grolier Award, 129
   and University of Minnesota School of Mathematics
      and Science Center, 140
McGuire, Erma, 155
McIlrath, Mrs. Mary Kellogg, *99*
McKay, John, *189*
McKillips, Nancy, 190
McKinley, William, 34
McKnight Foundation, 159
McKown, Blanche E., 99
McMonigal, Liz, *136*
McNally, Miles, 16
Mechanics and Apprentice Libraries, 25
Mechanics Library Association, 29
Meissner, Edie, 160
Melander, Enoch, 16

MELSA. *See* Metropolitan Library Services Agency.
Mercantile Library Associations, 25–28, 33, 48
Merchants Trust and Savings, 95
Merriam, John L., 28
Merrill, D. D., 28
Metropolitan Library Services Agency, 123, 156, 161
Metropolitan Museum of Art, 16
Metropolitan State Foundation, 190
Metropolitan State University, 150, 155, 160, 189–191, 199
   and Dayton's Bluff Branch Library, 191
Meyer, Scherer, and Rockcastle, 146, 150, 176, 190
Midway National Bank, 155, 160
Midway YMCA, 50
Millet, Larry, 176
Minneapolis Public Library, 18, 49–50, *53, 84*
Minneapolis Tribune, 30
Minneapolis YMCA, 29
Minnesota Department of Education, 75
Minnesota Federation of Women's Clubs, 103
Minnesota Foundation, 124
Minnesota Historical Society, 22, 26, 41, 49, 75, 138, 156, 160
Minnesota House Tax Committee, 192
Minnesota Library Association, 49
Minnesota Medical Society, 23
Minnesota Methodist Conference, 34
Minnesota Senate Tax Committee, 192
Minnesota Territory
   capitol, 15
   legislature, 22
   superintendent of schools, 22
Mrs. Hull's Millinery Store, 145
Mitchell, Bernard J., 113, *166–67*
Model Cities, 196
Moon, Amy C., *97*
Moore, Costello, and Hart, 155, 157
Moore, Pearl, *19*
Moore, Richard A., 155, 158, 160
Morgan, J. Pierpont, 63
   and Pierpont Morgan Library, *63*
Morrisey, Jay, 147
Mortinson, Severin, *121,* 123, *139*
Morton, J. Neil, 160
Mullaney, John P., *109*
Muppets, 111

National Popular Education Society, 21
Nattrass, J., 43
Neal, Mildred, *19*
Neighborhood House, 50
Neill, Edward D., *54–55,* 53–54
Nelleson, Elaine, 119
Nelson, Seven, *193*
Neve, Alice, 126–27, *127,* 129, 140, *140,* 150, 187–88, 195, 197, 200, *200*
New York Public Library, 25, 56
New York State Library, 77
Nicholson, Dick, *174,* 174–75
Nicholson, Nancy, *174,* 174
Nicholson Information Commons, *175,* 183
Nicols, John, 28
Niemeyer, James C., 145
Nobles Company, 190
Northern Pacific Railroad, 42
Northwest Area Foundation, 150
Northwestern Trust Company, 85
Norwest Center, 163
Norwest Foundation, 101, 116

Nowan, Gertrude, 127
Noyes, D. R., 59

Olds, Mrs. Robert E., 68
Olivier, Laurence, 138
Oman, Marie, *19*
Ordway, Lucius Pond, *61,* 61
Owens, Belle M., *19, 97*
Oz, Frank, 111

Parks, Gordon, *157,* 160, 198
Parson, Mary, 102
Paulson, Hulda, *19*
Pearce, Irving, 91
Pearson, Albin S., 138
Pearson, Peter, 151, 160–63, *161,* 173–74, 176, 183, 188, 191–92, *193,* 195
Penumbra Theatre, 196
Perrie Jones Fund, 119, 124, 155, 158, 160
Pershing, John Joseph, 63
Peterborough Library, 22
Peterson, Axel F., *109*
Peterson, Grace, *122*
Peterson, Karen Kol, *154*
Peterson, Robert, 132
Phillips, H. W., *99*
Pierpont Morgan Library, 63, *63*
Pillsbury, Charles A., 29
Pohling, Jack, 176
Pond, J. P., 28
Poole, William Frederick, *48,* 48–49, 62, 71
   and *Poole's Index,* 48
Pope, Emily, *19*
Pope, William C., 61
Porter, Truman W., *152, 152,* 155, *158, 158,* 160
Potts, W. S., 28
Powers, William, 18, 74, 76
"Prairie Home Companion," 160
Prescott, George W., 28
Prince of Wales, 16
Pusin, Miss, *93*
Putnam, Herbert, 30
Pyle, J. G., 51

Queenan, William, 158
Quie, Gretchen, 160

Rabendorf, Klein
   and *Little Crow's Village,* 20
Rahn, Lucy, *19*
Ramaley, R., 28
Ramsey, Alexander, 15, 22, *42,* 42
Ramsey County Agricultural Society, 23
Ramsey County Courthouse, 15, *45, 94,* 99
Ramsey County Historical Society, 160
Randall, Mrs. Edward. *See* Grace Spaulding.
Raspanti, Celeste, 187, *194*
Reform School of Minnesota, 27
Reid, Joe, 171
Reiter, Jim, *182*
Retman, Janice, *182*
Ricci, Ulysses, 66
Richardson, Harris, 85
Richardson, Walter J., 85
Ridder, Mrs. B. H., *109*
Ridgway, Ethel, 146
Robbins, Emma, 141

Robbins, Ortha Dorothea, *136,* 136–37
Robertson, D. A., 26, 28
Ronald M. Hubbs Center, 188
Rondo neighborhood, 132
Rosander, Lydia, *105*
Rossiter, Thomas P.
  and *Minnesota Prairie,* 31
Rumsey, Matilda, 21
Ryan, Carol, 161–162, *162*
Ryan, Joseph, 102
Ryan Hotel, 42

St. Anthony Park Elementary School, 177
St. Anthony Village Library Association, 22
St. John's University, 22
St. Louis Public Library, 86
St. Paul Athletic Club, 81
St. Paul board of education, 27
St. Paul Chamber of Commerce, 30, 44–45, 53–54, 60
St. Paul city charter, 53, 81, 103, 154
St. Paul City Council, 42, 54, 68, 76, 89, 93–94, 103, 156,
  161–63, 191–92, 196–97, 199, 203
St. Paul City Hall, 54
St. Paul Civil Service Bureau/Commission, 76–77, 83,
  89, 102, 106
St. Paul College, 188. *See also* St. Paul Technical-
  Vocational Institute.
St. Paul College Club, 107
St. Paul Commercial Club, 19, 55, 75
St. Paul Common Council, 55–56, 59–60
St. Paul Company
St. Paul Companies, 155, 160
St. Paul Department of Planning and Economic
  Development, 172, 196–97
St. Paul's first bookstore, *24*
Saint Paul Foundation, 124, 155, 157–61, 163, 174
St. Paul Garden Club, 108
St. Paul Heritage Preservation Commission, 151, 172
St. Paul Institute of Arts and Letters, 51, 67–68★
St. Paul Library Association, 28–31, 33, 41–43, 55, 89.
  See also Friends of the Saint Paul Public Library.
St. Paul Mercantile Association, 66
Saint Paul Public Library
  and bar-coding, 156–157
  and Jewish Book Week, 107
  and National Award for Museum and Library Service, 193
  and *Plan for Libraries,* 173
  and schools, 50, 84, 114
    Advisory Board, 89, 91, 101
    Advisory Committee, 85
    board, 54–55, 60, 74, 76, 85, 93, 107
    Bookmobile and library truck, 72, 77, 113–14, 118,
      133, 150, 165–66, *165–67,* 170, *179, 200*
    book sales, 133, 159
    book stations, 50, 72, 96, 118, 143
      at American Hoist and Derrick Company, 72
      at St. Paul City Railway, 72
    branches, 118, 172
      Arlington Hills, 74, 143–145
      Dayton's Bluff, *149,* 150, *186,* 192
        and Homework Help Center, 190
        and Metropolitan State University, 150, *186,* 190, 193
      Hamline-Midway, 84, 95–96, 125, *145,* 145–146, 169
      Hayden Heights, 116, 147–149, 156, 176
        and Cleveland Elementary School, 148
        and Hermann Miller Shoe Store, 148
        and St. Clair Branch, 148

Highland Park, 116, 134, *146,* 147–48, 153, 155, 176
  and Hillcrest Recreation Center, 148
Lexington Avenue, 123, 132, 147, 149–150, 155,
  187, *188–89,* 189, *194,* 195–98. *See also* Rondo
  Community Outreach.
Merriam Park, 84, 95–96, *145,* 145–47
  and deaf community, 147
  and Twin City Bungalow Club, 147
Rice Street, 116, 119, *146,* 147–48, 182, *182,* 189
  and reopening, 182
  and Rice Street Library Action Committee, 182
Riverview, *74,* 143–44, *144,* 189
Rondo Community Outreach, *149,* 150, 166, 192,
  197–98, 198–200, *201,* 203
  and Black History Collection, 200
  and Bookmobile, 150, 200
  and Homework Help Center, 200
  and Southeast Asia History and Culture Area, 200
  staff, *200*
Saint Anthony Park, 74, 116, 143–45, *144,* 176
  and children's wing, 177
  and remodeling, 144, 177
Sun Ray, 123, 128, *148,* 149–150, 153, 155, 173, 176, 189
West Seventh, *148,* 149–150, 165
  and West Seventh Community Center, 150
Carnegie libraries in St. Paul, 74, 123, 143–44, 148
  and National Register of Historic Places, 144
Central Library, *52,* 53–67, *64–66, 68,* 74, 78–79, *80,*
  85, 90, 94, 96, 99, *106,* 114, 125, 132, 134–35,
  143, 153, 155–56, 165, 172
  and James J. Hill Reference Library, 51, 54, 60, 67–68
  and remodeling/reopening, 169–185, *178,* 195–196
Art and Music, 169
Business and Science, 169
Cedar and Third Street location, 26
Children's department/program, 50, *73,* 90, 128
Circulation Room, *124,* 170
Classroom Department, *93*
Cochran Children's Room, 111, 124, 129, 134–35,
  138–141, 155, 165, *184–85,* 187
F. Scott Fitzgerald alcove, *168*
Film Bureau, 111–12
Fine Arts Room, 72
fire, 15–19, *17,* 75, 99
Great Books Program, 107
Greenleaf Clark Reference Room, *69, 73, 96*
House of Hope Presbyterian Church location, 18–19,
  75, 99, 138
Ingersoll Building location, 15, 26–27, *28*
Listening Room, 113
Marion Ramsey Furness Memorial Room, 111
Market House location, 15–18, *40,* 56, *57,* 75, 99, 138
Mississippi Room, *180*
Music Room, 112
Nonfiction Room, *181*
Paperback Book Room, 131
Periodical Room, *92*
phonograph collection, 72
puppet theater and shows, *102,* 110–11, 111, *115,*
  129–130, 165, *185*
"Races of Mankind" exhibit, *106*
Ramsey County Courthouse location, 15
Reading Room/programs, *65,* 96, 129–30, 165
Reference Room, *57,* 96, 170
Saint Paul Collection, *175*
School Services Division, 72
Science and Industry Room, *124,* 128

Skinner Room for Young People/Adults, , 108, *109,*
  110–11, 128, 131, 138, 155
  Social Science and Literature Room, 77, 159, 169
  Youth Services, 139, 178
Community Relations, 130, 169
electronic recordkeeping, 123, 170
fiftieth anniversary, *98*
head librarians. *See* Maggie Creek, Mary S. Creek, J.
  Archer Eggen, Edward Eggleston, Evan E. Edwards,
  Melanie Huggins, Josephine Kelly, Jennie T. Jennings,
  William Dawson Johnston, Perrie Jones, Gina La
  Force, Helen J. McCaine, Gerald (Jerry) Steenberg,
  Webster Wheelock, Carole Williams.
Home Bound Books, 114
Homework Help Centers, 149, 187–89
hospital library service, *104–05,* 104, 106
jade books, 16
Labor Management Committee, 171
lecture series, 41
Library Beacon, 95–97
Library Staff Doings (LSD) newsletter, 128–29
100th birthday, 159
organization of, 43
Plan for Libraries, 197
Spring Book Fair, 107
staff in 2000, *171*
staff with William Dawson Johnston, *79*
World Languages Committee, 164
St. Paul Public Schools, 155, 188
St. Paul–Ramsey Arts and Science Council, 155
St. Paul Seminary, 54
Saint Paul steamer, 68
St. Paul Technical-Vocational Institute, 188. *See also* St.
  Paul College.
St. Paul Warehouse and Elevator Company, 28
St. Paul YMCA, 16, 66
  free library, 25–28, 33
  free reading room, 23
Sanchez, Tom, 197
Sands, Phyllis, *106*
Savage, Louise, 111. *See also* Mrs. Arthur H. Savage.
Savage, Arthur H., 111
Savage, Mrs. Arthur H., 134–35, 138
Schaenzer, David, 200
Scheibel, James, 147, 161–62, 172, *188*
Scherer, Jeffrey, 146, 176
Schmidt, Alma, 16
Schrieber, Lona, 25
Schubert Club, 111
Schulz, Mrs., *96*
Schwarz, Lorraine, *96*
Science Museum of Minnesota, 171
Second National Bank, 27
Selby Avenue Community Development Corporation, 196
Sharood Shoe Store, 15
Shepard, David Chauncy, *59,* 59
Sherwin and Berwin, 67
Sigsbee, Charles, 18
Simonton, T. D., 25, 27–28
Skinner, James H., 95, 108. *See also* St. Paul Public
  Library, Central Library, Skinner Room for Young
  People.
Skinner, Mrs. James H., 95, 108, *109*
Skinner, William W., 95, 108, *109*
Slade, Charlotte Hill, 67
Slade, William, 21
Smith, Eva, 141

Smith, Mrs. Ida Wilson, *99*

Smith, Karen, 145

Smith, Milton, *93*

Smith, Scottie Fitzgerald, 160

Snider, Lizzie. *See* Edward Eggleston.

Society of Civil Engineers, 75

Sohlberg, Mrs. O. I., 108

Sonnen, Kathey, 158

Sorensen, Carolyn, *154*

Soule, Charles C., 61, 68

   and *How to Plan a Library Building,* 61

Spanish-American War, 19

Spaulding, Grace, 44

Spiess, Gerry, 160

Sprague, Marie, *19*

Stack, Kathy, 140, *158*

Staloch, Marika, 187

Stanton, Elizabeth Cady, 30

State Federation of Women's Clubs, 78

State Library Commission, 104

State Temperance Society, 27

Stavn, Ginny, 148

Steenberg, Gerald (Jerry), 124–25, 127–28, 134, *136, 152,*
   153–56, *154, 158,* 159–60, *161,* 162, 165, 169–170

   and University of Minnesota, 153

Stevens, J. Walter, 56

Stimson, Henry, 29

Strong, R. O., 26, 28

Stumpf, Peter P., 155

Sullivan, Louis B., 74, 143

Sullivan, Mary Margaret, 144

Swain, Edward, *117*

Swain, Tom, 174

Tax Reform Act of 1969, 157

Taylor, H. Knox, 28

Tedesco, Vic, *158*

Tews, Miss, *96*

Tews, Ruth, *86*

Thompkins, Clarence, 16–17

Thompson, Mrs. Horace, *109*

3M Company, 61, 190

Thune, David, 162

Toledo Public Library, 86

Tomasino, Mrs. Guy, *116*

Toomey, Dorothy, *96*

Toth, Susan Allen, 160

Toumley's Cigar Store, 15

Town and Country Club, 183

Treaty of Traverse des Sioux, 35

Twain, Mark, 15

Twin City Bungalow Club, 147

Uni-Dale Commercial Club, 132

Union Gospel Missions, 135

Universalist Church, 50

University of Minnesota, 18, 23, 28, 67, 77, 81, 101, 103,
   106, 113, 118, 123, 140, 143, 153, 160

USS *Maine,* 18–19

Valen, Linda, 146

Vall, Herman, 16

Vavoulis, Beverly, 156

Vavoulis, George, 156

Ventura, Jesse, 192

Verret, Paul A., 124, 157–60, *159,* 163

VISTA. *See* Volunteers in Service to America.

Vitz, Carl, 86

Volunteers in Service to America, 187, 189

Wagner, Elaine, 129–33, *130, 165,* 169

Wahl, Rosalie, 160

Walker, Donald, 197

Walker, Thomas Barlow, 18, *30,* 30

Wallace and Franke's Grocery, 143

Warner, Susan, 197

War on Poverty, 130

Waterous, Fred A. Jr., 158

Weiler's Drug Store, 50

West, Jean, 158

West, Mrs. William Jr., *108*

Western Initiatives Development Corporation, 196

West Seventh Community Center, 150

Wheelock, Joseph A., 76, 81

Wheelock, Kate, 81

Wheelock, Webster, 61, 76, 81–87, *83,* 90–92, 94–95, 101, 103

Wilcox, Linda, 120, 125–28, 136, 153, 169–70, 173, 176,
   183, 190

Wilder Foundation/Charity, 104, 106, 119

Wilder Infirmary, 138

Williams, Bill, 183

Williams, Carole, *136, 154, 165,* 169–73, *170,* 176–77,
   177, 183, 190, 193, *194,* 203

   and Sholom Hospice Care, 183

Williams, Fred B., 155

Williams, J. Fletcher, 27

Williams, Thomas Hale, 30

Williamson, Lee, 197

Williamson, Thomas S., 21

Willms, Debbie, 193

Winsor, Justin, *48,* 48, 71

Winsor/Faricy Architects, 151

Women's City Club, 113

Women's Civil League, 60

Women's Clubs of St. Paul, 78

World War I, 51, 63, 76, 78, 84, 104, 115, 146

World War II, 116, 120

Worscher, Mrs. Joseph, *117*

Wunderlich, Harold, 67

Yoerg, Anthony, 68, 76

Young, Mrs. E. A., 68

Zeigler, Lee Woodward, 67–68, 181

This book was designed by

Mary Susan Oleson
NASHVILLE, TENNESSEE